MW00618080

To Helen,
who also appreciates
Horney.
With fond regards,
Bernie

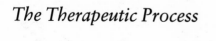

The Therapeutic Process

KAREN HORNEY

The Therapeutic Process

ESSAYS AND LECTURES

Edited with Introductions
by Bernard J. Paris

Yale University Press
New Haven &
London

Printed in the United States of America.

Horney, Karen, 1885–1952.
    The therapeutic process : essays and lectures / Karen Horney ;
edited with an introduction by Bernard J. Paris.
        p. cm.
    ISBN 0-300-07527-8 (c : alk. paper)
    1. Psychoanalysis.   I. Paris, Bernard J.   II. Title.
RC509.H674   1999
616.89'17 — dc21   98-11729
                                                      CIP

A catalogue record for this book is available from the British Library.

The paper in this book meets the guidelines for permanence and durability of the
Committee on Production Guidelines for Book Longevity of the Council on Library Resources.

10 9 8 7 6 5 4 3 2 1

For Marianne Horney Eckardt and Renate Horney Patterson

I should like to speak of psychoanalysis . . . as a sailor speaks of his boat. He knows its deficiencies and its assets, and loves it regardless of any faults it may have. . . .

Why do I love psychoanalysis? At first I thought I loved it because it gave an . . . almost aesthetic pleasure. There is, for instance, a pleasure in analyzing a dream, in understanding its meaning, and in explaining it to a patient.

Secondly, there is the therapeutic appeal of psychoanalysis. It can cure neurotic disturbances, such as alcoholism, depression, and fears of various sorts. And there is a great satisfaction when we succeed in helping a patient to become healthy.

These intellectual and therapeutic interests would intrigue me still today. But to stress them alone would appear to me like saying that you love a man because he is tall and handsome and has a nice voice, without considering other, deeper reasons why he is loved.

Now I see psychoanalysis as one of the most powerful aids in growth and development. . . . There is no good reason why we should not develop and change until the last day we live. Psychoanalysis is one of the most powerful means of helping us to realize this aim. It is a specific means of uncovering unconscious processes which are interfering with our development.

Karen Horney (1975)
Remarks made at a meeting of the Auxiliary Council of the Association for the Advancement of Psychoanalysis in 1942.

Contents

Preface

Karen Horney is best known as a psychoanalytic theorist. For some, her most important contribution is her earliest work, the essays on feminine psychology she wrote in the 1920s and early 1930s that tried to modify Freud's ideas about penis envy, female masochism, and feminine development while remaining within the framework of orthodox theory. Her emphasis on the cultural construction of gender put her far ahead of her time and made her the first great psychoanalytic feminist.

Others think of Horney primarily as a neo-Freudian member of the cultural school, the author of *The Neurotic Personality of Our Time* (1937) and *New Ways in Psychoanalysis* (1939). In these books, Horney developed a psychoanalytic paradigm in which culture and disturbed human relationships replaced biology as the most important causes of neurotic development. Although she paid tribute to Freud's genius, Horney rejected many of his premises and tried to shift the focus of psychoanalysis from infantile origins to the current structure of the personality.

In *Karen Horney: A Psychoanalyst's Search for Self-Understanding* (1994), I contended that Horney's most distinctive and enduring contribution is her mature theory. In *Our Inner Conflicts* (1945) and *Neurosis and Human Growth* (1950), she argued that individuals cope with the anxiety produced by feeling unsafe, unloved, and unvalued by disowning their real feelings and developing elaborate strategies of defense. In *Our Inner Conflicts,* she concentrated on the interpersonal strategies of moving toward, against, and away from other people and the neurotic solutions of compliance, aggression, and detachment to which they give rise. In *Neurosis and Human Growth,* she emphasized intrapsychic defenses, showing how self-idealization generates a search for glory and what she called "the pride system," which consists of neurotic pride, neurotic claims, tyrannical shoulds, and self-hate.

What I and others have tended to overlook is Horney's thinking about the therapeutic process. During her lifetime, Horney was reputed to be not only a great analyst but also a fine teacher and supervisor of analysts. She taught at the Berlin Psychoanalytic Institute in the 1920s, at the Chicago, New York, and Washington-Baltimore institutes in the 1930s, and at the American Institute for Psychoanalysis from 1941 until her death in 1952. She also taught at the New School for Social Research from 1935 to 1952. Many of her courses eventually led to her books, but there was one frequent topic of her teaching on which she never wrote at length: the therapeutic process. She included chapters on this topic in *New Ways in Psychoanalysis, Self-Analysis, Our Inner Conflicts,* and *Neurosis and Human Growth,* but these have often seemed incidental to the main focus of the books.

In addition to these chapters, however, Horney produced a substantial body of teachings about the therapeutic process. They are related to her ideas about the origin and structure of neurosis, as we shall see, but they are less determinedly systematic than her theoretical writings, and I think they will be of value to all clinicians, whether they subscribe to her theories or not. Characteristically lucid and intelligent, they are based on a wide experience and are full of wisdom and practical advice.

It is Karen Horney's teachings on the therapeutic process that I have collected here. I have divided the collection into three parts: Early and Middle Essays, Later Writings, and Lectures on Technique. All of the stages of Horney's thought are represented: the Freudian phase, the break with Freud and the development of a new paradigm, and the mature theory (see Paris 1994).

Part I begins with an essay from Horney's Freudian phase, "The Technique of Psychoanalytic Therapy" (1917). In the 1920s Horney devoted herself to writing about feminine psychology and the relations between the sexes, but in the 1930s she returned to clinical issues as she began to rethink the therapeutic process from the perspective of her new theoretical positions. The remainder of part I consists of five essays, one previously unpublished, that were written between her arrival in the United States in 1932 and the publication of her first book. These essays show Horney breaking away from Freud and beginning to develop the structural paradigm, with its emphasis on the present, that she expounded in *The Neurotic Personality of Our Time* (1937) and *New Ways in Psychoanalysis* (1939).

Part II presents Horney's hitherto uncollected writings on therapy from the 1940s and early 1950s, and these reflect her mature theory. There is an interval of ten years between the last essay in part I and the first in part II, during which time Horney published *The Neurotic Personality of Our Time* (1937), *New Ways in Psychoanalysis* (1939), *Self-Analysis* (1942), and *Our Inner Conflicts* (1945). In the last three of these books, there are chapters on the therapeutic process. In order to provide a context for the material in part II and to make this volume a more complete account of Horney's views on therapy, I offer an account of the relevant developments in her thought in the introduction to part II.

Part III consists of reconstructions of the lectures on psychoanalytic technique that Horney gave at the American Institute for Psychoanalysis in 1946, 1950, 1951, and 1952. I have been told by those who knew her that if she had lived, Horney's next book would have been on technique. Her lectures on the topic confirm this, since her books were typically preceded by courses in which she worked out the ideas about which she was planning to write. In 1947, 1948, and 1949, she taught courses relating to the contents of *Neurosis and Human Growth;* after that, she concentrated on therapeutic technique.

Although Horney did not live to write her book on technique, in the 1950s and 1960s her students and colleagues published eleven accounts of her teachings in the *American Journal of Psychoanalysis*. These were based on their notes from her courses and constitute, in effect, a version of her intended book. Together with the material in parts I and II, these accounts of her lectures give us a rich picture of Horney's ideas about the therapeutic process and establish her as an important thinker on the topic. There is some overlap with *Final Lectures* (Horney 1987), which consists of transcriptions of recordings of the course in 1952 that was interrupted by Horney's death, but the accounts in the *American Journal of Psychoanalysis* are more extensive and complete.

Horney's lectures are valuable, I think, not only because they give us insight into a previously overlooked aspect of her thought but also because they are highly pertinent to the continuing concerns of clinicians, both practical and theoretical. Once more ahead of her time, Horney saw therapy as a collaborative enterprise and developed an interactive model in which the therapist is open, frank, and supportive and experiences growth along with the patient. She was highly sensitive to the ways in which the therapist's personality can both facilitate and obstruct the healing process, and she had a great deal to say about the therapist's "neurotic remnants" and countertransference phenomena. She was operating within the framework of her theory, to be sure, but very flexibly. She anticipated continuous revision of her ideas by herself and others as a result of clinical experience.

Acknowledgments

Two items in this book have been previously unpublished. "The Misuse of Psychoanalysis" was among the Horney writings that I found in Harold Kelman's papers at the Postgraduate Center for Mental Health in New York. I am grateful to Natalie Jaffe, Kelman's niece and executor, who led me to this material and has kindly placed it in my possession. Horney's lecture "Pride and Self-Hatred: Solution in Therapy" is from her course "Pride and Self-Hatred in Neuroses," the notes for which were among her papers at the American Institute for Psychoanalysis. My thanks to the institute and to Jeffrey Rubin, who was dean at the time I did my research, for providing me with a copy of these notes.

The remaining pieces in this book are reprinted with the permission of their original publishers, who are identified in the headnotes. These include the *American Journal of Psychoanalysis* (Plenum Publishing Corporation), the *Journal of Nervous and Mental Disease* (Williams and Wilkins), *The Family* (Family Welfare Association of America), the *Newsletter of the American Association of Psychiatric Social Workers,* the *Psychoanalytic Quarterly,* and the *Digest of Neurology and Psychiatry* (Institute of Living, Hartford, Connecticut). Horney's essays from *Are You Considering Psychoanalysis?* are reprinted with the permission of W. W. Norton and Company. Morton B. Cantor has kindly allowed me to include his reconstructions of Horney's lectures on analytic technique and has given me permission to edit them.

I am grateful to Yale University Press for permitting me to use material from *Karen Horney: A Psychoanalyst's Search for Self-Understanding* (Paris 1994) in the introduction to part 2 of this book. My editor at Yale, Gladys Topkis, has contributed greatly to this project through her encouragement and her suggestions, and Lawrence Kenney has improved the text by his excellent copy-editing.

I have received assistance from other sources as well. Jaye Giancana has helped me to locate Horney material at the American Institute for Psychoanalysis, and Diane Kaplan has supplied me with photocopies of Horney's notes from her courses on analytic technique, which now reside in the Karen Horney Papers in the Manuscripts and Archives division of the Yale University Library. Sara Sheiner's daughter, Mimi Sheiner, has given me her mother's notes from her courses with Karen Horney, and I have consulted these when editing the reconstructions of Horney's lectures in part 3 of this book. As always, my wife, Shirley, has been my first reader, best critic, and chief source of emotional support. I am deeply thankful to her.

This book would not have been possible without the generous cooperation of Karen Horney's daughters, Marianne Horney Eckardt and Renate Horney Patterson, who, as her literary executors, have given me permission to publish her writings. From the beginning of my work on Horney in 1989, they have been extraordinarily kind and helpful. I dedicate this book to them in gratitude.

PART I

Early and Middle Essays

Introduction

Although she is known as a psychoanalytic rebel, Karen Horney was an orthodox Freudian for many years. After studying medicine at the universities of Freiburg, Göttingen, and Berlin, she entered analysis with Karl Abraham in 1910 and began seeing patients in 1912. She became a founding member of the Berlin Psychoanalytic Institute in 1920 and taught classical theory there for the next twelve years. Although she sought to modify Freud's views on feminine psychology, her early essays on this topic were written within the framework of his basic ideas.

Aware of the social construction of gender and influenced by the sociology and anthropology of her day, Horney gradually began to challenge Freud's emphasis on biology and to stress the importance of culture. This process was accelerated by her move to the United States in 1932. There she encountered a less repressive society, new intellectual influences, and patients whose problems were different from those she had treated in Berlin. In the early to mid-1930s, her essays reflected her new modes of thought.

The first essay in part I belongs to Horney's Freudian phase; the remainder belong to the period of transition during which she broke from Freud and began to develop a new psychoanalytic paradigm. In "The Technique of Psychoanalytic Therapy" (1917), Horney's first publication, she did not challenge orthodox theory in any way. She followed "Freud's own views" and dismissed "divergent procedures such as those of the Zurich school," "which continues to call its method 'psychoanalysis' in spite of its basic difference." Freudians were later to object to Horney's continuing to call *her* method psychoanalysis in spite of her basic differences from them. Because it deals with issues to which Horney frequently returned, this first essay provides a good point of departure for tracing the evolution of her ideas.

Although her courses on technique at the Berlin Psychoanalytic Institute were very popular, Horney published nothing on this topic from 1917 to 1934. She returned to it as her interest in feminine psychology waned and she began to explore the implications of her new ideas for the therapeutic process. The essays written during her early years in the United States prefigure *The Neurotic Personality of Our Time* and *New Ways in Psychoanalysis* in many important ways and are the earliest writings in which we see the paradigm shift that led to her mature theory.

In "The Technique of Psychoanalytic Therapy," Horney assumed a knowledge of Freudian theory and sought to delineate "the most important points of therapeutic technique." After describing how the physician arrives at a knowledge of the unconscious through the analysis of free associations and resistances, she observed that "this knowledge does not change the situation in the slightest." The patient's primitive infantile instincts must emerge so that they can be affirmed, rejected, tamed, or sublimated; but they are prevented from emerging by the conscious ego, which does not wish to admit their existence, and the unconscious, which does not wish to relinquish their gratification. The main task of psychoanalysis is to eliminate resistances, which are activated mainly by getting close to a repressed complex and by the dynamics of the therapist-patient relationship. Horney regarded this relationship as of the utmost importance and devoted much of her essay to an examination of it. Although she continued to maintain the centrality of the therapist-patient relationship, her conception of its dynamics underwent considerable change as her ideas evolved, and it is useful to measure that change from the orthodox position with which she began.

The most important feature of the relationship is the transference, in which aggressive and libidinal impulses that had been fixated on infantile models are cathected on the therapist. The transference "performs an invaluable service in therapy in that it actualizes and makes manifest those repressed and forgotten instincts," but it also obstructs therapy by generating resistances. The patient is embarrassed about tender or hostile feelings toward the analyst, which leads to silence; also, the patient wants the doctor to fulfill primitive wishes instead of analyzing them. Insight can help to resolve the transference, since infantile wishes "no longer strike us as desirable once they have become conscious," and "repression may be replaced by conscious condemnation." Many primitive desires "are so excessive, so fantastic and grotesque that they cannot stand up to the clear light of day."

As she did throughout her career, Horney warned against encouraging the patient's dependency on the therapist because the dissolution of the transference is essential for cure. She objected to the practice of trying to educate patients and of giving advice, for patients should develop autonomy and the capacity to make decisions for themselves. The analyst "will serve the patient better by limiting himself to simply helping the patient clarify the motives that drive him toward this or that decision." Horney later developed a more collaborative model of therapy, but in this paper she approved of Freud's advice for avoiding transference difficulties, such as sitting behind the patient and not sharing one's own inner experiences.

What Horney required of the analyst here is remarkably similar to her later teachings, except that it is cast in Freudian terms. In addition to having theoretical knowledge, the analyst must be free of unresolved repressions that will create blind spots in his perceptions. Because the connections the analyst makes are largely intuitive and unconscious rather than a product of ratiocination, he must have "no resistances within him against any insights." Horney advised not only that analysts be psychoanalyzed but also that they continue to analyze themselves so as to be "conscious of a possible countertransference or counterresistance."

There was an interval of sixteen years between "The Technique of Psychoanalytic Therapy" and "The Misuse of Psychoanalysis," an unpublished paper that Horney wrote in July 1933, less than a year after she arrived in the United States. Although she had moved farther and farther from Freud in her essays on feminine psychology, in "The Misuse of Psychoanalysis" she presents a view of transference which is virtually identical to that offered in her very first essay. This piece is interesting historically because it gives us a vivid sense of the ways in which psychoanalytic ideas had filtered into the culture. In her outline of the article, Horney referred to people showing off their psychological insight in "amateur parlor clinic[s]."

The paper is a satire on people who have acquired some psychoanalytic knowledge and employ it for bad motives and in irresponsible ways. There are compulsive truth tellers who conceal their own self-deceptions by striking at the most vulnerable points in others, omniscient people who must feel that they can explain everything, zealots who are in analysis themselves and must analyze everyone else, martyrs whose psychological knowledge helps them in their search for evidences of maltreatment, husbands who accuse their wives of wanting to castrate them, wives who taunt their husbands with their dread of women, and masochists who use psychoanalytic insights to flagellate themselves. Horney's account of these types is amusing, but she had a serious point: imperfectly understood ideas used without restraint can do damage to ourselves, to others, and to our relationships.

Horney reserved her strongest criticism for what she called "professional offenders," especially "wild analysts" who do not know how to manage the transference, which she still saw in largely Freudian terms. People would not dream of having an operation performed by someone not trained in surgery, "but they apparently have a notion that the soul is less vulnerable, and therefore do not mind going to a physician who is not specifically trained for analytical work." The greatest danger is that the untrained physician will "react emotionally to the patient's positive and negative" transferences, thus increasing dependency or driving the patient deeper into neurosis. The object of therapy is not the acting out of instincts but the replacement of repression by control. Psychoanalysis "is a wonderful therapeutic instrument, as long as it is recognized as a radical procedure" that requires a technique as precise as surgery if it is to be conducted successfully.

Although she expressed great respect for psychoanalysis when properly used, I cannot help suspecting that Horney was satirizing not only the abuses of psychoanalysis but orthodox theory itself because she presented a great many standard psychoanalytic explanations with a jocularity that suggests irreverence. This suspicion is supported by "Conceptions and Misconceptions of the Analytic Method," an essay published in 1935 based on a paper Horney presented at the Chicago Psychoanalytic Society in the fall of 1933. The title of her paper, "Misuses of Psychoanalysis in Daily Practice," suggests that it was a sequel to "The Misuse of Psychoanalysis." There is no surviving copy of the original paper, but Horney's published essay was devoted to her innovative ideas about how psychoanalysis *should be* practiced rather than to its misuses. She began, however, by attacking the misconception that there is no analytic method at all and describing the impression many psychiatrists have of psychoanalysis:

> The psychoanalytic procedure is based on the free-association of the patient. The analyst is dependent on what the patient chooses to tell him. The analyst usually veils himself in silence ("the myth of the silent analyst") and only now and then makes some wise-cracks which he calls interpretations. These interpretations chiefly concern connections which the analyst constructs between present actions, attitudes and symptoms of the patient, and childhood experiences mainly of a sexual nature and supposedly radiating from the so-called

Oedipus complex. The interpretations are of an arbitrary character both in content and sequence. There is no assurance of correctness and relevance and no guarantee against the analyst's power of suggesting thoughts alien to the patient. The analysis takes a long time, the outcome is difficult to estimate, and there remains a secret or expressed doubt whether or not the benevolent interest of an understanding physician for the same length of time might not have led to the same result. Testing the procedure is only possible after having submitted to the same process oneself as in an initiation rite.

Instead of defending psychoanalysis against these presumed misconceptions, Horney then stunningly asked whether, "allowing for some exaggeration," such a picture of analysis "should be called a misconception or approximates the true state of affairs."

Horney acknowledged that in the past psychoanalysis contained "too many arbitrary factors," but she observed that "a change is gradually taking place" as a result of the contributions of such people as Theodore Reik, Edward Glover, Ella Freeman Sharpe, and Wilhelm Reich. She then presented for the first time her structural paradigm, in which patients' associations are used to explore the "immediate causes" of their attitudes "and the function they perform in the present situation" rather than to recover infantile origins. Because we can observe the patient's attitudes, "we are on safe ground in interpreting them as long as we avoid all uncertain statements such as direct deduction about childhood situations." This procedure eliminates the arbitrary character of so many psychoanalytic explanations of the sort that Horney mocked in "The Misuse of Psychoanalysis."

Another reason for starting "from the patient's attitudes and the immediate motives for them" is that explaining the attitudes in terms of their origins in childhood means providing "the first and the last link in a chain with all intermediate links missing." The present is certainly an outgrowth of the past, but it is not a direct repetition of it. Instead, each step conditions the next, so that current attitudes and behaviors are the result of a continuous process of development. Thus "interpretations which connect the present difficulties immediately with influences in childhood are scientifically only half-truths and practically useless." Horney did not rule out exploring the past but felt that we can recapture it only by beginning with "the immediate motives for the observable attitudes of the patient" and then gradually tracing "the emotional causal chains which lead from the present symptoms to the earliest shaping influences."

A third reason for starting with the patient's current attitudes and their immediate psychological functions is that these attitudes can obstruct the therapeutic process. Although they may have their origin in childhood, they serve as a defense against fears in the present and cannot be relinquished un-less their protective function is understood and the current need for them is ameliorated.

Horney concluded by mentioning two difficulties that arise in the procedure she is recommending. The first is that the patient's attitudes may be "com-posed of contradictory trends." Much of her later work was devoted to explor-ing such contradictions. The second is that, given the cultural conditions in which we live, analysts, like their patients, may have "fears and defense reac-tions against them." These will "tend to blind [them] to certain aspects of the picture and cause [them] to see others in an exaggerated way." They can mitigate these problems by undergoing analytic training and by being ana-lyzed themselves. Horney now spoke of analysts being hampered by their defenses rather than by their repressions.

Horney explored another aspect of her new paradigm in "Restricted Ap-plications of Psychoanalysis to Social Work," published in October 1934. There are three sources, she observed, of neurosis: infantile fears, defenses against these fears, and actual conflict situations. Although she initially de-scribed infantile fears in Freudian terms, as the child's fears that its "primitive instinctive drives" will not be gratified, she said nothing about instincts in the remainder of the essay but instead offered an explanation of neurosis that she would develop much more fully later.

Neurosis arises not so much from the frustration of instincts as from the behavior of parents who treat the young child inconsistently and fail to give it "the feeling of warmth and protection" it needs to counteract its sense of helplessness. Feeling frustrated, intimidated, and confused by a "mixture of indulgence and harshness," the child responds with a "rebellious hostility." This provokes a "renewed intimidation" that forces the child to suppress its antagonistic behavior. The child's hostility can be lived out only in violent fantasies, but these are so threatening that they have to be repressed, and the child develops vague fears of both its buried explosive affects and possible retaliation from others. All this creates "anxiety states" (the precursor of Horney's concept of "basic anxiety") against which the child defends itself by developing "certain character trends," the function of which is to avoid fear-arousing behaviors. The child, and later the adult, adopts "protective measures" that result in inhibitions, emotional impoverishment, and loss of flexibility, but that provide a feeling of safety in an unreliable world. The protective measures may work smoothly for a while, but "situations will easily arise" in which they are ineffective ("the actual conflict situation[s]"), and then the individual is flooded with anxiety.

Horney's advice to psychiatric social workers was to refrain from exploring the underlying causes of the patient's disturbance, which can be treated only "by means of regular analysis," and to limit themselves to dealing with actual conflict situations. These can be eased as long as care is taken "not to stir up any of the deeper anxieties." The "numerous defensive strategies" should be left "untouched." These are the province of the psychoanalyst.

A year later, in 1935, Horney published another talk she had given to psychiatric social workers: "On Difficulties in Dealing with the Transference." Instead of warning them to stay away from deeper anxieties, as she had done before, she discussed the "explosive material" that is likely to emerge in the therapist-patient relationship and offered some advice for dealing with it. Horney used this occasion to formulate some of her new ideas about the transference.

She began by once again explaining transference in Freudian terms. The patient is compulsively acting according to an old pattern and is feeling toward the therapist as he or she had felt toward an important person or persons in early childhood. Horney no longer saw much benefit from pursuing this track, however.

The crucial issue, she argued, is not the possible infantile sources of the patient's behavior but "the dynamics which make the patient continue this attitude at the present time": "If for reasons that were adequate at that time, a patient suppressed his criticism toward his childhood surroundings, what forces are at work in his present life to keep him uncritical, naive, and immature?" We cannot "effect any change in the present difficulties" unless we understand "the current interplay of psychic drives." The object of therapy is "*not* to recapture childhood memories, but to change something in the present attitudes," and that can be done only by understanding their immediate defensive function.

In this model, uncovering and understanding the patient's reactions to the therapist and the therapeutic situation continue to be of great importance, not as a means of gaining access to primitive instincts and early object-relations, but as a way of grasping the current interplay of psychic forces. The patient's display of characteristic defensive strategies in the interaction with the therapist was now the most important aspect of the transference for Horney. The therapist will be able to see these strategies clearly because he or she has (or should have) an exact knowledge of the situation to which the patient is reacting, whereas the patient's accounts of what goes on outside of therapy are often distorted, incomplete, and self-justifying.

Although Horney paid tribute to Freud at the beginning and the end of this essay, she had traveled a great distance from his way of thinking. The patient who seeks affection is trying not to gratify primitive instincts that have been transferred from their original objects but to allay anxiety, perhaps in a way that had its origin in the past but that has a current function. In the case of a patient who had a history of being attracted to his mother and even of having slept in her bed, Horney attributed his "erotic phantasies" not to an Oedipus complex but to childhood anxiety: "He was desperately afraid of his mother and therefore assumed an affectionate attitude toward her." His efforts to get reassuring affection were a defensive strategy that grew out of the past and that he held onto not because of fixation but because he was still filled with anxiety. He brought this strategy into his relationship with the therapist, where he had a chance of understanding and relinquishing it. Patients will be reluctant to recognize their defenses and will try to protect them against the therapist because they need them in order to cope with their anxieties. For Horney, this is now the primary source of resistance.

In "The Problem of the Negative Therapeutic Reaction," published in 1936, Horney addressed another clinical issue from her rapidly evolving structural perspective. Once again she began with Freud, praising his definition of the phenomenon as set forth in *The Ego and the Id*. A negative therapeutic reaction occurs when a patient shows an increase in symptoms, becomes discouraged, or wishes to terminate treatment immediately following an improvement or a "real elucidation of some problem." This is accompanied by hostility and a disparaging attitude toward the therapist. Freud regarded the negative reaction as "a serious barrier to therapeutic endeavors" and "indicative of a bad prognosis," but Horney argued that it can be overcome if properly understood. She tried to explain it not in terms of a tension "between the superego and the ego, resulting in a sense of guilt and need for punishment," but as an expression of the defenses a patient employs to cope with anxiety. Horney did not have these defenses sorted out as yet, but we can relate them to her later formulations.

In patients who display a negative therapeutic reaction, the effects of progress or of a good interpretation are of five kinds, not all always present or equally strong. The first reaction is that of what Horney later called aggressive or expansive personalities. These people are compulsively ambitious, see everyone as a rival, and regard a good interpretation as a defeat at the hands of the analyst. Their "striving for absolute supremacy serves as a protection against an extraordinary anxiety: it insures safety through absolute power." A good interpretation makes the analyst seem superior, and the fact that they need help challenges their claims to self-sufficiency. Their defenses thus endangered, "they must express their hostility and their sense of defeat by belittling the analyst." The fact that they have benefited from the analyst's help "seems irrelevant" because, despite the fact that they are in therapy, they feel that they should not require any assistance.

The second type of reaction springs from patients' "grandiose ideas" about themselves, what Horney later called their idealized images and neurotic claims. Because a good interpretation "usually implies the exposure of some weakness, or what the patients consider such," it is a blow to their exalted conceptions of themselves. They make excessive demands on themselves "to be perfect, flawless, beyond reproach" (what Horney called their "shoulds"), so that the analyst's insight into their problems "strikes them as humiliation." They try to alleviate their distress by making "the analyst feel insignificant, preposterous, and ineffectual."

The third kind of reaction arises from what Horney later called compliant or self-effacing tendencies. There is a fear of success, a recoiling from all competition. Because people of this type feel safe only when they are humble, inconspicuous, unthreatening to others, progress in therapy seems perilous to them. They defend themselves by feeling "discouragement, hopelessness, despair, and the wish to terminate the analysis."

The fourth reaction derives from what Horney here called guilt and later described as self-hate. For people who are already full of self-loathing, "the analysis resembles a trial," and a good interpretation "is perceived as an unjust accusation." However delicately presented, it "is reacted to as if it were a total condemnation, the intensity of which is proportional to the existing feelings of self-condemnation." To defend themselves, the patients will counterattack, trying to prove the analyst wrong in order to make themselves feel better.

The fifth reaction is once again that of a basically compliant person, someone who has "an excessive need for affection and equally great sensitivity to any kind of rebuff." For such people, the analyst's uncovering of their difficulties seems like "an expression of dislike or disdain," and, feeling rejected, they react "with strong antagonism." Complicating the picture is the fact that the childhood situation of such people engendered anxiety and hostility with which they sought to cope by striving for power as well as for affection, since these are the two defenses most common in our culture. Hence they are full of inner conflicts, which manifest themselves in the therapeutic situation: "A move towards competition with the analyst is followed by increased anxiety and need for affection." Here again Horney touched on the kinds of conflicts it became her mission to explore.

Horney was at pains to distinguish between the child's need for affection and the neurotic cravings of the adult. We are accustomed to think of excessive cravings for affection as infantile, a continuation into the present of the child's dependency needs for "help, affection, and attention." Neurotic needs for affection (or for power) are not infantile, however, but defensive in nature and the product of a long, complicated development. Horney put her thesis in italics: *"The attitudes we see in the adult patient are not direct repetitions or revivals of infantile attitudes, but have been changed in quality and quantity by the consequences which have developed out of the early experiences."* She contended that negative therapeutic reactions are resolvable "only if the analyst persists in analyzing the immediate reactions in their immediate causations."

Horney insisted, however, that she gave no "less importance to childhood experiences than any other analyst. These are of fundamental importance since they determine the direction of the individual's development." Childhood experiences are more formative than later ones because they are the source of the basic feelings of anxiety and the initial defenses against them. All subsequent development is influenced by childhood experiences, but the ways in which they manifest themselves in adulthood are shaped by that development.

One can imagine Horney writing a much more systematic analysis of the negative therapeutic reaction once she had her taxonomy of defenses worked out, but she did not return to the topic, and this is her richest account.

Karen Horney's early and middle essays on therapy are of interest for their clinical insights and also because they constitute a chapter in the history of psychoanalysis and illuminate the evolution of Horney's ideas. In these essays more than anywhere else we can see her making the transition from orthodox thought to her own understanding of human behavior and the therapeutic process. Her development in the years from 1933 to 1936 was remarkably rapid. By 1937 she had expanded many of the ideas adumbrated in her essays into her first book, *The Neurotic Personality of Our Time*. I shall discuss that book in the introduction to part II, as part of the context for her later essays on therapy.

I

The Technique of Psychoanalytic Therapy (1917)

While she was in analysis with Karl Abraham from 1910 to 1913, Karen Horney began attending his "Freudian evenings," which in 1911 became regular meetings of the Berlin Psychoanalytic Society. She became secretary of the society in 1915. Among her friends in the society were Heinrich Koerber, a coworker at the Lankwitz Kuranstalt (a military neurological hospital), and Iwan Bloch, president of the Medical Society for Sexuality (Ärzliche Gesellschaft für Sexualwissenschaft) and coeditor of its journal, Zeitschrift für Sexualwissenschaft. *Bloch invited both Koerber and Horney to address the Medical Society on February 18, 1917, an audience of physicians, psychologists, and laypersons with little or no psychoanalytic training. Horney relied on Koerber's presentation, which preceded hers, to acquaint the audience with the basics of Freudian theory. She discussed psychoanalytic technique, presenting her ideas in a clear, easy-to-follow manner, much as she did later when lecturing to lay audiences at the New School for Social Research. Her paper was subsequently published in the* Zeitschrift für Sexualwissenschaft, *vol. 4, fasc. 6, 7, 8, 1917. I am using the English translation by Edward R. Clemmens, M.D., which was published in the* American Journal of Psychoanalysis 28 (1968), 3–12.

The discussion that followed Dr. Koerber's paper on psychoanalysis, an excellent paper, distinguished particularly by its poignant formulations, brought forth many objections and questions about the practical and therapeutic aspects of psychoanalysis. I, therefore, have assumed the task of delineating to you today the most important points of therapeutic technique. To become acquainted with the method is particularly necessary for the understanding of theory. Statements to the contrary notwithstanding, all psychoanalytic theories in their entirety have grown out of observations and experiences which were made while applying this method. The theories, in turn, later exerted their influence on psychoanalytic practice.

The intimate interrelationship of theory and practice makes it difficult to appreciate and understand one without the other. It also makes my paper hard to write. I cannot possibly present you today with the entire theoretical basis of psychoanalysis and must, therefore, assume that you are familiar with the theories. Hence you may look upon my paper as a supplement to the one presented by Dr. Koerber. In view of the abundance of the material, I have been forced to further limit my presentation. The restriction which you will regret the least is that I shall follow in the main Freud's own views and that I will only briefly mention divergent procedures such as those of the Zurich School. It is unfortunate that in the narrow frame of a paper I can present only scanty case material which might contribute so much to our understanding. I will also have to forego refuting the objections that have been raised against the procedure, but I hope that a fruitful discussion will provide me with an opportunity to deal with those criticisms. Finally, I have limited the historical material to a minimum and have only tried to present clearly the difference between the original procedure and today's practice. A discussion that took place last winter brought out that certain views that had already been given up are still being attacked.

When we consider the manner in which psychoanalysis was practiced in its beginnings, we must make a sharp distinction between two phases: The very first one in which hypnosis was used and the second one which renounced its use as a matter of principle. The gap between these two methods is so wide that Freud himself stated that the history of psychoanalysis begins with the technical innovation of the abandonment of hypnosis.

What the two phases had in common, as distinguished from today's practice, was that they started from the symptom and then attempted to retrace its steps to its origin without looking left or right. Today, on the contrary, we worry less about symptoms and rather take our departure from the psychological surface, wherever it may be. We then attempt to penetrate into the unconscious, layer by layer, with the justified expectation that the symptoms are going to disappear by themselves, as long as we penetrate deeply enough into the unconscious. Better than theoretical explanations, a comparison will illustrate this contrast. We may compare psychoanalysis with the excavation of a buried city, in which we assume the existence of valuable historical documents. According to the old method, we would be interested in these documents only and would dig in those places where we expect to find them. According to the new method, we would wish to uncover the whole settlement, i.e., the whole unconscious, and would remove layer upon layer of earth inside of the entire perimeter. The disadvantages of the old method are obvious: in the first place, its goals are much less comprehensive since we searched only for isolated objects. Also, one could never be sure that we were digging in the right places, and finally we ran the risk that our laborious diggings would be buried again overnight by landslides.

To repeat, the old system started from the specific symptom, e.g., an hysterical paralysis of an arm, and made the patient concentrate his thoughts, under hypnosis, upon the time when the paralysis had first appeared. Frequently, numerous affect-laden events would come up and the patient was urged to describe them in detail with all their accompanying affects. The symptom would indeed disappear when the patient had reached the provoking events, mostly with intense manifestations of affect. This was the so-called abreaction which is the only thing that still comes to many people's minds when they talk about psychoanalysis. In the early days we explained the improvement as a consequence of the release of a "strangulated" affect. Subsequent views hold that the abreaction of traumatic affects that had not been able to release themselves, does not play the main role in the dynamic of healing.

The second phase began, as indicated above, with the abandonment of hypnosis. Initially this move was in part involuntary, because not all patients could be hypnotized. It also seemed at first that an invaluable advantage was being lost, namely, the expansion of consciousness which occurs under hypnosis. Freud found a substitute for this loss in the patient's associations, i.e., his unplanned thoughts that occurred when he was urged to remember the time of the first appearance of the symptom. In the early days this insistence was further enhanced by a suggestive pressure on the forehead. In those days Freud was of the opinion that all symptoms could be traced back to psychic traumata which had not been admitted to or had been rejected by consciousness, i.e., repressed because of their embarrassing content. More recently this view has been considerably changed and deepened. The abandonment of hypnosis marked an important step forward because its use had obscured the finer mechanisms of the neurosis. Particularly the phenomenon of resistance, which is so basic for both theory and practice, became apparent only after hypnosis had been given up. The main differences between then and now are as follows:

1. The former was a purely symptomatic form of therapy which started from the symptom and searched for underlying psychic traumata.

2. In those early days suggestion still played a certain role, although not as simple injunctions or prohibitions, in contrast to most other psychotherapeutic methods which used them outright.

3. Indications for treatment used to be much more limited. They have become increasingly broader.

It might be quite instructive to observe the development of the method in its details. However, for the sake of clarity I shall immediately proceed to give a brief account of the technique as it is used today or as Freud advises it to be used. The first question which is usually asked reads as follows: How does the physician obtain knowledge of the patient's unconscious? The raw material of this knowledge is supplied by the patient himself through his associations. He is asked to give his associations to a dream which he has reported or to a memory which has emerged. He is told to say everything that occurs to him, no matter whether he considers it trite, ridiculous, absurd, indiscreet or, most important, whether it might be embarrassing to him. This request for the turning off of all conscious critiques of the associations, the so-called psychoanalytic basic rule, initially is the only thing requested of the patient. It is not an easy thing to do, as will become evident to everyone who tries it. As a rule the associations do not reveal the unconscious wishes directly, but they are distorted by a kind of censorship that anxiously watched over the illicit unconscious wishes to keep them from reaching the light of day. While it is true that according to the laws of association the patient must produce in his associations material that is relevant to a defect in his actual memory, there is at the same time a strong resistance against the re-emergence into his consciousness of the repressed piece of memory. After all, he did not repress the underlying wishes for nothing, but because they were incompatible with the rest of the content of his conscious mind. It is the identical force that in the past caused the repression, i.e., the expelling from the conscious mind, that we now encounter as resistance, as soon as we try to reverse the repression. This resistance causes the associations to be distorted in many varied ways. They may, e.g., occur in symbolic disguise, or the patient may produce the most important associations in a doubting way, or he may present them as insignificant, etc.

I want to talk about resistance separately later, about its origins, manifestations and its resolution in psychoanalysis. I shall address myself first to the question of how the physician arrives at an understanding of the unconscious instinctual forces. I wish to state right here that this task of the physician is the less important and the less difficult one, though to the uninitiated it appears as the real difficulty. At this point we can profit from the experiences of Freud and of others. They permit us to simply translate many statements made by the patient, as long as they are not excessively distorted by the resistance. Thus we know that in general there is a repressed wish behind every anxiety. When a patient tells us, e.g., that she is overly concerned about her husband, how she fears that something may have happened to him whenever he is delayed a few minutes, how she frequently leans over him at night to make sure that he is still breathing, we may suspect that she harbors intense but repressed death wishes against her husband. This in no way exhausts the phenomenon. We would ask further: What can these death wishes be traced back to?

At other times we are helped by our knowledge of symbolism, especially in our work with dream interpretation. Furthermore we may conclude without hesitation that associations which are contiguous in time belong together according to the laws of associations. Thus, when a patient associates to a dream figure and my person occurs to her, and immediately afterwards she thinks of two people who performed some services to her without charge or who gave her gifts, I can easily guess her underlying wish that I analyze her for free.

At other times our attention is directed to the workings of unconscious forces when we hear about wishes, decisions or opinions, the motivations of which are conspicuously weak. In such cases we know that the views in question must be based in the main upon unconscious wishes.

Furthermore, experience teaches the following: Whenever a doubt is expressed, the conclusion contained or implied in it may be disregarded and the statement taken in its positive meaning.

We derive further insight through symptomatic behavior on the part of patients; through actions that they perform automatically, unconsciously, without paying attention to them, and that they explain as unimportant when questioned; furthermore through mistakes that they commit, e.g., when they lose something, make a mistake in speaking or take the wrong trolley car. These faulty actions are the result of unconscious wishes that break through, often with great obstinacy. One of my patients, on her way to an analytic session, took a wrong turn on the street. Thereupon she carefully memorized the street map in order to avoid such mistakes in the future; in fact she reminded herself shortly before her next trip to pay close attention — and yet she took the wrong turn at the same spot.

Valuable clues are often supplied by symptoms that appear during the course of analysis. One of my patients who suffered from stomach attacks became nauseous every time she talked about her brother. The further course of analysis revealed that the symptoms were connected with childhood memories in which the brother played the main role. These are only a few typical modalities of expression of the unconscious which could easily be expanded on. They cannot be simply translated schematically, since they differ from case to case. The most important knowledge in this regard was given to us by Freud in his *Interpretation of Dreams*.

Nevertheless, as I said before, the solving of the riddle of unconscious motives does not constitute the main difficulty and the main art for two reasons. In the first place, it advances us only up to a point, particularly in complicated cases. As a matter of fact we would block our own road to new insights if we limited ourselves to the interpretation of the patient's statements according to analogous experiences. One psychoanalyst told me that he went so far as to meet every new case as if he had no analytic knowledge at all.

But even if I could interpret the patient's whole unconscious mental activity from his statements, this would not help him one iota. You may picture the situation as though the patient had locked his unconscious instincts, like strange animals, behind a high wall over which he no longer can look. He does not know the animals any more but he is bothered and frightened by their noise. The physician, on the other hand, is able because of his knowledge to distinguish the different voices, to identify the animals and to whom they belong.

This knowledge does not change the situation in the slightest, not even if he were to tell the patient exactly what animals are behind the wall. What is needed is helping him take down the wall little by little. That way the animals can get out, and he may tame them or put them in a cage where they no longer bother him. This means that he may admit to consciousness those instincts hitherto unknown, he may affirm them, reject them or sublimate them. The wall that bars access to his unconscious instincts is called resistance. This resistance wall, which in analysis we must laboriously take down brick by brick, is defended by the patient in two ways: by the conscious ego, which does not wish to admit those primitive infantile instincts, and by the unconscious, which does not wish to give up the gratification which it derives from the activity of its instinctual life. Hence it is the main task of psychoanalysis to remove those resistances by means of uncovering them. It is not always simple to recognize or to find a resistance. Freud established a very simple basic rule for this purpose: Everything that hinders the progress of analysis is a resistance, omitting of course purely external obstacles. We can assume resistance is present when a patient arrives late, when he does not show up at all for insufficient reasons; when nothing occurs to him; when he sins against the psychoanalytic basic rule, i.e., to say everything that comes up; when he no longer dreams or when he produces dreams of such a volume that their accounting occupies the whole hour, when he complains for half an hour about the lack of progress instead of using the time to get on with the work, and when he suddenly begins to talk about the furniture, etc. Some patients try to distract the doctor from themselves by involving him in critical discussions about psychoanalysis or other topics; other patients become tired or fall asleep. Insights that had been gained are later denied, which is one of the reasons why psychoanalysts are just as hard to analyze as other mortals.

Aside from these typical forms of resistance, most patients have their own individual way of manifesting it, and in each case it must be observed and studied anew. Hence, the first task is to recognize a resistance as such and not to overlook it. Then it is necessary to help the patient to the insight that we are dealing with a resistance, which fact had not been clear to him in most cases. Finally, we have to uncover the causes of the resistance and so eliminate it. In a schematic way, we may say that we have to dig in two directions for the sources of resistance. Firstly, resistances appear if we get close to a repressed complex, and more intensely the more forceful the repression has been. Secondly, resistances are encountered which are based upon the relationship of the patient to the doctor. These latter resistances are the more important ones. It is fair to say that they participate to a greater or lesser extent in every resistance. We must, therefore, briefly consider this relationship.

Every person, by this constitution as well as through childhood impressions, has acquired his own peculiar way of conducting his love life, of setting conditions for it, for choosing what instincts are to be satisfied and what goals are to be pursued. These unique tendencies will determine to a certain extent the character of each new relationship. In every person, but more so in the neurotic, a significant portion of these tendencies remains unconscious and unfulfilled. The patient whose need for love has remained largely unfulfilled moves toward every new person, including the physician, with expectations of being loved. He transfers on to the doctor not only conscious emotions such as liking, trust, etc., but also unfulfilled and unconscious love needs. This phenomenon, called transference, is not characteristic of analysis alone, but occurs with every psychological treatment of neurotics. With the other treatment modalities it simply is not uncovered as much nor traced back to its sources as it is in psychoanalysis. When we succeed, as treatment progresses, to free the libido which is fixated upon the infantile models, this liberated libido will now be cathected at first upon the physician. In most cases this is not a simple falling in love, but *all* instinctual tendencies are transferred to the doctor. Next to tender desires, and sometimes even covering them up, are hatred and defiance, thirst for power, and destructive impulses directed against the physician.

What role does transference play in analysis and what is its relation to resistance? This is a complicated subject and for reasons of brevity I will only be able to discuss some of its surface aspects. A moderate degree of transference is at first favorable for the progress of therapy, be it analytic or other types. After some time, however, it is this very transference which becomes the most powerful weapon of the resistance. This is so in regard to three main factors. In the first place, it is obvious that the patient feels embarrassed, at least consciously, about telling the doctor when tender or hostile feelings toward him rise to the surface. This often leads to silence on the part of the patient because he does not want to communicate these associations which, nevertheless, keep impinging upon his awareness. Still more frequently, those instincts which are in the process of being uncovered at that particular stage of therapy attach themselves to the person of the doctor even prior to their becoming conscious and demand fulfillment from him, again unconsciously. The content of the transference wishes thus changes with the stage of analysis, but the tendency remains the same, i.e., to transform them into actuality, as long as they are unconscious, and all this without any concern for reality. This leads to a resistance, a blockage, which may be expressed in the language of the unconscious as follows: I do not wish to be analyzed further, but rather want the doctor to fulfill my wishes. The physician will recognize the presence of a resistance, and if he focuses on presenting transference difficulties, he will successfully uncover from the patient's associations his transference wishes and so resolve them.

This amounts to a twofold gain: A further piece of resistance has been broken down and a piece of unconscious psychic life has become conscious, not only to the physician but also to the patient, and the latter is what counts.

It is, of course, the negative transference which in a very special way lends itself to resistance — hostile, defiant tendencies which, according to the infantile thought processes of the unconscious, do not wish to do the doctor the favor of making progress. Once such a resistance has been overcome by having made it conscious, therapy proceeds smoothly and the patient will spontaneously produce additional pathogenic material.

This is why I said earlier that the physician's ability at interpreting is not the most important skill, but rather his early recognition and removal of resistance. A resistance that has been overlooked and an unrecognized transference may easily lead to failure in therapy, while an incorrect interpretation tends to correct itself. The transference may be likened to a strong magnet which initially attracts the instinctual forces that are hidden in the depths where they do their damage. It performs an invaluable service in therapy in that it actualizes and makes manifest those repressed and forgotten instincts. It is therefore mainly in the area of the transference that the battle between the patient's unconscious and the physician is fought, the patient trying to realize those wishes that he unconsciously directs on to the physician, while the physician in turn forces him to content himself with insight only.

This gaining of insight leads at the same time to the gradual resolution of the transference. I have often been asked how mere insight can have such an effect. The answer is rather simple. Most of these wishes are infantile and they no longer strike us as desirable once they have become conscious. In consciousness powerful opposing forces are at work which generally are stronger than those primitive desires so that, to quote Freud, repression may be replaced by conscious condemnation. Furthermore, we must consider that particularly those desires that come out of the deepest layers of the unconscious are so excessive, so fantastic and grotesque that they cannot stand up to the clear light of day.

The instinctual forces that have been liberated from the unconscious should not remain forever tied to the physician, but must become free to be used in real life. Hence the dissolution of the transference is a further condition for a cure. For this reason we avoid all that might tie the patient more than necessary to the doctor or might even cause a permanent dependency.

The point of view, in particular is of utmost importance in therapy. Nevertheless, not all psychoanalysts do it equal justice. On the contrary, there are vast differences in viewpoint regarding it, both in theory and in practice. First of all, there is the question whether the doctor should try to influence the patient in an educational fashion or, as the problem is often expressed, whether analysis should be followed by synthesis. The next question is inseparable from the former, i.e., what attitude the analyst should take in relation to the patient's actual conflicts. The patient, in his infantile orientation toward the doctor, usually asks for advice. The analyst, on the other hand, reminds himself that most conflicts cannot be understood without bringing out in the open the instinctual forces that are unconsciously operating. He knows that he will serve the patient better by limiting himself to simply helping the patient clarify the motives that drive him toward this or that decision. This will enable the patient to make his decision all by himself.

By contrast, the Zurich School, which, without justification, continues to call its method "psychoanalysis" in spite of its basic differences, specifically deals with actual conflicts. Moreover, it wants to educate the patients so that they may become able to do justice to their "life tasks." Such a procedure, though beguiling at first glance, runs contrary to the basic tenets of analysis. It is precisely analytic investigation that has demonstrated how many neurotics have become sick while trying to sublimate their instincts beyond their capacity. By coaxing them toward sublimation they are driven more deeply into the conflict from which they had escaped into the illness.

Freud offers several suggestions for the avoidance of unnecessary transference difficulties which seem to relate to mere externals, but only apparently so, e.g., that the physician ought to sit behind the patient; that he have the physical examination done by a colleague; also that the analyst should abstain from telling his own inner experiences which he hopes might facilitate some possible confession on the part of the patient. Several other such pointers derive their inner justification from these same considerations.

Transference is not the only factor that helps in therapy. Also useful are the slowly developing intellectual interest in the procedure and the conscious wish to become free from the suffering of the neurosis. This latter point, in particular, acts as such a strong incentive that subjective improvement and a sense of well-being during therapy often are detrimental to the course of the analysis, since motivation from this source decreases.

Subjective improvement is not easy to evaluate. Frequently it is nothing but a transference success and therapeutic reverses may simply be expressions of resistance. Even after therapy has been terminated, improvement often does not occur immediately but manifests itself after some time. The reasons for this are manifold. A real difficulty blocking a definitive cure is the patient's gaining an advantage from his illness which he does not wish to forego, e.g., when a woman who is married to a callous husband will obtain more consideration from him by virtue of her suffering.

It is well known that a course of psychoanalytic treatment requires a long time. Freud figures that in general it takes six months to a year, possibly longer in severe cases, with one treatment a day. It certainly would be highly desirable to shorten the duration of treatment. Nevertheless, Freud expressly warns against any optimism in this regard by pointing out that profound psychological changes simply cannot occur overnight. The length of treatment also is hard to estimate in advance, even after a trial period of two or three weeks. This brief trial treatment, which Freud makes every patient undergo before advising him to enter analysis, is of particular diagnostic value, especially in order to separate unsuitable cases of schizophrenia from other psychogenic illnesses. The cost of treatment is rather high, in keeping with the length of time spent on it by the doctor. Nevertheless, it seldom reaches the amounts that are habitually spent for hospitalization in private sanatoria or for other forms of treatment. Nothing is asked of the patient at first but complete candor and adherence to the basic analytic rule. The chance of being lied to in analysis is not particularly great for two reasons. Firstly, most patients have a strong conscious desire for honesty. If, however, the patient tries to introduce a lie, it will have to be conceived of as another product of the psyche and no harm is done if we analyze it in the same way in which we analyze dreams. In the further course of associations the lie invariably is revealed.

The question now arises as to when we should first tell the patient anything about his unconscious wishes. Freud has given us a precise rule to answer this question: Not before a workable transference relationship has been established and then not until resistance has for the first time taken over the transference. For the first communication to the patient as well as for all subsequent ones we make it a rule to proceed with the utmost caution and to say something only when the patient has arrived near the repressed complex through his own insight. Otherwise we provoke unnecessary resistances or meet with a complete lack of understanding. It is as though we were to confront a person in his everyday life with his unconscious motives, e.g., if we were to tell an overprotective mother that she harbors death wishes against her children. This would lead to nothing but bitterness which would be all the greater the more accurate our evaluation. But since in analysis we do not say anything until the patient can almost grasp it with his own hands, we have a chance to talk about sexual topics, for example, without hurting the patient, and much more easily than is the case in a non-analytic setting. The reaction that occurs upon such a communication has to be well understood. There may be an immediate insight which the patient admits with a feeling of relief. Or, agreement may manifest itself by the sudden disappearance of a symptom which had occurred during treatment. In other cases the patient may confront the doctor with a conscious "no" and yet bring in relevant associations that lead him to the proper insight. In some cases where the physician has not hit the mark, the patient's criticism may be awakened which reveals that the patient knows better, and after a few associations will bring about the solution to the riddle.

There is a remaining question to discuss concerning what doctors and what patients are suitable for analysis. What we demand of the physician besides theoretical knowledge is that he be free of unresolved repressions. If he harbors within himself resistances against the recognition of his own complexes, he will overlook these complexes in his patients or at least evaluate them wrongly. Every unresolved repression in the doctor, according to an apt expression by Stekel, amounts to a blind spot in his analytic perception. Thus Freud rightly demands that whoever wishes to practice analysis must first undergo an analysis himself or at least undertake a serious self-analysis, particularly of his own dreams. Furthermore, it is necessary that the analyst continue to analyze himself so that he be conscious of a possible counter-transference or counterresistance. We might also think that the analyst ought to have a splendid memory in order to retain the thousands of details and associations of his different patients and to utilize them at the proper moment. This, however, is not the case. The physician accomplishes his task by allowing all the patient's productions to reach him with an equal interest without making a selection. The psychological situation that results makes the physician absorb the patient's communications via his own unconscious, so that he unconsciously recognizes the connections. Thus he is able at the proper moment to reproduce all associations, dreams or data pertaining to an association. He is able to do this only if he has no resistances within himself against any insights.

Finally, we now come to the question as to which patients are suitable for analysis. This question about indications cannot be answered exactly yet, which is not surprising for a relatively new method. Quite generally we may say that we require of patients a certain level of intelligence and of ethical standards. Furthermore, patients over fifty are unfavorable, because older people generally are neither willing nor able to transform all values as occurs in analysis. However, some patients over fifty who suffered from depression have been successfully analyzed.

Furthermore, the patient must be capable of a psychologically normal state, from which the pathological material may be tackled. In other words, he must not be permanently confused or severely melancholy. It also seems that a pronounced degenerative constitution acts as a barrier to the effectiveness of analysis. However, a definitive statement cannot as yet be made about the meaning of constitutional factors.

As far as specific indications are concerned, we will consider as positive all cases of chronic psychoneuroses, particularly those without stormy or threatening symptoms, since analysis cannot concern itself for some time with the possible continuation of symptoms. Hence we include all kinds of obsessive neuroses, obsessive ideation, compulsions, phobias, anxiety states, somatic manifestations of hysteria or, to avoid the loaded concept of hysteria, psychogenic somatic manifestations.

Full-fledged perversions generally are not numbered among the treatment possibilities of psychoanalysis. Experiences with the analysis of manic-depressive states and milder cases of schizophrenia are no doubt encouraging, but clear guidelines for therapeutic indications are still missing. It would appear that the patient's ability to establish a workable positive transference with the physician is a major prerequisite for the success of therapy.

However, cases of the above-mentioned forms of psychoneurosis have been cured after they had resisted all other forms of therapy. Obviously, those cases that come to analysis at the present time are the most severe ones, after having already unsuccessfully tried other forms of therapy. What is unique about the effect of analysis is that not only does it free patients of their symptoms, but it removes all their inner difficulties which they had in dealing with life, and it especially helps them properly to adjust to the environment. Many a marriage that might have floundered because of the neurosis of one of the partners has become healthy through analysis, because the patient became able to direct all his forces toward his marital partner, forces that previously were fixated upon infantile models. Obviously, not even analysis can change constitution. It can liberate a person whose hands and feet were tied so that he may freely use his strength again, but it cannot give him new arms and legs. But it has shown us that many factors that we had believed to be constitutional are no more than consequences of blockages of growth, blockages which can be resolved.

2

The Misuse of Psychoanalysis (1933)

At the invitation of Franz Alexander, Karen Horney moved to the United States in September 1932 to become associate director of the newly formed Chicago Psychoanalytic Institute. She had studied English in school, and in November 1932 she presented her first paper in America, "Psychogenic Factors in Functional Female Disorders." "The Misuse of Psychoanalysis" is dated July 20, 1933. Undoubtedly given as a talk, it was never published, although an accompanying outline describes it as an article. Horney's English is quite good considering how recently she had begun writing in that language, but the paper seems to be a draft, and it has numerous imperfections. I have edited it slightly to improve its coherence and readability. I found this essay among Harold Kelman's papers at the Postgraduate Center for Mental Health and have placed the original in the Karen Horney Papers, located in the Manuscript and Archives division of Yale University Library.

The widespread interest aroused by psychoanalysis certainly is justified because it offers an excellent means of understanding not only our own conflicts and conflicts in family life, but also problems of such general importance as the motives of crime or of suicide, or the attitudes we assume toward social phenomena like economic depression and political or revolutionary movements.

When I have read an analytical paper to a lay audience, I am often left with a dubious feeling, however, wondering whether or not the information which has been received with apparently so much enthusiasm is more of a benefit or a danger.

We human beings are a queer sort of mixture of god and animal, and the animal within us seizes every opportunity to make mischief, to reach its own goals, independent of our godlike side. It might therefore be a wise thing for me once to play the role the fool plays in Shakespearean drama, and to show the opposite side of the picture, the misuses of psychoanalysis.

First of all I am thinking of people who feel the pathological urge always to tell the truth, pathetic people who are deceiving themselves on some fundamental trends in their lives and therefore have to be compulsively honest on the surface. Certainly they are very unpleasant companions. Knowing something about analysis, such people may, for instance, tell an overprotective mother who constantly worries that her child may be drowned while swimming, or might have some accident when crossing the street, "To tell you the truth, I think you are only torturing that child; you must have very intense death wishes against it." Or they may tell a very prudish woman who does not dare to seek any company without her husband, "My dear girl, I know what is the matter with you, you must have a strong wish to be unfaithful to your husband and are afraid of it." Or to a woman who pretends that her husband does not want to go out without her, they may explain that this is probably a disguise for her terrible jealousy. Or to a father who considers no man good enough to marry his daughter and who ascribes it to a highly developed sense of paternal responsibility, they may say that he in reality wants to keep the daughter for himself and is jealous of every man approaching her. Or to a girl who sacrifices her life for her mother and finds a deep moral satisfaction in doing so: "You must have terribly deep feelings of guilt toward your mother and certainly must hate her. All your sacrifice is nothing but making good for these impulses." Or when they happen to meet other people who likewise make a fetish of truth-telling and are proud of what they consider their sincerity, they may say, "You do nothing but indulge in your sadism."

Such unpleasantly disposed people have always existed, but analysis might lend them more dangerous weapons than they had before. If they happen to have some intuitive understanding, it might help them to pounce upon the most vulnerable point in others. What may occur in these cases is, at best, that the others think them to be fools. At worst, they may stir up acute feelings of guilt or anxiety.

This could easily happen if someone were to be made abruptly aware of unconscious motives. A woman I have seen in my analytical practice believed that nothing was as alien to her as jealousy. There was an intense mutual attachment between her and her father, and during puberty the girl went through an intense period in which jealousy of the mother was identical with wanting to kill her, so that jealousy meant for the daughter the culmination of all evil. Note that these death wishes toward the mother did not remain wholly in the realm of phantasy. The mother suffered from a severe heart disease, the girl had often heard people say that sudden excitement could really kill her, and she was tempted to cause such excitement. This situation naturally produced a deep feeling of guilt, a repression of all jealous feelings, and the creation of an ideal of being perfectly devoid of jealousy, which served to cover up her most intense fears.

How are we to proceed in her analysis? For a long time our only care will be to create a feeling of security because such a woman, condemning these trends in herself so vehemently, will automatically assume that everyone else must condemn them in the same way. But in time she will gradually realize the possibility of aggressive drives existing in all of us, even toward beloved persons; and she will slowly understand how she could not help being driven into these conflicts, how she fought against them, and how they influenced her later life. But all this will be the work of long months if the analysis is to liberate her from the pressure without shattering her, as a bald analytic observation from a friend might do.

Likewise, it may be quite dangerous to interpret dreams when people describe them in company. A professional analyst often feels very much embarrassed on such occasions and finds a more or less adequate excuse for remaining silent. But dreams often have such a transparent symbolism that some people cannot resist interpreting them, and thus they reveal in public the most primitive drives of the dreamer.

Several motives may be active in these compulsive truth-tellers. They may be seeking an outlet for their own aggressions. They may feel it is their function to bring illumination to their friends, an activity that is usually not appreciated because people have good reasons for wanting to keep their illusions. . . . Or they may aspire to be omniscient. For these people, a situation in which they do not know everything better than others is a serious threat to their self-confidence. Analyzing other people is a harmless sport, so long as they keep their superior knowledge to themselves, but very dangerous if they want to impress other people with it.

The people who aspire to omniscience will expect analysis to fulfill all of their secret hopes: to be perfectly good, perfectly happy, and master over life and death. For instance, knowing that an illness *may* have psychological causes, they will expect an analysis to protect them from ever getting sick, and they will resent any indisposition of the analyst as a deep flaw. Since they project their own desire for omniscience upon the analyst, these people have an uncomfortable feeling when an analyst enters the room, as though a strange power enabled him to look into the most secret corners of the heart.

Some people use their psychological knowledge as a justification for their own lack of pity and social responsibility. Knowing that illness *may* be caused by a wish, they may say to someone, "You only have gotten ill because you wanted to spoil my pleasure or to spite me." Realizing that an accident *may* be induced by an unconscious need for self-punishment, they will assume that the victim has induced it himself and is deriving satisfaction from it. Or being aware that failing to find a job *may* be the result of certain infantile trends, they will generalize such possibilities and think that people who are out of work only have a childish desire to be taken care of.

A perfect nuisance in this respect are those who are starting to go through their own analysis. They often are dangerously enthusiastic. They know for sure that appendicitis is nothing but an expression of a conflict, that a person who is short of breath certainly is not right in his sexual life, that a heart attack undoubtedly is a fit of acute rage, that a Communist certainly is a person who wants to kill his father and enjoy common possession of the mother-soil, and that a monarchist is one who has adopted a passive attitude toward his father. They know that the only thing to do is to analyze the appendicitis or the Communistic tendencies and are convinced that everybody around them ought to be analyzed. This is nothing new. Their zeal is similar to that of religious converts, and they contribute something to the reputation of psychoanalysis as a religious sect.

Others for whom analytical half-knowledge may be dangerous are those who play a martyr role. Their psychological structure is, roughly speaking, like this: They have suffered a great deal from some sort of unjust treatment in childhood and have consequently accumulated an explosive amount of bottled-up rage within them. They feel guilty about this rage and repress it, but unsuccessfully, since it keeps seeking an outlet. Because of their feeling of guilt, it cannot come out directly, so they have to seek some justification for it. And they find a justification for aggression in being treated badly themselves. They are convinced that other people have been cruel and nasty and that they, the innocent ones, are perfectly justified in blaming them. Such people either have a talent for provoking others to treat them badly without being aware of it, or they may be very keen in discerning evil intentions and hostile motives in others.

Insofar as analysis involves the capacity for guessing fundamental attitudes by means of trivial signs, martyr-types use their knowledge to reveal the dreadful hostility which the world shows toward them. A wife, for instance, will feel that she is modest in her claims and that her husband certainly is culpable for not fulfilling the few little wishes she has, like coming home on time for dinner or mailing a letter. Knowing that coming late or forgetting something *may* be an expression of antagonism, she will make violent reproaches and tell her husband that these little trifles just show all his concealed hatred for her. The mistake such people are making is that they analyze only their partners, in a one-sided way, and are not aware that they have provoked them by their own nagging and have exaggerated the signs of hostility. Such a mistake is facilitated by the fact that all of us see more clearly the mote in the eye of the other than the beam in our own.

In marriage, an underlying hostility will often betray itself in money matters. A husband may consider himself generous because he gives luxurious presents but feel upset when his wife asks him for a reasonable amount of money. If such a husband has looked into Freud's papers, he may point out to his wife that all women want to castrate men and that asking him for money is just her way of doing so. Before she acquired psychoanalytic knowledge, the wife may only have thought him somewhat queer, but now she may think of the title of one of my papers which implies that men have dread of women ["The Dread of Woman"] and point out to him that this is certainly an expression of his fear of women, thus hurting his masculine pride. Such controversies have always existed in marriage, but sometimes it seems as if the addition of a little analytical knowledge has made them more poisonous.

I have said that usually we see the weakness of others more clearly than our own, but there is an exception to this rule. Some people are always hunting for faults within themselves. I remember, for instance, a patient who, after his wife left him, fell into a depression. Apparently the wife had been sadistic, pleasure-seeking, and unfaithful to him. But he accounted for the failure of his marital life by saying that she was young, beautiful, had been educated in a different way, and had been seduced by her environment. The real fault was his. He had identified himself with his father and had tried to be a tyrant toward her. Not only that, but he had not gotten enough affection from his mother and was love-hungry and sensitive to every denial. He managed in this way to overcome all the underlying rage he had toward women in general and his wife in particular. This rage and his fear of it were shown clearly during analysis of his earlier memories and phantasies. But he had put his self-analysis into the service of repressing his hostility, and thus creating a false picture of the whole situation. He became more and more overwhelmed by feelings of guilt, which he succeeded in overemphasizing.

Speaking of feelings of guilt makes me think of the possible danger of an analytical half-knowledge when used by the Catholic Church in confes-

sion. . . . Neurotic persons very often suffer from too strict demands of con-
science, not realizing the truth of the saying that good people are those who
only have evil thoughts, while bad people act upon them. They condemn their
thoughts, their feelings, their phantasies, as though they were doing evil by
having them. . . . I don't want to discuss the value of confession. It certainly has
its psychologically good side, and it has its very dangerous side, but I am afraid
the danger might be immensely increased if analytical knowledge enables the
priest to dig up every secret and hidden impulse — particularly since he is in
authority and therefore has the power to awaken feelings of guilt.

Psychoanalysis is misused when it is attempted by people who are not well
trained for it (wild analysis). People avoid going to a surgeon who has not
learned the proper technique, but they apparently have a notion that the soul
is less vulnerable, and therefore they do not mind going to a physician who is
not specifically trained for analytical work. There is a certain justification for
that attitude in so far as a bad analysis usually doesn't kill anyone, while a bad
operation might do so.

The main danger in a wild analysis is the misuse of the emotional relationship which is established between the analyst and the patient. There is a widespread misunderstanding about that relationship, as though the patient always fell in love with the analyst or as though he had to fall in love with the
analyst if the analysis is to be successful. What happens in reality is this: the
patient will carry over those emotional attitudes which he has established in
his ordinary life into the analytical situation. If he has a fear of getting attached
to someone, he will show the same fear towards the analyst. If he has a fear of
being deceived and cheated, he will have the same fear in regard to the analysis. If he is liable to repress his criticism by a facile enthusiasm, he will react
the same way in analysis.

Thus far there is nothing particular in the situation, nothing which doesn't
happen in the same way in relation to a teacher or to a maid, to a husband or to
any authority. Yet there are factors which give the emotional relationship in
the analytical situation a specific character and strength. Because the patient is
asked to display an unusual degree of sincerity and to say everything that
passes through his mind, the infantile character of his reactions will eventually
appear, and the part of his personality which has not gone through processes
of social adjustment will emerge. In the emotional relation to the analyst
infantile trends will appear in their crude forms of love-demands, hatred,
destructive impulses, mistrust, spite, etc. The relation of the patient to the
analyst will thus be very dramatic and highly charged with emotion. A strong
bond will be built up by powerful positive or negative feelings being "transferred" to the analyst. Because the analyst does not reject him but feels a wish

to understand him apart from the "transference" reaction, the patient will express many thoughts which he has never told to anyone and has not even admitted to himself. Furthermore, he will become tied to the analyst by expecting from him a fulfillment of all his secret infantile hopes, though consciously he may have only a reasonable wish to be cured of his symptoms. These tendencies account for the exceptional emotional bond in the analysis.

This may seem to be an unnecessary difficulty in the analysis, but it is, in fact, not only unavoidable but also indispensable. It is, in a well-conducted analysis, one of the chief means of cure insofar as the patient really experiences emotional drives within him which otherwise he never recognizes, seeing only their results in the reactions he elicits from the outside world. The foremost law for the analyst is not to react emotionally to the patient's positive and negative feelings but to use them as a means for uncovering the driving forces at work in him. There is great danger in an analytical treatment in which the doctor is not master of the situation. Instead of being cured, the patient may slide into a lasting dependency on the analyst or may be pushed deeper into his neurosis. Analysis, as well as surgery, requires knowledge and experience in a specific technique.

Psychoanalysis is easily open to misuse since it deals with human relations. The findings of analysis have led to a particular stress on the conflicts we experience in childhood. When analyzing any form of neurosis, any inhibition or character deviation, we can always trace back these manifestations to some conflict situation in childhood. Prophylaxis being the most noble branch of medicine, we naturally wonder if we cannot prevent later neuroses by applying analytical knowledge to child-rearing. . . . Realizing that every child suffers from some conflicts and that such conflicts *may* lead to a neurosis, some people claim that every child ought to be analyzed, a conclusion which seems premature, since a certain amount of conflict, if it is not excessive, may be indispensable for further development.

Another unfortunate influence of psychoanalysis may be observed in some parents. If they have heard something about the bad consequences of repression, they feel that they are caught between the devil and the deep blue sea. On the one hand, they know that children must adjust to society, implying repression of primitive drives, while, on the other hand, they are afraid of making children neurotic by thwarting their vital demands, so that they are liable to be too indulgent. Or if parents have heard of the fear and spite reactions of children toward grownups, they may try to descend to an infantile level themselves and thus create a false situation.

The fear of repression is not confined to children alone. Surveying historical periods, we find ourselves going through extremes of various kinds. Twenty or thirty years ago, there was an undervaluation and repression of sexuality. Nowadays, there is an overvaluation of sexuality and an almost pathological fear of repression. Much bewilderment has been caused by confusing repression with control. Repression means overcoming impulses by banishing them from our conscious mind. Control means facing the impulses existing within us and mastering them. Control, by the way, is the aim of analysis.

The kinds of problems I have cited are not peculiar to psychoanalysis. Every new remedy and every new philosophy goes through stages of being overvalued, undervalued, and indiscriminately employed. Analysis has been a fad for some time now, for it is a means of talking about sex in what seems to be a scientific way. This has led to the impression that analysis deals only with sex, while in reality it has to do with human conflicts in general. It is a wonderful therapeutic instrument, as long as it is recognized as a radical procedure requiring exact knowledge in order to be conducted successfully.

As far as casual applications are concerned, we should be aware of what may be stirred up in another person and realize the danger that we may be using, or misusing, psychoanalytic insights in the service of our own primitive, uncontrolled tendencies. For people who cannot desist from casual applications, I should like to emphasize in closing that this requires kindness and tolerance. The sentence *Nihil humani a me alienum puto* — "I think nothing human is alien to me" — should stand in the background of every analytical application.

3

Conceptions and Misconceptions of the Analytical Method (1935)

This essay began as a paper entitled "Misuses of Psychoanalysis in Daily Practice," presented to the Chicago Psychoanalytic Society in the late fall of 1933, probably as a sequel to "The Misuse of Psychoanalysis." Horney delivered an expanded version, now entitled "Concepts and Misconcepts of the Psychoanalytic Method," to a combined meeting of the New York Neurological Society and the Society of Neurology and Psychiatry of the Academy of Medicine in New York in January 1934. A summary of that talk was published in the Archives of Neurology and Psychiatry *32 (1934), 880–81. Horney revised the paper again and published it as "Conceptions and Misconceptions of the Analytical Method" in the* Journal of Nervous and Mental Disease *81 (1935), 399–410.*

This essay marks the first appearance of Horney's unorthodox ideas about therapy. With its emphasis on understanding the patient's behavior in terms of its function within the present structure of the personality, it constitutes a major departure from the Freudian method of trying to connect current behavior directly to its early origins. It is difficult to say how long the ideas in this essay had been gestating. There is evidence that Horney began to develop them while she was still in Germany. In New Ways in Psychoanalysis, *she writes that during the time of her "dimly perceived doubts as to the validity of psychoanalytical theo-*

ries," she was stimulated and encouraged by two of her colleagues in Berlin: Harald Schultz-Hencke "questioned the curative value of infantile memories and emphasized the necessity of analyzing primarily the actual conflict situation"; and Wilhelm Reich "pointed out the necessity of analyzing in the first instance the defensive character trends a neurotic has built up" (1939, 12).

We cannot say whether Horney taught such ideas in Berlin, but we know that she began to do so soon after she arrived in Chicago, liberated, perhaps, by her new environment. She herself credits "the greater freedom from dogmatic beliefs" that she found in the United States with alleviating "the obligation of taking psychoanalytical theories for granted" and giving her "the courage to proceed along the lines" that she "considered right" (1939, 12). Notes from her courses at the Chicago and Washington-Baltimore institutes are in the Karen Horney Papers at Yale. Her first biographer, Jack Rubins, has provided the following account of her students' recollections of her courses in Chicago:

> [They were] exciting and innovative. They combined the old and the new. She continued to use such classical concepts as transference, unconscious oedipal feelings and defenses against them, death wishes, castration anxiety, and oral or anal needs. In combination with these, she introduced newer interpersonal and culturally oriented defensive stances like unemotionality, intellectualization, seeming obedience and compliance, propitiating attitudes and needs for superiority. In her technique, she would start analyzing the more conscious, on-going attitudes and gradually penetrate to the deeper, earlier childhood ones, always emphasizing the need to seek each and all intermediate attitudes responsible for the preceding [sic] one. Resistances had to be analyzed — or at least worked on — first. Behavior manifested toward the analyst had to be considered first in terms of unconscious present feelings toward others. Only then could they [sic] be seen in terms of infantile attitudes toward parents, now being transferred onto the analyst. (1978, 181)

Within a few years, Horney had almost completely abandoned the old ideas in this mixture and had set out to reinvent psychoanalysis. According to Franz Alexander, he and Horney did not get along in Chicago because he felt that she was too radical: "Hers was a revolutionary approach which implied the repudiation of so many of Freud's fundamental concepts" (quoted by Rubins 1978, 185). Her colleagues at the New York Psychoanalytic Institute were to be even more disturbed by her ideas.

From a scientific point of view, it seems useless to discuss gross individual misconceptions of psychoanalysis which arise from lack of knowledge or a reluctance to follow in detail a psychological approach which is not only complex but also foreign to customary medical thinking. It might be of value, however, to discuss the basic misconception that there is no psychoanalytic method at all, a misconception which one encounters in psychiatrists who have been open-minded enough to read a great deal of psychoanalytic literature and to make their own attempts at analyses, but have supplemented the knowledge they have gained from books only by fortuitous and not always accurate information received from the remarks of patients and other analysts.

The impression which they usually obtain from these sources may be summarized in this way: The psychoanalytic procedure is based on the free-association of the patient. The analyst is dependent on what the patient chooses to tell him. The analyst usually veils himself in silence ("the myth of the silent analyst") and only now and then makes some wise-cracks which he calls interpretations. These interpretations chiefly concern connections which the analyst constructs between present actions, attitudes and symptoms of the patient, and childhood experiences mainly of a sexual nature and supposedly radiating from the so-called Oedipus complex. The interpretations are of an arbitrary character both in content and sequence. There is no assurance of correctness and relevance and no guarantee against the analyst's power of suggesting thoughts alien to the patient. The analysis takes a long time, the outcome is difficult to estimate, and there remains a secret or expressed doubt whether or not the benevolent interest of an understanding physician for the same length of time might not have led to the same result. Testing the procedure is only possible after having submitted to the same process oneself as in an initiation rite.

Allowing for some exaggeration, we may raise the question whether such a picture of analysis should be called a misconception or approximates the true state of affairs. In fact, some ten or twenty years ago, analysis did not present a very different aspect. It contained, so far as the activity of the analyst was concerned, too many arbitrary factors to deserve to be called a method. There was a vagueness about the procedure which showed itself, for instance, in the fact that when discussing a case three analysts might have three different concepts about its structure.

As a result of efforts from several angles, a change is gradually taking place, and psychoanalysis is becoming a describable and teachable method. My aim in this paper is not to give a detailed description of the technique but only to select certain points which are of methodological importance.

Analysis is based on the free-association of the patients. The patient is asked to acknowledge and to express every slight detail which occurs to him. This implies the working hypothesis, not yet contradicted by the facts, that the content of verbal associations or emotions which come up in close temporal relation have an inner connection of some sort even though there is no apparent logical link between them. If, for instance, a patient tells us that she does not like to go to parties or social gatherings and then immediately thinks of several examples of how hypersensitive she is to every criticism in past and present time, we feel justified in suspecting that her dislike for parties has something to do with her fear of being exposed to criticism.

By listening carefully and attempting not to select particular elements in accordance with preconceived ideas or theories, we may gain a preliminary impression of what factors play a rôle in the life of each personality. In other words, the verbal statements of the patient represent the first kind of data on which we base our knowledge.

Assuming that the patient does not lie consciously, these data are, however, subjective and incomplete in two respects: (1) There may be a distortion of *facts*. For instance, if a patient tells us that she has been maltreated by her mother, at first, we cannot verify the extent to which this is true, nor judge how far the patient exaggerates from a need for self-justification. Also, we cannot judge how cruel the mother really was and how far the punishments were provoked by the patient herself. Or if a patient tells us that all the teachers in her school are homosexual we do not know whether this statement is true or is merely the result of observations tinged by her own homosexual tendencies. If a patient tells us that all men are brutes and all women are treacherous, we would discount such avowals in an analytical hour just as we would in outside conversation. We would in both cases only think that the person must have emotional reasons for seeing certain aspects of life in this particular way.

Another reason for the unreliability of the verbal statement is the fact that the patient, as well as every other human being, is liable to deceive himself about his own *feelings* or *motives* for having certain feelings. One may hear at the beginning of an analysis that the patient considers himself very happily married, but some time later he realizes that he hates his wife intensely and has not dared to admit it to himself. Or a patient may come to the analysis with the conviction that she is deeply devoted to her mother and it may take some time to be able to discriminate how much genuine attachment there really is, and how much the attachment is an over-compensation for some violent hatred which has been instigated by feelings of guilt and fear. Or a patient may tell us with subjective honesty that she has no desire other than to have an affair with a man or to marry, while a closer investigation later may reveal a marked antagonism against men and certain non-sexual motives for being impelled toward them.

On the basis of these experiences we would be inclined to say, in contrast to assertions made in defense of the dependability of the questionnaire method as opposed to analysis, that these direct statements of investigated persons are in no way reliable.

Fortunately we can supplement them by other kinds of data which are more dependable, namely, our own observations of the patient's behavior as it is shown in his manner of associating and in his attitudes in the analytical situation.

The manner in which various patients associate is very different. Some patients do not associate freely at all but deliberately choose topics and control their emotions. Others try to give an organized report of their life or to follow systematically and intellectually certain problems which come up. Some talk in a rather unemotional and detached way as though they were interested onlookers. In other cases, one becomes aware, after some time, that they never talk about their present life situation and never mention anything about their relations to the analyst. The type of association may also vary, during one and the same analysis, from stammering, punctuated with long pauses, to a flight of ideas, and from an emotional outpouring to abstract philosophizing or theorizing embellished with analytical terms.

Also there are very precise, observable differences in the attitudes which the patient shows in the analytical situation including attempts to keep the relation quite impersonal and to have an impenetrable politeness, a more or less covert attitude of suspicion, a general apprehensiveness or an overt fear, a demanding attitude, amorous behavior, hostility or hostile aggressiveness, a provocative attitude, a careless attitude, or a tendency toward deceitfulness.

We may particularly observe *emotional changes* in reaction to the analyst's behavior or statements. To select a very simple example, one may observe different reactions to the analyst's cancelling an hour or being late. One patient may react to it with over-jealousy. Another one may suddenly become very critical of the analyst, while pretending not to have any objections to the cancellation at all, but on the contrary, to be glad about the additional free time, thus revealing a characteristic denial of disappointment and an ignorance of the hostility which was a reaction to the disappointment. Or to give a more complex illustration, one may observe that a patient who has done quite well suddenly becomes desperate, fills his time with complaining that he is unable to accomplish anything not only in the analysis but in his work, that the analysis is of no use at all, and that he might just as well quit and reconcile himself to the idea of remaining neurotic all his life, and finally he ends by expressing the conviction that the analyst is thoroughly bored with him and dislikes him.

In contrast to the patient's verbal statements, these moods have the advantage of being directly observable, and training in making observations quickly and accurately is possible.

In a case like the last one mentioned, I have learned from experience to distinguish clearly between the various elements just as a person trained in microscopic observation will see the details of tissue structure and recognize their importance, where I would only see an accumulation of cells. What I see in this situation is: something must have happened which has made it particularly necessary to a patient that I like him, something which has increased his need for affection from me. On the other hand, some obstacle must be in the way, so that he cannot reach out frankly for my affection but jumps directly to the conclusion that I dislike him. It is probably some feeling of guilt which gives him the conviction that he is utterly unlovable. Having a particular need for my affection and feeling at the same time that he does not want it, he probably has become very antagonistic toward me. But the same feeling of guilt which accounts for this dilemma also hinders him from being openly antagonistic. It forces him to express his anger in disguised ways: he does not cooperate, he tells me practically in so many words, "Look how miserable you have made me." This reproach probably is at the same time a relief inasmuch as the patient now puts the blame on me and in addition pays for his guilt by suffering.

This much I would deduce from having observed these single trends: veiled antagonism + veiled accusation — feeling dislike — a self-depreciative attitude — suffering + disposition to accept the suffering as an unalterable fate. This tentative picture is an artificial construction but its plausibility is confirmed by the fact that in a great number of similar reactions the connecting links are more evident and show just this dynamic structure.

If now — as in the case I am thinking of — I know from the preceding parts of the analysis that it is a fact that this patient has strong guilt feelings, that he does always reach out for affection or approval as a reassurance against this feeling, and that he does very easily feel rejected and does respond with hostility, then I feel justified in interpreting tentatively the observed picture in the indicated way. In this case, the patient confirmed it by telling me that some days ago an infantile memory had come up containing an anal fantasy accompanied by sharp feelings of guilt, and that this guilt had been reinforced by his not having told it to me in the subsequent interviews. This gave me access to an understanding of his guilt feelings on the basis of surviving fantasies. Both kinds of data, the communications of the patient and our own observations, supplement each other. The observations alone, though accurate, give us no clue to the reasons why a patient acts in a certain way. The patient will never tell us directly, so we use the content of his associations to explain his attitudes or, more precisely, we discern the immediate causes for them and the function they perform in the present situation.

It is important to understand these attitudes because we rely on them for further interpretation for the following three reasons: (1) Because we can observe these attitudes, we are on safe ground in interpreting them as long as we avoid all uncertain statements such as direct deduction about childhood situations. Take the case of a patient who is very eager to bring everything to my attention which he considers important. After some time it strikes me that his attitude toward me is utterly impersonal, he has no affection, no antagonism, no fear — just a complete blank. He has told me in the meantime about his deep antagonism against his mother, mostly disguised by a fine understanding between them but sometimes coming out in unexpected outbreaks of hatred which could not be accounted for by the given situation. He also has told me that his opinion about himself vacillates between considering himself unusually gifted and feeling exceedingly stupid, especially when he has to encounter new situations. He also tells me how readily he becomes conscience-stricken and how he has to take pains to do everything correctly. The first thing I recognize is that the efforts which the patient apparently makes to meet the analytic demands are dictated by the motive of having to act correctly and living up to expectations. The next thing I do is to draw his attention to his impersonal attitudes and in response to this I learn of his apprehensions about being regarded as stupid. My interpretation restricts itself to showing him the connection between his attempts to be rational and impersonal and his fear of being ridiculed and disliked. I leave aside all interpretations which would imply a similarity between his attitude to his mother and to me for the simple reason that I do not know enough about the implications of his relation to his mother.

(2) The second reason why we start from the patient's attitudes and the immediate motives for them is that it is useless for a patient who wants to have nothing to do with women to get the idea that this is because he was disappointed by his mother or intimidated by his father. It may be true but it would mean giving him the first and the last link in a chain with all intermediate links missing. The intervening facts may be that he has withdrawn from girls as a little boy, that he has developed a rich fantasy life, that he has masturbated with considerable guilt feelings, that as an older boy he became aware that he could not fight with other boys, and could not approach girls the way the other

boys could, and that he then felt thoroughly inferior, and developed a compensatory ambition in mental fields with a tremendous need to be superior there to such a high degree that other more primitive satisfactions no longer matter much to him. If one sketches this one possibility of how a life may really develop, each step conditioning the next one, then it is apparent that interpretations which connect the present difficulties immediately with influences in childhood are scientifically only half-truths and practically useless. The practical outcome will be only that the patient will leave the analysis with a great deal of interesting knowledge about himself in particular and about analysis in general without any of his attitudes really changing.

There is still a third reason why we have to start from understanding the patient's spontaneous attitudes: if we do not, they may serve as an impediment to further understanding. One may observe this very clearly in analyses which are undertaken without sufficient training. To give one of many examples: a younger colleague of mine who was a beginner in analysis had started to analyze a woman with phobias of touching objects which were touched by other persons, a phobia which eventually confined her to bed. He had obtained certain data of her history. Her father had been very violent and had preferred her brother to her. Her mother had neglected her and had had affairs with men. In her adolescence she had been maltreated by an aunt. She had been capable and ambitious until she had become paralyzed by her phobias. The attitudes which she now showed were rather alarming. She was domineering, extremely demanding, and displayed a very destructive hostility against the analyst, wishing to ruin his reputation and to put him into embarrassing situations. At the same time she made love to him in a very demonstrative way, exposing herself and asking him for sexual attentions. These attitudes were so prominent for a period of several months that the analysis became completely stagnant. The psychiatrist had failed to understand the immediate causes for these attitudes but had tried to interpret them partly as revenge against all the injury which she had suffered from her father, and partly as an identification with the mother. Such was the state of the analysis when the case was brought to my attention. It was clear that as long as these attitudes persisted in dominating the situation nothing could be accomplished. We therefore focused our attention upon understanding the truest reasons for them. Omitting technical details, the result was as follows: My colleague had not seen that all these attitudes were designed to offset the patient's intense fear that the analyst would get rid of her if he discovered that something was wrong with her. All her life she had been afraid. When she married she had concealed severe abdominal pains from her husband because she was afraid he might reject her.

All her life she had asked, "Am I all right?" She had worked hard and tried to accomplish something in order to justify her existence. We came to understand that the immediate function of all her alarming attitudes represented different ways of defending herself against this fear. Her domineering and exacting pose served her as means to intimidate others and thus prevent an expected attack, while her love-making served as a desperate means to bind the analyst emotionally to herself and thus to change him from a condemning judge into a condoning lover. Her hostility really meant an attempt to destroy him, since this was the only radical way of getting rid of an enemy by whom she feared to be detected and destroyed herself. Her behavior was that of an animal who will kill another animal by whom it feels attacked. After we understood in what way and to what degree her seemingly contradictory behavior was dictated by an intense fear, the reasons why she was so afraid could then be tackled and gradually came out.

The same applies to all attitudes. As long as a patient, for instance, has the tendency to be submissive and obedient to the analyst, (this particular type has been described by Clara Thompson in " 'Dutiful Child' Resistance") he will be liable to accept everything which the analyst says in order to please him, without ever questioning his conviction. Or if a patient is fundamentally suspicious he must necessarily receive every interpretation with the secret suspicion that it is all sham and suggestion. It is therefore not only a matter of scientific honesty but of practical interest to start from understanding the surface attitudes. If one constantly proceeds in this way, always analyzing only the immediate motives for the observable attitudes of the patient, one traces gradually the emotional causal chains which lead from the present symptoms to the earliest shaping influences in infancy.

How this may be done is illustrated by the following fragment of a case, in diagrammatic form. For the sake of clarity I am condensing the material which appeared in five months and am leaving out all details and intermediate vicious circles. It concerns a patient who was afraid to go out alone and to stay anywhere where she could not leave at a moment's notice. Of her history, she gave the following data: her father had spoiled her by lavishing presents and admiration on her; she had been queen in the sorority; she had always had admiring men surrounding her. Her breakdown had occurred after her father and her husband suffered financial losses which put an end to her being spoiled. The attitude which she had toward life consisted in being very self-righteous and demanding, as she herself expressed with the words, "I have a divine right to receive." These excessive claims were the first to show in the analysis. She expected to get well without revealing her difficulties. She made special claims as to time, wanted to have her hour changed, come on Sundays, etc. She expected the analyst to admire her. She expressed a claim to have the best analyst in the world. Her whole family had to make sacrifices in order to make her analysis possible. Very soon she showed signs of intense anger and resentment. She complained bitterly that the analyst treated her as if she did not amount to anything, and she showed her resentment by an increase of her symptoms for which she held the analyst responsible. This anger represented a reaction to the denial of her claims, "the rage of a thwarted queen." After having observed this reaction in the analytic situation, she could understand that this reaction was typical of her in every situation where she felt thwarted. In diagrammatic form:

excessive claims → *hostility*

The next thing which came up was envy toward the analyst in the form of a resentful pondering on his alleged privileges and superiority, also accompanied by intense hostility. After this reaction was uncovered, she confirmed it by giving a great deal of data about how she was intensely envious of people who had any real or alleged advantage. For instance she said that she wanted to kick every woman who was better dressed than she was. In diagrammatic form:

excessive claims → *hostility*
↘   ↗
envy

At the same time we were able to understand part of her apprehensiveness as a retaliation fear in reference to her hostility. In addition to this it was observable that when she felt hostile to the analyst, without becoming fully aware of her hostility or the reasons for it, she spontaneously felt apprehensive. This connection shed light upon the anxiety she felt in the presence of other women. Both had the same origin in her awakening hostilities. The inexorable law of retaliation led her to suspect aggressive impulses on the part of those whom she herself wanted to injure. In other words we are able to understand part of her apprehensiveness as a retaliation fear in reference to her hostility. In diagrammatic form:

claims → *hostility* → *fear (of retaliation)*
↘   ↗
envy

After this surface attitude had been worked through in detail the whole insecurity which was hidden behind the queenly attitude appeared. While at the beginning she had talked of her husband in a very condescending way, she realized now that she actually felt very inferior to him and that she was full of self-reproaches for having failed to be a good wife. In the analytic situation this insecurity showed in the form of hypersensitivity to alleged criticism. We understood then that her queenly attitude was not only the direct result of her being spoiled by the father but more a superstructure grounded on deep inferiority feelings.

$$
\begin{array}{l}
\textit{excessive claims} \;\rightarrow\; \textit{hostility} \;\rightarrow\; \textit{fear (of retaliation)}\\
\qquad\qquad\qquad\searrow\quad\nearrow\\
\qquad\qquad\nwarrow\quad\textit{envy}\\
\qquad\textit{feelings of inferiority and insecurity}
\end{array}
$$

When this increasing fear came up in the analysis she expected every moment to be found out, and to have the analyst discover what was in the background. She wanted to quit the analysis. She had ideas of suicide which at the same time involved a threat of ruining the analyst. The hostility which appeared on this level had the function of a counterattack because she resented the analysis as an attack on her secret guilt feelings. After the hostility had been interpreted in this way she was able to talk. Gradually the content of her guilt feelings became apparent, which I must indicate here only summarily. We learned that she had always been afraid that something was wrong with her as a woman, that she was not like other girls, that she had had a vaginal discharge in her high school years, had been wetting her bed until twelve years of age and had been greatly distressed by the first menstruation, taking the bleeding as a proof that something had been damaged. This later led to the admission that she had deep fears about being damaged by masturbation. All her intense feelings of unworthiness appeared, and fear about the consequences of mas-

$$
\begin{array}{l}
\qquad\qquad\qquad\textit{claims} \;\rightarrow\; \textit{hostility}\\
\qquad\qquad\textit{claims} \;\rightarrow\; \textit{hostility} \;\rightarrow\; \textit{fear (of retaliation)}\\
\qquad\qquad\qquad\searrow\quad\nearrow\\
\qquad\qquad\uparrow\;\textit{envy}\\
\qquad\textit{feelings of inferiority and insecurity}\\
\qquad\qquad\uparrow\\
\textit{vague feeling of guilt} \;\rightarrow\; \textit{fear of discovery and punishment} \;\rightarrow\; \textit{hostility as}\\
\qquad\swarrow\qquad\qquad\qquad\uparrow\qquad\qquad\qquad\qquad\textit{counter attack}\\
\qquad\qquad\swarrow\quad\textit{fear of being damaged}\\
\textit{attitude of}\qquad\qquad\uparrow\\
\textit{self-righteousness} \;\leftarrow\; \textit{destructive fantasies}\\
\textit{as a defense.}
\end{array}
$$

turbation, and the feeling that she had deserved to get sick. On the basis of this we understood her attitude of self-righteousness, her compulsive striving to be perfect as a defense against these guilt feelings. Gradually the origin of her feelings of guilt was traced to destructive fantasies against every member of the family.

Described in this fashion, psychoanalysis may give the impression of being a rather simple procedure. One must not forget however that this highly schematized presentation is intended to point out principles only and not to deal with technique, with its endless variety of difficulties. To mention only two outstanding ones: there are difficulties in recognizing the real feeling of a patient whose surface attitude is smooth and unrevealing, and difficulties in understanding and integrating them.

If, for instance, a patient brings an abundance of material, takes the treatment seriously and considers her analyst to be an ideal person, one may easily be induced to return the compliment and consider the patient as an ideal patient, overlooking the danger which is involved in such an idealization. (Woe to you if you are not quite perfect.) Just as one may miss other trifling indications of underlying mistrust and fear, one may fail to see that the patient's ideal behavior is dictated only by the wish to please and appease the analyst, and thereby one fails to uncover the most important defense against her fears, and so leaves these fears untouched. A similar difficulty is presented by those patients who deliberately or automatically keep all emotions out of their relations with the analyst, and instead offer long dreams, childhood memories, speculations on later conflicts — in short, all the material they expect an analyst to be interested in. Here again, the danger of overlooking the problem of detachment and aloofness is very great, although it may be the central problem of the patient.

A difficulty in understanding the patient's attitudes although they are actually presented arises when they are composed of contradictory trends. For instance a destructive attitude and a wish for love-making both occurred in a confusing manner in the case in which I have referred. One may be in doubt as to the real meaning of this emotional display. The patient whose reactions to guilt feelings I have mentioned made every effort to please the analyst, entertain him and bring him something which might interest or impress him, yet he was constantly obstructing the analysis and remained unable to let himself go emotionally and kept back all relevant material. Again it was difficult to understand these apparently contradictory trends. By paying enough attention, and insisting actively enough upon analyzing these trends, one found out that the patient was in the following dilemma: On the one hand, he was very apprehensive and therefore was trying constantly to appease the analyst or to impress him with interesting material. On the other hand, to bring out his infantile fantasies and their influence on his present life meant for him exposing himself to an unbearable humiliation.

Mention of these difficulties introduces the question: if the patient does not convey his attitude clearly and beyond doubt, are there not too many subjective factors entering into the judgment? There is no doubt that such subjective factors cannot be excluded. There may be errors in the observations of the analyst due either to insufficient training or to emotional factors within himself which tend to blind him to certain aspects of the picture and cause him to see others in an exaggerated way. Analytical training serves to diminish these factors; and discussing the analyses with others sharpens the observation. Being analyzed oneself helps to mitigate blind spots. The didactic analysis, therefore, is no mysterious prerequisite but is only necessary because we live under cultural conditions in which a straightforward development is very rare. If we had no particular fears and defense reactions against them, we would not need a didactic analysis. It would then be only a more impressive way of teaching, and preferable, also, because analyzing cannot be demonstrated. To make the observations accurately and to evaluate them correctly can be taught without it.

What there is of novelty in this presentation does not lie in any additions or subtractions that it makes to the complicated technical steps which have to be taken in each individual analysis. The novelty consists in the systematic formulation of well-known and well-tested devices. Thus we come to handle the analysis in anything but arbitrary, dilatory or vague, and unscientific fashion. We know that the associations of the patient flow back and forth blending present and past events. The analyst has often felt it proper to follow the patient with his interpretations here and there according to the recommended systematic technique. On the other hand it keeps the conduct of the analysis in the hands of the analyst who proceeds in an orderly fashion using from the diverse material of the associations only that part which is relevant for the surface emotional layer of the patient. The analysis proceeds thus, surely and certainly, step by step, keeping always to the observed material from each emotional layer to the next.

4

Restricted Applications of Psychoanalysis to Social Work (1934)

In spring 1934 Horney moved from Chicago to New York and began teaching at the New York Psychoanalytic Institute. According to Jack Rubins, she made contact with the United Jewish Aid Society, soon to become the Jewish Family Service, from which she received referrals. The society was seeking psychiatric consultants to help supervise its social work staff, which dealt mostly with refugees. The director, Rose Landers, recalled that Horney was "approachable, understanding and helpful to both the social workers and patients. She seemed so down to earth, able to meet the patients on their level. They felt at home with her and peaceful. She was dynamic and full of life. Our social workers all worshipped her" (quoted by Rubins 1978, 190). The present essay, originally a talk given to the social workers, appeared in The Family *15 (1934), 169–73.*

The essay contains the germ of some of Horney's most distinctive ideas. It prefigures her account of the structure of neurosis in The Neurotic Personality of Our Time *(1937), a book that emerged from the courses she began to teach at the New School for Social Research in 1935.*

There is little disagreement that psychoanalytic knowledge can be helpful to social workers in dealing with certain cases that are otherwise inaccessible. There is, however, an open question — in fact an uncertainty that borders on bewildered confusion — regarding the possibilities and the limitations of the applications of psychoanalysis to social work. This manifests itself in both an incredulity concerning excellent results as well as an easily aroused feeling of discouragement toward failures.

It may lead, if not to clarity, to a tentative formulation of points of view, if one revisualizes what factors constitute a neurosis. Regarding their origin in time there are, very schematically speaking, three sources: infantile fears, their residues in the personality (*i.e.,* mainly defense reactions against the fears), and actual conflict situations which give rise to definite, neurotic manifestations. As it is a prerequisite for understanding to have a clear picture of what is meant by these terms, I will briefly indicate their content.

1. Infantile fears may arise on the following basis: an infant shows at a very early age certain primitive instinctive drives for which it wants satisfaction and indulgence. Neurotic parents fail to declare their own demands with consistency and fail at the same time to give the infant the feeling of warmth and protection necessary to the child on account of its utter helplessness. Instead it feels exposed to frustrations and intimidations or — still worse — to an inconsistent mixture of indulgence and harshness. The chld responds with a rebellious hostility which is in proportion to the degree of intimidation and may or may not show on the surface. Expressions of their rebellious spirit, however, such as temper tantrums, feeding difficulties, bed-wetting, and so on, meet with renewed intimidation. By far the larger amount of the antagonistic impulses have to be repressed and can be lived out only in fantasies which, no longer checked by reality, assume and retain an archaic character (such as fantasies of eating up, crushing, and tearing to pieces). These fantasies again are quickly banished from conscious awareness; but repressing them does not keep them from existing and inevitably has one consequence: that of creating fears of being attacked in the same way. The structure of the anxiety states that are so frequent in infancy may be understood on the basis of such retaliation-fear, with the only addition that the fear is shifted from persons of the environment to animals, burglars, ghosts, or fantastic figures.

2. No human being can stand living under the continuous stress of vague fears; automatically, reflex-like, we build up certain defenses the aim of which is to protect us against having these fears aroused. The ways in which we obtain protection against fears are manifold: We repress those impulses that would lead to fear reactions if we indulged in them. We avoid situations in life where they might be stirred up. We stress and favor the development of certain character trends which are likely to check the dangerous impulses.

To give a very gross and simplified example: let us assume that the emotion a certain person is most afraid of is jealousy, because jealousy for him is connected with hostile impulses of a destructive character. Such a person may later on repress the affect of jealousy to such a degree that he is subjectively convinced that jealousy is quite foreign to him. Moreover, he will avoid approaching women for whom he might have to compete with other men. If a competition situation arises he will be inclined to withdraw or to be excessively broad-minded or to be absolutely blind against all evidence of disloyalty. He may even avoid developing a strong attachment to any women in order not to incur the danger of jealousy. Furthermore he may develop homosexual tendencies — thereby avoiding women altogether and being on good terms with men.

All these protective measures may work quite well. The life of such a person will be necessarily narrowed down in intensity and expansiveness. The more impulses are hidden this way the more a life will be impoverished; and the more rigid these protective attitudes are, the less flexible a person will become in his responses to situations. Thus far the result will be a personality with inhibitions and limitations, and one has to be careful when thinking of inhibitions to avoid the simplification of thinking only of gross, visible ones. They may also be subtly ramified and not easily perceptible to the untrained eye.

3. With all these limitations life may go on quite smoothly and it may go on so forever. However, situations will easily arise which for such a person are unsolvable: this is precisely what I call the actual conflict situation. To take up the simple example of the repressed jealousy: let us imagine that this man has married and his wife is unfaithful to him. He will first try to protect himself with blindness but after a while the situation becomes so obvious that he cannot help facing it. He then tries being broad-minded and making friends with the lover, but the lover rejects him. When this protection also proves ineffectual, repressed murderous impulses associated with jealousy flare up. They do not reach consciousness but are sufficiently potent to arouse a definite anxiety. He may now develop neurotic symptoms such as a phobia of touching knives, hypochondriac fears, or others.

The actual conflict situation is not necessarily of such a gross nature. A neurosis may break out because a person is criticized by his superior, because he loses money, because he is thinking of marriage — in short, in all sorts of circumstances which usually will not throw a person off his feet. The effect seems to be out of proportion to the cause but it is not: persons with the above-sketched development, if only their limitations are sufficiently far-reaching and rigid, are like people wandering on a very high, narrow mountain trail with a precipice on each side. Any accident, such as a storm, a fog, an unevenness of the trail, may throw them down.

Thus visualizing the structure of a neurosis, one can approach the first practical problem relevant to the question of chances of a short-cut in psychoanalytical work: what indicates the severity of a neurosis?

The disagreeableness and alarmingness of the symptoms are deceptive. Also a practical, healthy person may have a breakdown with suicidal ideas and any sort of alarming symptoms if he is hit by a series of traumatic events and he will recover his mental peace spontaneously in a limited time.

There are, however, three factors which are likely to give quite a good tentative picture:

1. A time factor: it makes a difference whether the difficulties started one to two years ago, or fifteen to twenty years ago. The lapse of a great length of time indicates first of all the impossibility of a spontaneous solution. Furthermore one is safe in assuming that, if a neurotic disturbance started long ago, secondary changes will have taken place which in their entirety increase the healing difficulty.

2. The nature of the circumstances or events stimulating the manifest neurotic disturbances: one must keep in mind that a severe, incisive experience such as the death of a beloved person, betrayal of friendship or love, and so on, can also threaten the equilibrium of a well-poised individual. A wholesome individual, however, will not be seriously disturbed by puberty, marriage, childbirth, menopause, or by reading a certain book, having a bad dream, being criticized, and so on. Hence the less realistic weight or the more symbolic weight these stimulating factors have, the greater the probability of a severe neurotic understructure.

3. The diffusion of the inhibitions: a person with widespread inhibitions subtly imbibed into his whole personality is likely to be one with widespread underlying fears toward which he has to be on his defense. For practical purposes it suffices to investigate roughly these four areas of life:

(a) How are his contacts with people? Has he difficulties in making contacts, difficulties in keeping friendships, and so on?

(b) How is his sexual life? Has he sexual relations, are they satisfactory, is he able to have a lasting good relationship with a partner?

(c) How is his attitude to money? Is he able to earn money under favorable circumstances? Is he able to spend money in proportion to his earning capacities? Is he apprehensive or inconsistent in regard to money?

(d) How is his attitude to work, accomplishment, ambition? Can he concentrate on his work, enjoy it? Is he afraid of competition? Can he stick to one job? Is his expansiveness or his ambition in proportion to his presumable capacities?

If one finds, apart from the outspoken symptoms, widely ramified inhibitions, one may safely assume a severe neurotic entanglement. To form a tentative opinion about the seriousness is important because this factor determines the chances of good therapeutic results, and also the way of therapeutic approach. While this is valid for the psychoanalyst it is of still more practical importance for the social worker, because first of all one has to recognize the impossibility of dealing analytically with a severe neurosis otherwise than by means of a regular analysis. The recognition of this fact and a good training in discriminating between different types of cases would help to avoid failures and discouragements.

This does not imply that one is to keep hands off altogether if there are deeply rooted neurotic troubles. There may be in these cases actual upsetting conflict situations in addition to the chronic disturbances. And one may tackle these with good results if one takes painstaking care not to stir up any of the deeper anxieties. This danger can be avoided by leaving the numerous defensive attitudes untouched. How to detect them, how to estimate their intensity, and how to avoid them should be part of the analytical training of the social worker.

The most fertile soil for psychiatric social work, however, is found in those cases in which the contribution of the actual conflict situation is very great in comparison with the neurotic background. Analysts usually are inclined to underestimate the frequency of these lighter cases because the great majority of cases who come for analytical help are of the severe type. Here is one of the reasons why analysts so often have a tacit or outspoken belief that "real" help can be given only by the extensive psychoanalytic procedure. What has to be done in these lighter cases — the uncovering of the precise conflict situation plus the connection it has with the symptom — can be done in a limited time and does not require a command of the intricate psychoanalytic technique.

As far as young children are concerned it will often suffice and even be preferable to discuss the situation only with the mother, to make her understand what the child is up to, to make her see how far she or others have contributed to the conflicts and what changes in her attitude would be helpful. One does not "cure" a neurosis in this way but nevertheless the help can be of decisive and lasting value.

I shall give a simple example in order to illustrate what can be accomplished in this fashion and what not:

A mother came to ask my advice about the feeding difficulties of her two-year-old daughter. The girl refused to eat. The mother had tried everything, punishment, kindness, disregard of the difficulty—nothing had helped. Finally the mother had sat down for hours with the girl trying to persuade her to eat. Some questioning showed that this difficulty had started soon after the birth of a younger sister some months ago. The child achieved two purposes with the eating strike: she let the mother feel her resentment against the new family situation and she succeeded in absorbing a great deal of the mother's time. I explained to the mother the probably existing fears and wishes of the child, and how both were expressed in the feeding difficulties. On the basis of this understanding we figured out what to do about the situation and decided that the mother should pay no attention whatever to the feeding but otherwise give to the child a great deal of affection and warmth in order to calm down the fears of losing the love of the mother.

The mother understood the situation well and in a few days the child ate in a normal way and was much more cheerful.

What has been achieved by this simple procedure? (1) Disappearance of the symptom. (2) Preventing the following vicious circle from developing: growing resentment from the side of the mother against the older child, turning with more affection to the baby, growing resentment from the side of the older girl, and so on.

What has not been achieved? There is no guarantee that the girl will not later on develop other neurotic symptoms. Not every two-year-old girl will be seriously disturbed after the birth of a younger sibling. If a girl reacts to such a situation with neurotic symptoms, it indicates that there must be an atmosphere of conflict in the house. In fact, in this particular case the mother was a neurotic person. It is probable, therefore, that we have helped only in one situation and not fundamentally in the way of prophylaxis.

In dealing with grown-ups the principles are the same. Here, too, the understanding co-operation of the environment will be valuable. The main task, however, will naturally be to let the patients themselves see their problems.

A woman came to ask my help for a depression that had started some months ago, after she had learned that her husband had been unfaithful to her for years. As this woman until her depression was comparatively well adjusted, it was not difficult to discuss and clarify her actual conflict situation. It consisted chiefly in her not daring to admit to herself the deep resentment that she felt against her husband.

What was accomplished in this case was an immediate help concerning the neurotic manifestation: the woman lost her depression and was able to work again. Moreover she was able to deal with her husband in a sensible way, and to get a divorce.

What was not accomplished? The disaster in her marriage life, so far as the patient's own share in it was concerned, was determined by her own very complicated attitude toward men. She really was seeking the son in the man and had turned away from the husband after her son was born. This background could not be changed in a few interviews. In an analysis one would have had to work through all these deeper problems in order to enable her to choose a more adequate mate.

TO sum it up: While with the available tools one cannot expect to change the neurotic structure of a life, one can give very effective help in actual conflict situations even though these may arise on a neurotic foundation. I suppose that this does not exhaust all the possibilities — only further experience can show us further indications.

Still a word about the psychoanalytic training of social workers. The question has been raised as to whether or not a personal psychoanalysis of the social worker is a necessary prerequisite to the application of psychoanalytic skills. Again lack of experience forbids my giving a definite answer. Tentatively I assume that an actual psychoanalysis is indispensable only when there are disturbing character difficulties.

It would be necessary, however, for the social worker to acquire a solid knowledge about various neurotic structures and about the phenomena occurring in the inter-relations between patients and therapists. A clear technique regarding the handling of interviews cannot yet be taught, because it has to be different from the usual psychoanalytic technique. The best ways of proceeding should be worked out in co-operation between social workers and analysts on the basis of discussing the cases in great detail.

5

On Difficulties in Dealing with the Transference (1935)

This essay was originally a paper given at the dinner meeting of the American Association of Psychiatric Social Workers, National Conference on Social Work, Montreal, June 1935. It was published in October in the News-Letter of the American Association of Psychiatric Social Workers *5 (1935), 1–12. In this essay, Horney redefines transference, resistance, and the therapeutic process in the light of her evolving structural model. She emphasizes the need to understand the patient's behavior not in terms of childhood fixations and object relations but in terms of current defenses and conflicts. The ideas introduced here, as in the preceding two essays, received much elaboration and refinement in Horney's subsequent writings.*

Psychiatric social work is a new field and it is only natural that there still are many uncertainties and many unsolved problems. Among the problems relating to therapy, the main ones seem to be those of interpretations and limitations, questions of technique, and problems of possibilities for treatment.

Among the technical problems, there is one which seems to be particularly surrounded by mystery and apprehensiveness — that is, the problem of how to understand and deal with the emotional reactions of the client to the worker. The reality sources of this apprehensiveness are easy enough to understand:

when dealing with emotional problems in neurotic persons, the worker may feel that she is working with explosive material. In spite of the worker's best efforts to be helpful, the client will react at times with outbreaks of defiance, suspicion, vengeance, or still worse, the worker is distinctly aware that these reactions are present and affecting the client without his being aware of it and without the worker being able to tackle them. Or, in spite of the worker's endeavors to keep emotionally detached herself, and to keep the client from getting dependent on her, she is not able in some cases to prevent a reaction of utter dependency, desperate clinging and violent demands for any sort of affection. Experiences like these naturally create a feeling of uncertainty and even helplessness, with a subsequent tendency to keep hands off altogether.

As is well known, Freud was the first one to put his finger on this bothersome problem and to show how one could not only understand it but also make use of it for the benefit of a cure. The essence of Freud's discovery was that these reactions are not only stimulated by the immediate situation but also conditioned by earlier emotional experiences, particularly those that have occurred in childhood. He called these reactions "transference" because the patient often seemed to revive certain attitudes toward persons of the early environment and to "transfer" them to the analyst. It may serve to dispel the mystery surrounding this concept if we point out two frequent misunderstandings.

The first misunderstanding consists in the notion that something exceptional is going on in the psychoanalytic situation. The truth is such emotional reactions occur in any human relationship in which factors similar to those in the psychoanalytic situation are present; that is, in any situation in which one person accepts something from another, in which one person is stronger than the other, and in which the weaker person is full of anxiety. Similar situations are constantly occurring in our culture between parents and children, teachers and children, employers and employees, directors and staff members, physicians and patients, social workers and clients, husbands and wives, etc. In all of these situations one may find the same irrational, emotional reactions of infatuation or hostility. In short, one can say people feel and behave just as irrationally outside the analytic situation as inside. It has been pointed out that the emotional reserve of the analyst constitutes a frustration which is not present in other situations. This, however, is true only to some extent. Neurotic persons have always, on the basis of their anxieties, needs and demands which are partly excessive, partly contradictory in themselves, so that they are bound to meet with frustration and disappointment all the time. The frustration, due to the objective attitude of the analyst, differs from this only in being more consistent.

The only real difference to any other situation in life is that these reactions are expressed in the analytic situation and that their complete expression is encouraged (free association). It is only the extent of this freedom of expression that makes them appear more dramatic and disproportionate. The very extent of this expression allows a rather unique opportunity for accurate observation of the reactions. It was a stroke of genius to discover and to utilize this very simple fact.

The second misunderstanding arises from simplifying the Freudian concept of transference and, therefore, in not knowing how to apply it. The observations on which this concept is founded are that there are often striking similarities in the infantile and the present reactions, and that pointing out to a patient that he was compulsively acting according to an old pattern often brought some relief. This idea often is carried into practice with the expectation that it is sufficient to point out to a patient this repetitive pattern, to tell him, for instance: "You love me now because you love your sister"; or, "You are spiteful and suspicious toward me just as you were toward your father"; or, You are afraid of me because you were afraid of your mother." Proceeding in this way would, in the majority of situations, constitute a short cut from which the patient or client will benefit but very little because it remains an intellectual concept. It has this value, however: it may make the patient realize that his reactions of infatuation, spite, suspicion, etc., were once an adequate reaction to some difficult childhood situation, but that they are no longer warranted by the present situation. Furthermore, if the patient realizes that his emotional upset is a repetition of earlier feelings, the analyst may help the patient to achieve a greater emotional detachment toward the analyst and thereby render him willing to cooperate with him.

Such a simplification of technique overlooks one important question: what are the dynamics which make the patient continue this attitude at the present time? If, for instance, a patient has been spoiled in his childhood and has been the center of attention and admiration, what makes it impossible for him to give up his excessive demands for affection in his adult life? If for reasons that were adequate at that time, a patient suppressed his criticism toward his childhood surroundings, what forces are at work in his present life to keep him uncritical, naive, and immature? Not understanding the current interplay of psychic drives, makes it impossible to effect any change in the present difficulties. Without this understanding the question "Why is the patient apprehensive or suspicious or affectionate just at this time" will remain unanswered, and will prevent insight into the structure of the present conflicts and their implications, and consequently will keep the analyst from helping the patient to become aware of them. Self-evident as it is, it seems necessary in the face of certain misunderstandings to emphasize that the therapeutic aim in the psychoanalytic therapy or in any kind of treatment akin to it is *not* to recapture childhood memories, but to change something in the present attitudes. The knowledge of childhood experiences, therefore, is valuable only insofar as it serves to throw light on the present difficulties. With this therapeutic aim in mind, the pertinent question concerning the technique is: how can we understand the present conflicts of the patient?

The answer is: observe how he is acting and try to understand first of all what are the immediate reasons for his acting just the way he does. For this, the psychoanalytic situation offers the best possible opportunity. One of the reasons for this I have mentioned already. The patient is encouraged to express his reactions. He will not always be able to express his real feelings, but the analyst, trained in making accurate observations and deductions will be able to recognize what is going on. In addition, the analyst in the psychoanalytic situation is able to know by observation what is going on between him and the patient. He may learn a great deal from what the patient is telling him about his reactions to other life situations, but it is difficult to judge these situations as accurately. He does not know the person with whom the patient has to deal, and the patient may give a one-sided account of a situation. The patient may have a deep need to present all his reactions as being adequate to the situation or as being justified by the behavior of other persons and may therefore instinctively pick out only such examples as will prove his point. All these possibilities of error are absent in the psychoanalytic situation. The analyst knows what he has felt or said or done, and how he has said or done it — at least he is supposed to know — and therefore he has an exact knowledge of the conditions to which the patient is reacting, and a very good basis for estimating the irrational factors in these reactions. This, however, is not only important for his own understanding, but is also a prerequisite for conveying this insight to the patient. While otherwise the patient may make the mental reservation that the analyst is going on an assumption of some kind, here he is presented with interpretations based on evidence and even if he does not like to accept these interpretations he cannot help getting a feeling of conviction. If, for instance, a patient tends to explain the fact that she becomes easily infuriated because everyone has disappointed her and fails to do his duty toward her, the analyst may think in his own mind that possibly this patient is making excessive demands without realizing it and becomes indignant at everything which falls short of a 100% fulfillment of these demands because of her disappointment, but neither will the analyst have evidence of this, nor will the patient be convinced. If, however, the patient gets infuriated when she comes ten minutes too early for the appointment and has to wait, and if the analyst makes a series of similar observations of her behavior in relation to him, then he can show her that she is in fact over-exacting and reacts with rage toward any person or situation in which her demands are not fulfilled to the last item and at once. Or, if a patient tells the analyst how people have turned against her because they envy her, the analyst cannot be sure how far this is a correct observation of herself, or how far there are subjective factors in the patient herself which make her see envy when it is not present, or at least make her over-rate it. If, at the same time, this patient has one failure after the other in life, the analyst may guess that she may have a fear of envy, a fear of such intensity as to let her instinctively arrange failures in order to avoid that fear. But he can be sure of these dynamics only if he observes that this fear of envy is coming up towards him too, and that she presents herself as helpless and inefficient to him in order to shield herself against his assumed envy. The analyst then can show her her share in incurring failures, and if he has worked through with her the connection between fear of envy and incurring failures, he may proceed to work on the problem of why she is so afraid of envy.

There is another good reason for following up very carefully and uncovering the patient's reaction to the analyst in the psychoanalytic situation. If he does not uncover these reactions as they come up, the patient's affect will accumulate and not only cause him suffering which might have been avoided, but also render it extremely difficult to cope with. Take, for instance, a patient with excessive demands like the one mentioned before. He will feel constantly hurt and infuriated — and without knowing that he is so — because he has only a limited time allotted to him, because the analyst has other interests besides him, because he does not solve for him every problem on the spur of the moment, because he uncovers shortcomings of his instead of admiring him, and so on. If he does not uncover these reactions, they will be bottled up and he will become so resentful against the analyst that any cooperative work will be impossible. Or, he will react to his increasingly bottled-up rage with an increasing anxiety which makes him suffer and likewise renders the analyst's work futile.

Or, take a patient who, because he is so filled with anxiety, tries to get reassuring affection from him. He does not get as much as he needs at the moment, the analyst's kind interest and sympathy does not reassure him sufficiently, so he makes renewed and desperate efforts to secure his love. He will bring him presents and be more and more convinced that he is in love with him. If the analyst does not understand and uncover the dynamics present in the particular situation, that is, in this case the fact that he is not really in love with the analyst, but is in need of reassurance because he has anxieties, his infatuation will increase and make any real work illusory, either because he insists on love and refuses to work with the analyst, or because he gets furious at what he feels is a rebuff.

It is this kind of accumulation of affect which more than anything else has brought the transference into disrepute, while it is only a wrong technique which is to be blamed.

Does this kind of procedure in any way diminish the importance of childhood influences? By no means; there is nothing to be detracted from what Freud has said about the molding influences of childhood. It only means one should not try to make the patient reconstruct memories too early. They will come up in their time quite spontaneously and be helpful for the understanding of his problem. Take, for instance, the example I gave of a patient seemingly falling in love with the analyst, and assume that such a patient tells you he has felt attracted to his mother, has slept with her in the same bed beyond puberty. If, following this lead from the past, the analyst would tell him, "You love me now because I represent the mother for you," it would be only half true. In the first place, he loves the analyst now, or thinks that he does, because he is full of anxiety and therefore feels a particular need for his affection as a means of reassurance and protection. It might be much more truthful that his erotic phantasies concerning his mother were built on the same pattern: that is to say, that he was desperately afraid of his mother and therefore assumed an affectionate attitude toward her. Furthermore, that he found this device effectual in childhood and therefore is trying it out on the analyst. If now the analyst does not uncover the anxiety behind this seeming infatuation in the present situation, he will cut off his way for seeing and analyzing the patient's anxiety, and this is what he has to get rid of.

These considerations contain implicitly the answer to two questions which are raised frequently: how active or passive should one be in carrying on an analysis or therapeutic case work? And, what material should one tackle and what material should one leave alone at any given monent?

If the analyst realizes the importance of understanding and uncovering the patient's reactions toward himself and toward the psychoanalytic situation, then consequently he has to consider it his foremost, immediate task to tackle these reactions. In order to be able to do so, he has to observe carefully and minutely, in order not to let any disguised expression of these reactions escape his attention. He has to be trained for such observation in order to know what to look for. And here is the answer to the question of activity or passivity on the part of the analyst: in tackling these important reactions, he has to be very active. The patient will not present them to him as a rule. On the contrary, he will do whatever he can to defend himself against the analyst's prying into his real motives. As a rule, a patient will willingly admit that he is spiteful toward the analyst as he was toward his father, but it will require all the analyst's observation, energy and consistency to prove to the patient that he is spiteful just now because he has not complied with his demand to see him three times a week instead of twice or with whatever demands he may have made. This does not mean any mysterious "resistance" on the part of the patient, but a very understandable fight which he puts on in order to maintain his ways of protecting himself against his anxieties. Let it suffice here to indicate only this connotation of the "resistance" because it would require a discussion of the structure of the neuroses duly to evaluate this phenomenon. Let me rather stress not only the necessity of being active in this procedure, but also of being consistent. It is not sufficient to clarify an irrational reaction of the patient once, but it must be done consistently, without letting oneself be distracted from this track until all the implications of the patient's reactions are discovered and worked through thoroughly. Dealing with the transference phenomena in this way will still remain a difficult task, but it will remove the feeling of mystery and even uncanniness which has surrounded it. The therapist will no longer feel that he is walking on bombs which may explode at any moment, but will feel safe ground under his feet with every step he takes. This change of feeling is something which happens in ghost tales: the ghost loses his power and vanishes if one has the courage to address him, and one will be able really to appreciate what Freud has said of the value of transference phenomena as the most effective tool we have for the therapy of neuroses.

6

The Problem of the Negative Therapeutic Reaction (1936)

This was the first paper Horney presented at the New York Psychoanalytic Society, in November 1935. Her audience may have influenced her deference to Freud at the outset and her insistence at the end that she did not attribute less importance to childhood experiences than other analysts. She emphasized this, she says, "because misunderstandings have arisen." Given her unorthodox thought, her relations with her conservative colleagues at the New York Psychoanalytic were bound to be difficult. Fortunately, she found more receptive forums in which to work out her ideas, at the Washington-Baltimore Institute, to which she commuted from New York for several years, and the New School for Social Research, where she taught from 1935 until her death in 1952. After presenting her paper to the New York Psychoanalytic Society, she delivered it to the Berlin Psychoanalytic Society in December when she returned to Germany to visit her daughters, Brigitte and Renate. (She was still considered an overseas member of the Berlin Psychoanalytic.) The paper was published in the Psychoanalytic Quarterly *5 (1936), 29–44. Like the preceding papers in this group, this essay introduces many ideas that Horney was to develop systematically over the next fifteen years. It remains her fullest discussion of the negative therapeutic reaction.*

There are many reasons for an impairment of a patient's condition during analysis; their common denominator is the arousal of anxiety, with which either the patient or the analyst is unable to deal adequately.

What Freud has called the "negative therapeutic reaction" is not, indiscriminately, every deterioration of the patient's condition; but the fact that the patient may show an increase in symptoms, become discouraged, or wish to break off treatment immediately following an encouragement or a real elucidation of some problem, at a time, that is to say, when one might reasonably expect him to feel relief. In fact, the patient very often actually feels this relief distinctly, and then after a short while reacts as described. Freud considers this reaction indicative of a bad prognosis in the particular case, and, as it is a frequent occurrence, a serious barrier to therapeutic endeavors in general.

When Freud first published these observations many questions arose concerning the specific nature of such an impairment, among them, Are we so sure in our expectation of what should bring relief to the patient? I remember my own scepticism on the subject. But the more experience I gained, the more I came to admire the keenness and the importance of Freud's observation.

Since there is nothing to add to Freud's description of the phenomenon, let me cite an example. A lawyer with widespread, subtle inhibitions in almost every life situation had not got on in life in proportion to his abilities. During the analysis the possibility arose of his getting a much better position. It took him quite a time even to perceive his opportunity. On this occasion for the first time we discussed his ambition, which he had repressed to an unusual degree. He could not even dream of ambitious aims, nor see possibilities in reality, nor take any step towards attaining such goals. However, when we indicated the possibility that he really was intensely ambitious, he recalled flashes of fantasy in which he was reforming the system of justice in the whole world. He came to see the discrepancy between his actual dull resignation and his hidden ambitions.

He must have felt relief for a brief time, but immediately he went into reverse gear, saying to himself, "You don't think you feel better after this!" Then he showed an increase in symptoms along the whole line. At the same time the disparaging attitude towards the analyst of which Freud speaks as belonging to the picture was manifest in his scarcely being able to listen to me and in his telling me: "You think you are smart. Any dummy could have told me that. These are all very trivial results."

In principle, this sequence of reactions is invariably present: first, a definite relief, then a shrinking back from the prospect of improvement, discouragement, doubts, hopelessness, wishes to break off, utterances like: "I had rather stay as I am — I am too old to change" (this from a twenty-four-year-old man).

"If I should be cured of my neurosis I could break a leg and still have something to worry about." At the same time a definite disparaging, with intense hostility. One patient of mine had to think and express one thought throughout the hour — "you are no good". The patient whom Feigenbaum describes thought of gangsters and charlatans in transparent reference to the analyst. The impulse to berate the analyst more often comes out indirectly: doubts of the analyst; increasing complaints with a tendency to show the analyst that he is of no help — all indicating a hostility which may be so strong that if repressed it may show itself in suicidal ideas.

The only point one might add to Freud's description is that anxiety may arise during the phases of the negative reaction either openly or in disguised form. In the latter event the increase of anxiety may reveal itself in an increase of those symptoms which are the characteristic expression of anxiety in the particular person, such as the feeling of being rushed or having diarrhœa. The more hostility reactions are repressed, the more likely is anxiety to appear.

You will recall how Freud accounts for the phenomenon of the negative therapeutic reaction — in his opinion the attitude of spite and the impulse to show superiority towards the analyst represent only a surface reaction, or, as Feigenbaum calls it, a "by-product." The real dynamics, he believes, lie in the particularly great tension of these patients, between the superego and the ego, resulting in a sense of guilt and need for punishment in order to avoid anxieties concerning the superego. The suffering in the neuroses, therefore, has too valuable a function to be given up.

The negative reaction, implying as it does essential frustration of therapeutic effots, presents a sharp challenge. It is an intricate problem, of which we must learn much before it is solved. Its interesting theoretical implications, however, I shall not touch, but merely suggest a way in which the whole problem may eventually be solved — that is, steps from the technical side which will lead to this goal. To illustrate these technical suggestions I present the description and interpretation of the phenomena in cases of a certain character structure which, tentatively, I am inclined to call the masochistic. I wish to show how the negative therapeutic reaction follows out of this structure with such necessity that it can be predicted; and finally, how by understanding its underlying trends one can overcome it.

A description of this intricate structure would far surpass the frame of a paper. I shall, for the sake of presentation, take up only those points which bear directly on the reaction, omitting many ramifications and interrelations, intricate and difficult to follow, and trace the main line only.

In the first place, we see these reactions stimulated by a good interpretation — by which, to repeat, I mean an interpretation that either states clearly a problem of the patient's current difficulties or offers a partial solution of it, or throws light on hitherto incomprehensible peculiarities of the patient. We see, moreover, that the negative reaction follows regardless of the special content of the problem or solution offered. That is, the reaction does not primarily express a resistance against some particular insight.

The question then is: What effect has such a good interpretation on the deeper emotional layers? In persons with the character structure in question, the effects of a good interpretation are of five kinds. They are not always all present, nor are they all always equally strong, but they may exist in combinations of varying intensity.

The first reaction is that these patients receive a good interpretation as a stimulus to compete, as if the analyst, by seeing something they had not seen, is proved more intelligent, clearersighted, or more articulate than the patient — as if the analyst had asserted his superiority over the patient. The patient is resentful and expresses his resentment in different ways. Very rarely he expresses it directly. For instance, a patient of this type began to ponder whether he would have been able to see the particular implication or to express it as clearly as I. Much more often the resentment is revealed in subsequent attempts of the patient to reëstablish his superiority by belittling the analyst, as in the examples already cited. Connected with this impulse to disparage the analyst, there is much rage of which the patient may or may not be aware: but he is never aware that the rage was provoked by the skilfulness of the interpretation. The rage may be disguised, as above, or may determine a complete refusal to coöperate.

The vehemence of the disparaging impulses in these cases raises the question whether they are not more than a surface attitude, that is, dynamically speaking, an essential element in the whole picture. To answer this question we must consider the rôle played by competitiveness, rivalry and ambition in the entire make-up.

In order to get an adequate estimate of the specific importance of this attitude for these individuals, we must remind ourselves of the enormous rôle played in our culture by competitiveness — a trait so general that we tend to consider it an ingrained trait of human nature. However, a knowledge of other cultures proves that such a view indicates only our insufficient detachment from the peculiar conditions under which we live in our civilization. Our culture is pervaded by competition, not only in the business and political fields, but in social life, love life, marriage, and other fields as well. In fact, the entire picture as manifested in the character structure described is culturally conditioned, although, of course, through the channels of particularly unfortunate individual conditions in childhood. On the basis of this situation we must expect a certain amount of competitiveness in every analysis; and experience shows it to be a constant factor in the patient's relations with the analyst. Consequently we may limit our question to special features in our patients' competitiveness.

1. The competitiveness may exceed the average in quantity. Persons so affected constantly and automatically compare themselves with everyone they meet, even in situations which involve no actual competition. Their sole standard of values seems to be that of being ahead of or behind some other person. Their feeling towards life is that of a jockey in a race; they are dominated by the question, am I ahead? They have, in addition, fantastic expectations of their capacity for accomplishment. They fancy themselves the most popular person, the best physician, etc., in the world. They expect blind admiration.

When they start to paint they expect to be masters like Rembrandt immediately; their first play they expect to be at least as good as one by Shakespeare: the first blood count in the laboratory must be perfect — with inevitable repercussions of despair and depression. In the moral sphere these extraordinary demands express themselves in having to be perfect, encountering here the same exasperations at everything short of perfection. These ambitions, however, exist only in fantasies, which may or may not be conscious. The degree of awareness differs widely in different persons. There is, however, never any clear realization of the powerful rôle these ambitions play in the patient's life or of the great part they play in accounting for his behavior and mental reactions.

2. The second special feature is the amount of hostility involved in these ambitions. Such a person's attitude may be characterized thus: "No one but I shall be a good musician, read a good paper; no one but I shall be attractive, praised, or get attention and care when sick." Combined with this is the impulse ruthlessly to brush aside all possible competitors. One patient who was writing a paper nearly destroyed the paper of a friend because he considered it good, although it dealt with an entirely different subject from his own. This reaction was followed by despair of ever accomplishing anything, which was another expression of his demand that he alone should be able to accomplish anything.

Rationalizing in one way or another such persons compulsively disparage every competitor; or repressing, they overcompensate by exaggerated admiration. They cannot endure the idea of the analyst's having other patients besides themselves, and often protect themselves by shutting the other patients entirely out of their minds.

This attitude of hostile rivalry generally (in my experience always) is entirely unconscious. These patients know only that they are inordinately sensitive to any kind of criticism. They may go so far as to react with anger to any advice or offer of help—so far as such an offer implies an insinuation of any possible imperfection or lack of self-sufficiency—even when they recognize that the offer is kindly meant.

They are aware, in addition, of certain subsequent reactions which are the outcome of the anxiety connected with their rivalry attitude, into which I shall go later. The origin of this compulsive rivalry may be traced back to childhood. It is sufficient to say here that this kind of striving for absolute supremacy serves as protection against an extraordinary anxiety: it insures safety through absolute power. Hence, if this position is endangered the patients react with anxiety, hostility, or depression. This attitude is usually evinced during analysis by the patient's regarding any progress as a triumph of the analyst—a possible feather in the analyst's cap. The fact that the patient himself will profit from such success seems irrelevant.

With these implications in mind we understand now the impact of the reaction to a good interpretation: the patients feel endangered in their own position and react with rage when the analyst dares have a better grasp of the situation than they themselves. They must express their hostility and their sense of defeat by belittling the analyst.

In the cases considered so far, the negative therapeutic reaction not only did not depend upon the content of the interpretation, but in addition the interpretation did not even have to be correct—only skilful or brilliant.

The second type of reaction to a good interpretation is somewhat more closely connected with the content, although only in a very general way. So far as a good interpretation usually implies the exposure of some weakness, or what the patient considers such, it means what one might call a narcissistic blow, or merely descriptively speaking, a blow to the patient's self-esteem. The demands of these patients to be perfect, flawless, beyond reproach, are so excessive that everything that falls short of absolute admiration strikes them as humiliation. They feel humiliated, therefore, if one uncovers nothing more than the fact that they are in a dilemma, that they have certain anxieties, and that there are irrational elements in their expectations. They react as if they automatically translated the analyst's reference to "anxiety" into "cowardice," "sensitivity" into "effeminacy," etc. In fact, they will tell the analyst that they understand him that way, if their reactions are discussed and if they are able to grasp them.

It has always hurt the patient to be dimly aware of flaws in his personality. But he feels humiliated if the analyst brings these flaws to his attention. As long as he is not aware of his reaction he can only express a vague resentment, such as feeling scolded by the analyst, or feeling a diminution in his self-esteem since the start of the analysis. But no matter whether the feeling of humiliation is closer to or farther from conscious awareness, the patient will instinctively retaliate by trying to humiliate the analyst. He may do so frankly, or subtly try to make the analyst feel insignificant, preposterous, and ineffectual.

This impulse to humiliate the analyst merges with the disparaging tendency in the first reaction. Both reactions arise on the basis of strong competitiveness: while the first reaction is a direct expression of rivalry, the second springs from the grandiose ideas and the need for admiration which is a later product of the excessive ambitions. The self-esteem of these persons rests on the shaky ground of (unconscious) grandiose illusions about their own uniqueness and therefore collapses like a card house at a light touch.

I proceed now to describe *the third reaction:* in so far as a good interpretation means the unravelling of a knot or the elucidating a problem from which the patient has suffered, it brings definite relief. This relief may be felt for so short a time that it scarcely figures in awareness. But it may be quite outspoken and definite, although always of short duration only. The essential point in this third reaction is, however, not the relief in itself, but the immeasurably swift realization that such a solution means a move towards recovery and success; the anticipation that more solutions of this kind will eventually lead out of the neurosis.

It is this realization and anticipation that is followed by a feeling of discouragement, hopelessness, despair, and the wish to terminate the analysis. In order to understand the dynamic problem we must consider the further consequences of this particular kind of ambition, which as we have seen contains definite elements of hostility towards others. Success is equal to crushing others, and maliciously triumphing over the crushed adversaries, an attitude necessarily leading to a fear of retaliation with two aspects: a fear of success and a fear of failure. The fear of success might be phrased: "If I attain success I shall incur the same sort of rage and envy that I feel towards the success of other persons"; and the fear of failure: "If I make any move towards ambitious aims and fail, then others will crush me as I would like to crush them." Any possible failure, therefore, comes to connote a danger to be avoided at all costs.

The device to ward off this danger might be formulated: "I had better stay inconspicuously in a corner, or remain sick and inhibited." To express this more generally, there is a recoiling from all aims that involve competition. This is accomplished by a constant, accurately working process of automatic self-checking, with inhibitions as a result. Thus, one patient gave up painting when she married, although it was her sole satisfactory activity, because she was a better painter than her husband and she feared his envy. This same patient observed that when she spoke to a stupid person she automatically acted even more stupid; and that when she played with a bad musician she played worse than her partner. Any success these persons achieve, such as progressing in their studies or winning a game, is felt as a peril.

Dreams show this tendency very clearly and often reveal the conflicts quite early in the analysis. These patients dream of being defeated by a competitor, of incurring failures, or being humiliated. They do not even dare to dream of plain wish fulfilments or ambitions; even in dreams (as in life) they feel safer when they imagine that they are humble or defeated. After these patients have thoroughly recognized their fear of success, their dreams change in character.

This attitude entails an automatic curb on any progress. The self-checking process is not limited, however, to activities involving ambitions, but is expressed principally in an undermining of self-confidence, the prerequisite for all accomplishment.

In this context their self-belittling operates to exclude them from competition. Women of this type will say, for instance, that they feel so utterly unattractive that it would be absurd for them to dress nicely, or that they feel utterly incapable and incompetent. While the fact that they are actively engaged in self-belittling is unconscious, they are aware of the results, namely, intense feelings of inconsequence or even of worthlessness.

As a result of these inhibiting forces failures ensue, which even if not complete, cause a discrepancy between accomplishment and potentialities, not to mention an even greater discrepancy between grandiose ideas and feelings of inferiority. A realization of this discrepancy is essential for an understanding of the vicious circle in which these persons are moving. To omit again the originating childhood factors, the circle looks much like the following diagram:

Anxiety-hostility
    Ambitions $\Big\{$ expression of hostility
                 defense against anxiety
      Self-checking as defense
        Inhibitions against success and failures
          Real failures
            Envy towards less inhibited or more fortunate persons=increase
              of hostility
            Increase of anxiety.

Though the ambitions may not have been so fantastic and so hostile at the outset, these qualities grow and increase. This development in a vicious circle accounts for the intensity of the emotions with which we are now confronted.

Bearing in mind the ruthless energy with which persons of this structure must turn from any progress they make, we understand the third type of negative therapeutic reaction: progress means danger, so it must be averted. From this point of view *the negative therapeutic reaction is a special form of the fear of success*. The discouragement and hopelessness which accompany it are apparently genuine feelings, arising from a deep-lying realization of being caught in a dilemma from which there is no escape.

This third reaction almost coincides with the factor Freud pointed out as the main source of the reaction, with the difference in emphasis that where Freud stresses feelings of guilt I have emphasized anxiety. The two feelings, however, are closely akin. In fact, in the cases I have in mind, sometimes one and sometimes the other is in the foreground. A second difference consists in my ascribing a special content to these feelings of guilt and anxiety, namely, hostility on the basis of rivalry.

Especially in those cases in which the guilt feelings are more in the foreground, there is *a fourth reaction* to a good interpretation: it is felt as an accusation. This reaction may be so strong as to dominate the picture for some time. More precisely, the interpretation is perceived as an unjust accusation, for the same reason given by Freud, namely, the sense of guilt is unconscious. The patient therefore feels constantly put on the defensive, so that the analysis resembles a trial. An interpretation, however kindly and considerately given, so far as it arouses a sense of guilt or merely proves the patients wrong in some respects, is reacted to as if it were a total condemnation, the intensity of which is proportional to the existing feelings of self-condemnation. The patients express this reaction by making a counterattack on the analyst: to prove him wrong by exaggerating his statements, by picking out some expression of the analyst's which was not altogether correct, by telling him directly or indirectly (for example by symptomatic doubts and anxieties) that he is keeping them from getting well or actually doing them harm.

To repeat: This reaction is in the foreground only in those cases in which the anxiety concerning the outside world is internalized to a particularly great extent.

The fifth reaction to a good interpretation concerns the patient's feeling of personal rejection on the part of the analyst, due to an excessive need for affection and equally great sensitivity to any kind of rebuff. Seen from this angle the patient takes any uncovering of his difficulties as an expression of dislike or disdain by the analyst and reacts with strong antagonism.

Wilhelm Reich has pointed out this factor as constituting the whole picture of the negative therapeutic reaction. I consider it a very important factor, indeed, but only one element among others, and one to be understood only on the basis of the whole character structure.

In the life history of these patients we find, generally speaking, that in childhood they endured an atmosphere lacking in all warmth and reliability but rife with frightening elements, such as fights between parents, injustice, cruelty, over-solicitousness, etc. The outcome was the engendering of hostility and anxiety. There are probably many ways of dealing with such a situation. The two most frequent in our culture seem to be the striving for power and the striving for affection, both representing a protection against anxiety — "If I have absolute power you cannot hurt me" and "If you love me you will not hurt me". These two strivings are, however, incompatible, for the ambitious striving contains a definite destructive element. This is in fact the main conflict in persons of the character structure under discussion.

Here I must make a reservation to a statement previously made, namely, that the attitude of hostile rivalry "necessarily" leads to fear of retaliation. Probably such a fear always will be present, although in varying degrees, but the simple fear of retaliation may function as a whip, driving the person on to gain more success and more power. What accounts for the recoiling from ambition is an additional anxiety, namely, an ever-lurking fear of loss of affection. One might venture the guess that in those persons capable of factually pressing their "no one but I" ambition, the positive emotional relationships to others were earlier and more deeply disrupted. These people no longer believe in affection. The patients I have in mind, on the other hand, are continually wavering between rivalry and affection. In the analytical situation one has an opportunity of seeing the interplay of these two sets of motives. A move towards competition with the analyst is followed by increased anxiety and need for affection. The feeling of being rebuffed by the analyst is followed by a renewed rivalry.

We may observe the same wavering in the patient's life history: for instance, being offered a position that implies leadership, recoiling from it out of fear, and then rushing into some love affair; or the other way around: being disappointed in a love relationship and suddenly developing a highflown ambitious attitude.

Why does the patient feel rebuffed so easily and react with such intense hostility to the rebuff?

These questions are easily answered if we have a full understanding of the implications of the patient's need for affection. We are accustomed to think and talk loosely of it as an "infantile" attitude, as a revival of the situation in which the child because of his helplessness needs help, affection, and attention from the mother. These infantile elements may be included in the excessive need for affection we see in neurotics, and may be expressed in dreams of longing for the mother, as well as otherwise. But there are elements in the neurotic need for affection — and these, dynamically, the essential ones — which make it a phenomenon entirely different from that existing in childhood.

Children certainly do need help and affection. But the healthy child, at least, is content with a reasonable amount of affection, or with the help it needs for the time being. The neurotic on the other hand, needs affection for quite a different reason, to reassure him against a double anxiety — anxiety concerning awareness and expression of his own hostility, and anxiety concerning retaliation from without. Because of his own repressed hostility he scents hostility — deceit, abuse, malice, rejection — in every move of the other person, as may be observed in his reactions to the analyst. The fact that he has to pay fees, for example, is a definite proof to him that the analyst wants only to abuse him. Even kindness may have only the effect of strengthening his suspicions. The reassurance he requires is unconditional love; which means that the other person should have no gratification or advantage in the relationship, but offer him a complete sacrifice of all he loves or cherishes. The other should always be admiring and compliant, however the neurotic behaves. Needs of this kind will hardly ever be met, and the analytic situation certainly means their continued frustration.

These implications being clarified, we can now answer the above question: getting affection protects the patient against his own lurking hostility and fear; as soon as he feels frustrated or rejected in these protective needs his hostility springs up. On this basis it is to be understood that a good interpretation is bound to evoke hostility, implying as it does an acute frustration of the patient's excessive need for affection, so that he feels it to be a direct criticism and a direct rejection.

I shall now try to summarize the different points made here, disregarding detailed trends: It is inherent in the character structure concerned that intense hostility from various interrelated sources is easily provoked. It is provoked unavoidably in the analytical situation, particularly by good interpretations. This hostility turns against the analyst and in its entirety constitutes a definite impulse to annihilate the analyst's efforts.

On the other hand, growing out of the same conditions these patients have a definite dread of any move forward: progress, success, or recovery. One part of the patient definitely shrinks from recovery and prefers illness. Different as the two currents are, they coöperate, and this is what makes the negative therapeutic reaction so difficult to conquer.

The main difference in my concept of the negative therapeutic reaction from Freud's then would be: In those cases in which I can observe the negative reaction the hostility towards the analyst is no surface attitude, unessential by comparison with the patient's recoiling tendency. Both attitudes are, on the contrary, from the same sources, inseparably entangled, and of equal importance.

To deal adequately with the negative therapeutic reaction it is necessary in the first place to recognize it as such. This is not difficult in cases in which it comes out in rather dramatic form as described by Freud, or as I have presented it here. Yet even so, an inexperienced analyst may become uncertain and discouraged, without recognizing in a detached fashion that this is the very effect the patient designs to produce in him. The same forces in the same combinations may, however, operate in an insidious manner, skilfully masked in pseudo coöperation; or behind a recognition and admiration of the analyst, including calling attention to some superficial improvement made. There will, however, be a discrepancy between recognition plus gain in intellectual insight and the lack of proportionate changes in the patient's personality. As soon as the analyst notices such a discrepancy he must confront the patient with this problem.

If one recognizes the negative therapeutic reaction in its various manifestations one must agree with Freud that it is a frequent occurrence, perhaps, as Freud points out, a feature of every severe neurosis — to which I should like to add only: in our culture.

The technical principles applied are pretty much the same as those presented in a recent paper. They are, roughly speaking, the same principles we all follow, namely, observing and uncovering carefully the emotional reactions of the patient to the analyst, with emphasis on two points:

1. As long as the negative reaction persists I select out of the material offered by the patient those parts which I can relate to his reaction to the analyst, and interpret those only.

2. As long as the negative therapeutic reaction governs the picture I refrain from making any construction of the past nor do I make direct use of one offered by the patient. The reason lies in the fact that *the attitudes we see in the adult patient are not direct repetitions or revivals of infantile attitudes, but have been changed in quality and quantity by the consequences which have developed out of the early experiences.* The "no one but I" ambition, for instance, is not a direct repetition of any infantile rivalry situation, nor is excessive craving for affection a simple repetition of the wish to be sheltered by the mother. Hence a direct interpretation in terms of the œdipus complex is of no avail in as much as it skips the intermediate steps of development, and therefore cannot resolve the vicious circle in which the patient is moving. The negative therapeutic reaction is — if at all — soluble only if the analyst persists in analyzing the immediate reactions in their immediate causations.

It is needless to say — and I say it only because misunderstandings have arisen — that this procedure does not mean that I attribute less importance to childhood experiences than any other analyst. These are of fundamental importance since they determine the direction of the individual's development. In fact, memories pertinent to the present situation do arise if the upper layers are carefully worked through, and do their share in helping understand the entire development.

If one persists in this way the negative therapeutic reaction can be overcome: to put it with more reserve — this has been my experience in cases of the described structure. This, of course, does not mean that we can cure all severe neuroses, but it means that the negative reaction as such does not imply a bad prognosis. The criteria for the therapeutic chances of a neurosis seem to lie in a series of factors and it would be desirable to get a more precise picture of the nature, weight and combination of these factors.

Later Writings

Introduction

At the beginning of "The Technique of Psychoanalytic Therapy," Horney pointed out that all psychoanalytic theories have grown out of observations made while applying the psychoanalytic method and that "the theories, in turn, later exerted their influence on psychoanalytic practice." In *New Ways in Psychoanalysis*, she proclaimed that her "desire to make a critical reevaluation of psychoanalytical theories had its origin in a dissatisfaction with therapeutic results" (1939, 7). The established theories and the methods of treatment derived from them "offered no means of solution" for many of her patients' problems. Her frustrations as a clinician led her to develop theories that more adequately described the phenomena she was encountering, and these theories, in turn, influenced her therapeutic practice.

The interaction between theory and practice continued throughout Horney's life, leading to a continual evolution of her ideas about both neurosis and treatment. I have traced the development of her theories in detail in *Karen Horney: A Psychoanalyst's Search for Self-Understanding*, and I shall offer a condensed account here to provide a context for her teachings about the therapeutic process. I believe that Horney has much practical wisdom to offer clinicians who differ from her theoretically, but her views on therapy cannot be fully understood without a knowledge of her ideas about personality disorders.

As we have seen, she began to articulate these ideas after she came to the United States in the essays she wrote on clinical issues. In the ten years between 1936 and 1946, Horney published four books: *The Neurotic Personality of Our Time* (1937), *New Ways in Psychoanalysis* (1939), *Self-Analysis* (1942), and *Our Inner Conflicts* (1945). In these books, she systematized and refined her ideas about the defenses against anxiety and the conflicts between these defenses. In her first book, she said little about the implications of her new psychoanalytic paradigm for the therapeutic process, but *New Ways in Psychoanalysis* concludes with a chapter on the topic, and she discussed it at length in *Self-Analysis,* which is as much about what happens in dyadic therapy as it is about analyzing oneself.

In *The Neurotic Personality of Our Time* and *New Ways in Psychoanalysis,* Horney stated her disagreements with Freud and began to develop her own version of psychoanalysis. Its distinguishing features were a greater emphasis on culture, a conception of neurosis as a set of defenses devised to cope with basic anxiety, and a focus on current character structure rather than infantile experience.

Horney argued that because he overemphasized the biological sources of human behavior, Freud had incorrectly assumed the universality of the feelings, attitudes, and kinds of relationships that were common in his culture. Not recognizing the importance of social factors, he attributed neurotic egocentricity to a narcissistic libido, hostility to a destruction instinct, an obsession with money to an anal libido, and acquisitiveness to orality. But anthropology shows that cultures vary widely in their tendency to generate these characteristics and the Oedipus complex as well, and Horney's experience of cultural difference after she moved to the United States confirmed this point of view.

Horney rejected Freud's derivation of neurosis from the clash between culture and instinct. In Freud's view, we must have culture in order to survive, and we must repress or sublimate our instincts in order to have culture. Horney did not believe that collision between the individual and society is inevitable; rather, she argued, it occurs when the environment frustrates our emotional needs and inspires fear and hostility. Freud depicts human beings as inherently insatiable, destructive, and antisocial, but according to Horney these characteristics are not expressions of instinct but neurotic responses to adverse conditions.

Horney did not reject the significance of childhood in emotional development, but she emphasized pathogenic conditions in the family that make children feel unsafe, unloved, and unvalued rather than the frustration of their libidinal desires. As a result of these conditions, children develop "basic anxiety," a feeling of being helpless in a potentially hostile world, which they try to reduce by adopting such strategies as the pursuit of love, power, or detachment.

Horney felt that these defensive strategies are doomed to failure because they generate "vicious circles" in which the means employed to allay anxiety tend to increase it. For example, frustration of the need for love makes that need insatiable, and the demandingness and jealousy that follow make it less likely than ever that the person will receive affection. People who have not been loved develop a feeling of being unlovable that leads them to discount any evidence to the contrary. Being deprived of affection has made them dependent on others, but they are afraid of that dependency because it makes them too vulnerable. Horney compared the situation created in this way to that "of a person who is starving for food yet does not dare to take any for fear that it might be poisoned" (1937, 114).

Although Horney devoted much of *The Neurotic Personality of Our Time* to the neurotic need for love, she also gave a good deal of space to the quest for power, prestige, and possession that develops when a person feels hopeless about gaining affection. She also discussed detachment and some of the intrapsychic strategies of defense, such as guilt, neurotic suffering, and self-inflation. She was to examine these in much greater detail later.

Horney's paradigm for the structure of neurosis is one in which disturbances in human relationships generate a basic anxiety that leads to the adoption of strategies of defense that are not only self-defeating but in conflict with one another. This paradigm formed the basis of Horney's mature theory.

Horney's early books also contain what became the foundational idea of her thought: neurosis is a process in which one becomes alienated from his or her "real self." The real self consists of inherent talents, capacities, and predispositions, which can develop fully only in an atmosphere of warmth, security, and acceptance. If one feels unsafe, unloved, and unvalued, one develops a basic anxiety that inhibits spontaneity and forces him or her to adopt defensive strategies. These strategies help to allay anxiety, but at a great price because they lead to self-alienation. A vicious circle develops in which self-alienation makes one feel weaker and more anxious, and this in turn forces one to cling all the more compulsively to the defenses that are alienating one from one's real self.

Among the most significant aspects of Horney's new version of psychoanalysis was her shift in emphasis from the past to the present. She replaced Freud's focus on genesis with a structural approach, arguing that psychoanalysis should be less concerned with infantile origins than with the current constellation of defenses and inner conflicts. In *New Ways in Psychoanalysis*, she distinguished between her own "evolutionistic" thinking and what she called Freud's "mechanistic-evolutionistic" thought. Evolutionistic thinking presupposes that "things which exist today have not existed in the same form from the very beginning, but have developed out of previous stages. These preceding stages may have little resemblance to the present forms, but the present forms would be unthinkable without the preceding ones." Mechanistic-evolutionistic thinking holds that "nothing really new is created in the process of development," that "what we see today is only the old in a changed form" (1939, 42). For Horney, the profound influence of early experiences does not preclude continued development, whereas for Freud later reactions or experiences are considered repetitions of earlier ones.

According to Horney, at the heart of Freud's conception of the relation between childhood experiences and the behavior of the adult is the doctrine of the timelessness of the unconscious. Fears and desires or entire experiences repressed in childhood remain uninfluenced by further experiences or growth. This gives rise to the concept of fixation, which may pertain to a person in the early environment, such as father or mother, or to a stage of libidinal development. Because of the concept of fixation, later attachments or other behaviors may be regarded as repetitions of the past, which has remained encapsulated and unchanged in the unconscious.

Horney did not attempt to refute the doctrine of the timelessness of the unconscious or the cluster of concepts related to it, but rather built her own theory on a different set of premises. The "non-mechanistic viewpoint is that in organic development there can never be a simple repetition or regression to former stages" (1939, 44). The past is always contained in the present, but through a developmental process rather than through repetition. In Horney's model, early experiences profoundly affect us not by producing fixations that cause us to repeat earlier patterns but by conditioning the ways in which we respond to the world. These in turn are influenced by subsequent experiences and evolve into adult defenses and character structures. Early experiences may have a greater impact than later ones because they determine the direction of development, but the character of the adult is the evolved product of *all* previous interactions between psychic structure and environment.

Another important difference between Horney and Freud is that Freud saw the determining experiences in childhood as relatively few in number and mostly of a sexual nature, whereas Horney thought the sum total of childhood experiences is responsible for neurotic development. Things go wrong because of all the things in the culture, in the relations with peers, and especially in the family that make the child feel unsafe, unloved, and unvalued and that give rise to basic anxiety. This anxiety leads to the development of defensive strategies that form a neurotic character structure, and it is this character structure from which later difficulties emanate. Horney saw sexual difficulties as the result rather than the cause of personality disorders.

As we have seen, Horney said that her desire to reevaluate psychoanalytic theory originated in a dissatisfaction with clinical results. In *New Ways in Psychoanalysis* she redefined transference, countertransference, and the goals of therapy, and in *Self-Analysis* she developed an account of the therapeutic process as conducted in accordance with her new paradigm. She refined her ideas about therapy in subsequent writings, especially in her lectures on technique (see part III), but the focus on structure rather than genesis remained the same.

According to Freud, analysis fosters regressive reactions, leading the patient to transfer onto the analyst feelings that derive from childhood. Horney's view of transference was that patients behave toward analysts in accordance with their character structure, and the analyst can use the transference to understand patients' defenses and inner conflicts. Like transference, countertransference is a manifestation not of infantile reactions but of character structure, in this case that of the therapist. Analysts must understand their own defenses lest they be blind to or indulgent of similar defenses in their patients. Hence the importance of a good didactic analysis and of "never-ending self-analysis" (1939, 303).

Horney focused on recognizing patients' defenses and discovering their functions and consequences. The purpose of therapy is "not to help the patient to gain mastery over his instincts but to lessen his anxiety to such an extent that he can dispense with his 'neurotic trends.'" Patients' defenses not only distort their relations with others but lead to a loss of contact with their spontaneous individual selves. The ultimate goal of therapy is "to restore the individual to himself, to help him regain his spontaneity and find his center of gravity in himself" (1939, 11).

Except for her lectures on technique, *Self-Analysis* contains Horney's fullest account of the therapeutic methods she developed on the basis of her new paradigm. To relinquish neurotic trends and achieve self-realizing growth, one must recognize one's trends (or defenses), explore their implications, and see how they are interrelated. Success in this painful and difficult process requires powerful incentives and ruthless honesty. It also requires both patient and analyst to assume specific roles and responsibilities. In self-analysis, the individual must try, as far as possible, to be both patient and analyst.

Horney recommended beginning with the patient's most conspicuous neurotic trend. Some patients will present their "need for absolute independence," others their "need to be loved and approved of," and yet others their "highly developed power drive." The trend that appears first is not necessarily the strongest or most influential, but it will be the least repressed and the one that "jibes best with the person's conscious or semi-conscious image of himself" (1942, 74–75). The more repressed trends will emerge later. The analysis must go through three stages: recognition of the neurotic trend; "discovery of its causes, manifestations, and consequences; and discovery of its interrelations with other parts of the personality, especially with other neurotic trends" (89).

These steps must be taken for each neurotic trend, they are not always taken in the same order, and each has "a particular therapeutic value" (89). Recognition of a neurotic trend does not usually produce radical change, but it diminishes people's sense of being powerless and at the mercy of intangible forces; it also gives them hope that they can do something about their suffering. Exploring the unfortunate consequences of the trend leads to an appreciation of the "necessity for change" (92). Because each trend is bound up with other, often contradictory, trends, people cannot work on one without taking up the others and trying to understand how they are all related. They must face the fact that their conflicts are paralyzing them or tearing them apart.

"The matter of incentive [is] crucial" in therapy (19), for patients must be strongly motivated if they are to endure the pain and struggle of working through their trends and changing their personality. Incentive is even more important in self-analysis, in which one has no help in overcoming resistances. There are two sources of incentive: the desire to suffer less from one's problems and the desire to unfold one's potentialities, "to live as full a life as given circumstances permit." Horney posits "an incentive to grow" that motivates a person "to come to grips with himself despite all the ordeals he may have to go through" (22–23).

For Freud, urges toward self-development emanate from narcissistic self-inflation. For Horney, narcissistic tendencies are not primary but reactive. They lead us to abandon our real selves and to try to actualize a "phony self." As the phony self "evaporates" through the process of analysis, we get in touch with our real self, which "is or should be, the most alive center of psychic life. It is this psychic center to which appeal is made in analytical work" (291). The desire to find ourselves, to develop ourselves, to realize our potentialities "belongs among those strivings that defy further analysis" (23). It is a given of human nature.

Horney presented the therapeutic process as an "exquisitely cooperative enterprise" (1946, 187) in which analyst and patient "work actively toward the same goal" (1942, 301). If the therapist assumes "an authoritative attitude," patients may develop "the paralyzing feeling that [they are] more or less helpless," whereas the object is to foster their "initiative and resourcefulness." In Horney's model, both patients and analysts have responsibilities. The three main tasks of patients are to express themselves as completely as possible, mainly through free association, to become aware of their unconscious driving forces and their effects on their lives, and to change the patterns of behavior that disturb their relations to self and others.

In *The Neurotic Personality of Our Time,* Horney had raised the question of whether her theory can be called psychoanalysis. If one believes that psychoanalysis "is constituted entirely by the sum total of the theories propounded by Freud, then what is presented here is not psychoanalysis. If, however, one believes that the essentials of psychoanalysis lie in certain basic trends of thought concerning the role of unconscious processes and the ways in which they find expression, and in a form of therapeutic treatment that brings these processes to awareness, then what I present is psychoanalysis" (1937, ix). Horney has often been accused of having discarded psychoanalytic conceptions of the unconscious, it is important to understand what she meant by unconscious forces or processes. By and large, she was not referring to drives that were repressed in early childhood and are still pressing for fulfillment. For her, the main repressed early affect with which we need to get in touch is hostility, which we may still be afraid to own. The repressed material with which she was primarily concerned derives from neurotic trends that are in conflict with our predominant trend or our conscious conception of ourselves, or whose full implications we do not want to recognize.

When we gain insight into an unconscious factor, we may recognize something that has been entirely repressed, as when "compulsively modest or benevolent" people discover that they actually have "a diffuse contempt for people." Or we may recognize the extent and intensity of a factor of which we have partial awareness, as when consciously ambitious people realize that their ambition "is an all-devouring passion" that determines their lives and contains the "destructive element of wanting a vindictive triumph over others." Or we may discover a relationship between seemingly unconnected factors, like the patient who was preoccupied with impending disaster because his "grandiose expectations" had been thwarted and he had "an underlying wish to die" (1942, 111–12). In each of these examples the unconscious factors are part of the current character structure.

Because of our resistances, insight into unconscious factors is difficult to achieve. Part of us wishes to maintain "the illusions and the safety afforded by the neurotic structure," while another part seeks to change and grow (267). The part that wants to maintain the status quo is threatened by every insight and seeks to block the analytic process. This is why incentive is so crucial.

Horney advocates an accepting attitude toward our resistances because we are not responsible for the forces behind their development. The defenses they are protecting have given us "a means of dealing with life when all other means have failed." They should be regarded as "given factors," "organic developments" (284–85). To achieve such self-acceptance, we must recognize that we are as we are for reasons beyond our control and that our parents "too were caught in conflicts and could not help harming" us (1939, 284). An understanding of genesis can be very important here. Accepting the inevitability of our neurosis does not mean approving of it, however, or giving up the effort to change.

Horney believed that if we can overcome our resistances, insight can have a therapeutic effect, especially if it is not just intellectual but is felt "in our 'guts'" (1942, 111). In facing the truth of our feelings, we liberate the energy that was needed for repression and open the way for action. Once we have seen what is going on in ourselves, we can envision a "way out of [our] distress," and this is a source of hope, even if our initial reaction was "one of hurt or fright" and we are not immediately able to change (114).

The most challenging task of patients is to change the factors within themselves that interfere with development. Horney did not provide a precise account of the mechanics of change, but she was quite clear on what she wanted to see happen. She hoped that patients would gain "a more realistic attitude" toward themselves "instead of wavering between self-aggrandizement and self-degradation"; that they would develop "a spirit of activity, assertion, and courage" instead of being paralyzed by "inertia and fears"; that they would become "able to plan instead of drifting"; that they would find "the center of gravity" in themselves "instead of hanging onto others with excessive expectations and excessive accusations"; and that they would develop a "greater friendliness and understanding for people instead of harboring a defensive . . . hostility" (118).

Therapists contribute five components to the healing process: observation, understanding, interpretation, help with resistances, and "general human help" (123). In observing, they try "not to select any one element prematurely" (126) but to pay equal attention to everything the patient presents. They then try "to grasp the red thread that passes through the apparently amorphous mass of material" (127). They interpret repetitive themes, overreactions, dreams and fantasies, resistances, evasions and omissions, and transferences (134–37). They solicit the patient's free associations as an aid to interpretation, which is a cooperative process. They make "suggestions as to possible meanings" if patients are ready for them, and "both try to test out the validity of the suggestions" (138).

As we have seen, in Horney's conception of transference, patients uncon-sciously display "in analysis the same irrational emotional factors, the same strivings and reactions" they manifest in other relationships (136–37). Since (ideally) the analyst has been well analyzed and engages in continuous self-analysis, the patient's patterns of behavior are not a response to peculiarities in the analyst and can be more readily traced to the patient's character structure. "By his very presence," therefore, the analyst "gives the patient a unique op-portunity to become aware of his behavior toward people" (142–43).

Horney assigned to analysts an active role in dealing with resistances. They must recognize them, help the patient to recognize them, and try to find out, "with or without the patient's help, what it is that the latter is warding off" (139–40). They can help patients overcome their resistances by offering en-couragement and emotional support.

For Horney, providing "human help" is a major part of the analyst's role. When the analysis is conducted in an atmosphere of "constructive friendli-ness" (1939, 299), anxiety is reduced and patients become better able to recog-nize and relinquish their defenses. Because they are self-alienated, patients have trouble taking themselves seriously — their real selves, that is, rather than their "inflated image" of themselves, which they take too seriously. The ana-lyst's friendly, serious interest helps patients to regard their growth as impor-tant and gives them the courage to be on friendly terms with themselves. If the analyst proves reliable as a friend, "this good experience may help the patient also retrieve his faith in others" (1942, 144–45).

The therapist's support is particularly valuable in helping patients deal with discouragement, anxiety, and the realization of painful truths about them-selves. It assists them in overcoming fear or hopelessness, giving them a sense that their problems can be resolved. Patients will feel profoundly threatened when, "bereft of glory," they realize they are "not as saintly, as loving, as powerful, as independent as [they] had believed." At this point, they need "someone who does not lose faith" in them, even though their "own faith is gone." In the course of therapy, patients must confront not only their loss of glory, but also the unsavory characteristics that are destructive to themselves and others. They tend to react with unconstructive self-hate, rather than with the self-acceptance that will enable them to grow. The therapist perceives that they are "striving and struggling human being[s]" and "still likes and respects" them as a result (145). This encouragement counteracts patients' self-hate and helps them to like and respect themselves.

Self-analysis is much more difficult than analysis because we must play not only the patient's role but also that of the therapist. It is harder to understand our behavior toward others without the well-analyzed analyst on whom to play out our neurotic patterns of interaction. But Horney felt that we "can develop an amazing faculty of keen self-observation" if we are bent on understanding our difficulties (146). The biggest problems in self-analysis are overcoming resistances and maintaining a hopeful and constructive attitude toward ourselves in the absence of human help. Despite these obstacles, Horney believed that self-analysis can be quite successful if the person has had prior analytic experience. Her prime example was a patient named Clare, who I have argued elsewhere is a fictionalized version of Horney herself (Paris 1994). As Horney's fullest case history, her account of Clare provides excellent illustrations of many of her ideas about the therapeutic process.

After *Self-Analysis,* Horney's next book was *Our Inner Conflicts* (1945), which contains important refinements of her theory. I shall consider that book in due course, but first I should like to discuss the opening essays in part II of the present collection: "What Does the Analyst Do?" and "How Do You Progress After Analysis?" These were Horney's contributions to *Are You Considering Psychoanalysis?,* a volume of essays by various hands she edited in 1946. Because these essays address topics Horney had taken up in *Self-Analysis* — the role of the therapist and the possibilities of self-analysis — it seems appropriate to comment on them here. They repeat some of her earlier points but add new material as well.

In "What Does the Analyst Do?" Horney argued that analysts should not try to suppress their emotions, which play an important role in the therapeutic process. Patients may be alarmed at the thought of analysts letting their "own emotional reactions come into play," but analysts cannot choke off their "impatience" or "discouragement without also inactivating [their] sympathy and blunting [their] sensitivity to what is going on," both in the patient and in themselves. Their discouragement, for example, might alert them to a patient's "hidden strategies" for defeating the analyst, or it may be a sign of their own ambition and need for glory, in which case it needs to be analyzed lest it disrupt the therapeutic process. Analysts should not "discard [their] feelings," which are "the most alive part" of themselves.

This essay elaborated Horney's idea that one of the therapist's roles is to provide human help to the patient. She endorsed neither Freud's prescription of analytic neutrality nor the contention of "some modern analysts" that "the very friendship the analyst extends to the patient is essential in curing him of his disturbances in human relationships." Although sometimes she had seemed to be advocating the second position herself, she was uncomfortable with the term "friendship." In a sense, the relationship between therapist and patient "is friendship at its very best," but it differs from "real friendship" in that it lacks the essential ingredients of "spontaneity and mutuality." Horney cited John Macmurray's characterization of friendship as a relationship in which we engage "because it is natural for human beings to share their experience, to understand one another, to find joy and satisfaction in living together, in expressing and revealing themselves to one another." Whereas friendship "has no purpose beyond itself," the relationship between patient and analyst "is essentially a functional one": "Your analyst and you may mutually like and respect each other. Yet you enter into the relationship for a definite purpose: to free you from your neurotic shackles and thereby create better conditions for your growth as a human being." The emphasis in the relationship should be "on the work to be done."

The friendly attitude of the therapist is, nonetheless, a crucial part of the healing process. It is the therapist's "consistent focus on the patient's best interest that eventually helps him to gain the latter's confidence." The patient needs "repeated, concrete evidence" of the therapist's reliability: "With all his anxieties, suspicions, and defensive hostilities — conscious or unconscious — he needs proof after proof before he can dare take the risk of really trusting someone." The therapist's acceptance of patients in spite of their problems helps them to become interested in themselves as they are, rather than being concerned mainly with what they should be. And the therapist's belief in patients' potentiality for growth helps them to regain their faith in themselves.

Horney's theory and practice intersected here, for her belief in her patients' potentialities for growth was based on her model of human nature, in which there are innate constructive forces pressing toward self-realization. That model, she contended, grew out of her clinical experience and was confirmed by it. With "rare exceptions," we see patients' "forward moving forces . . . come to life during analysis." Horney saw therapy as creating a safe, reassuring environment in which patients' anxiety would gradually subside, reducing their need for defenses and helping them get in touch with their genuine thoughts and feelings. Although she believed in innate constructive forces and the possibilities of growth, Horney was no facile optimist, for she had a vivid sense of how difficult it is to change and of the obstacles that lie on the path to self-realization.

In "How Do You Progress After Analysis?" Horney reaffirmed her belief in the value of self-analysis for someone who has been in therapy. She offered an example of a former patient who had success with the practice. As a result of her therapy, the patient, an interior decorator named Eileen, "had already recognized to what an extent she was glorifying her appeasing, conciliatory attitude." In her self-analysis, she investigated her tendency to put up with too much and gradually came to despise the unassertiveness she had originally attributed to her "goodness." The fact that she still could not change led her to the realization that "her desire to become stronger was paralyzed by her un-conscious feelings of being entitled to a soft and easy life." Only by recognizing and relinquishing her magical "claims" could she free herself to make efforts on her own behalf. Eileen has a "compliant" personality that is similar in many ways to that of Clare in *Self-Analysis;* and, although there are no identifiably autobiographical details here, as there are in the Clare case (Paris 1994), I cannot help wondering if Horney was not again fictionalizing some of her own "never-ending self-analysis."

Before discussing how we progress after analysis, Horney took up the inter-esting question of when analysis should be terminated. When psychotherapy was primarily concerned with the alleviation of symptoms, treatment was terminated when the symptoms disappeared, but now it "deals with person-ality as a whole" and helps us develop our potentialities. Because our growth as human beings "is a process that can and should go on as long as [we] live," "analysis as a means of gaining self-knowledge is intrinsically an interminable process." If patient and analyst "focused their attention entirely on what re-mained to be done, they would be tempted to go on and on forever."

Therapy can be terminated, Horney felt, when patients are ready to continue on their own. There are three main criteria for this. They must have clear and constructive objectives and not still be looking for a magical solution to their problems. They must be interested in seeing themselves as they are and could be "instead of trying to live up to a phantastic notion of what [they] should be." And they must take responsibility for their difficulties and want to work on themselves — they must realize "that heaven and hell are within" them.

In addition to the two essays from *Are You Considering Psychoanalysis?*, part II of the present collection includes two forewords — one to an article en-titled "Gymnastics and Personality" and one to a letter from a patient on the topic of finding the real self — and a number of abstracts of talks that Horney gave between 1946 and 1952. The letter and Horney's foreword to it are classic statements about the real self; the other items supply interesting details about Horney's thought and activity. The remaining major items in part II are a set of lecture notes dating from 1947 dealing with the question of how to resolve the conflict between pride and self-hatred in therapy; and an essay entitled "The Goals of Analytic Therapy," published in German in *Psyche* in 1951. These writings and the lectures in part III should be seen in the context of Horney's mature theory (for a full exposition, see *Karen Horney* [Paris 1994]).

Although Horney formulated her mature theory in her last two books, many of its elements were present earlier. In *The Neurotic Personality of Our Time,* she discussed two of the strategies people employ to cope with basic anxiety, the pursuit of love and of power, and she made reference to detachment, which became an important defense in *Our Inner Conflicts*. In *New Ways in Psychoanalysis,* she included chapters on narcissism and perfectionism, which are not mentioned in *Our Inner Conflicts* but appear as major solutions in *Neurosis and Human Growth*. In her first two books, she also introduced what she later called intrapsychic strategies, such as self-inflation, self-recrimination, over-conformity to inner standards, and neurotic guilt and suffering. Her list of ten neurotic trends in *Self-Analysis* contained an assortment of interpersonal and intrapsychic strategies that she systematized in her last two books.

The movement of Horney's thought was toward greater inclusiveness, a more sophisticated taxonomy, and a fuller elaboration of each solution. In *Our Inner Conflicts* and *Neurosis and Human Growth,* she organized defenses into systems of interpersonal and intrapsychic strategies, she described the constellations of character traits, behaviors, and beliefs that accompany each strategy, and she showed how defenses and inner conflicts give rise to complex and infinitely variable character structures.

Because Horney's thought was still evolving at the end, there are significant differences between her last two books. In *Our Inner Conflicts* her focus was on our relations with others, while in *Neurosis and Human Growth* it was on our relation to ourselves. Although she identified disturbances in human relations as the source of our difficulties in *Neurosis and Human Growth,* her emphasis was on the intrapsychic strategies that accompany self-idealization. Horney named the major neurotic solutions differently in each book, calling them compliance, aggression, and detachment in *Our Inner Conflicts* and self-effacement, expansiveness, and resignation in *Neurosis and Human Growth.* The two sets of terms can be confusing, but they clearly overlap and can often be used interchangeably. Horney described compliance, aggression, and detachment primarily in interpersonal terms, while in her discussions of the self-effacing, expansive, and resigned solutions she combined the interpersonal and the intrapsychic. The account of Horney's mature theory that follows synthesizes the teachings of *Our Inner Conflicts* and *Neurosis and Human Growth.*

In the introduction to *Neurosis and Human Growth,* Horney distinguished between healthy development, in which individuals realize their potentialities, and neurotic development, in which they become alienated from their real selves. The subtitle of the book is *The Struggle toward Self-Realization,* and her concept of the real self was now the foundation of her understanding of both health and neurosis.

The real self is not a fixed entity but a set of intrinsic potentialities — including temperament, talents, capacities, and predispositions — that are part of our genetic makeup and need a favorable environment in which to develop. It is not a product of learning because one cannot be taught to be oneself; but neither is it impervious to external influence, since it is actualized through interactions with an external world that can provide many paths of development. People can actualize themselves in different ways under different conditions. Everyone requires certain conditions in childhood, however, to achieve self-realization. These include "an atmosphere of warmth," which enables children to express their thoughts and feelings, the good will of others to supply their various needs, and "healthy friction with the wishes and will" of those around them (1950, 18).

When their neuroses prevent parents from loving the child or thinking "of him as the particular individual he is," the child develops a feeling of basic anxiety, a sense of the world as threatening and unreliable. Such a feeling prevents him "from relating himself to others with the spontaneity of his real feelings, and forces him" to develop defensive strategies (1950, 18). Horney divided these into *interpersonal* and *intrapsychic* strategies.

According to Horney, people cope with their basic anxiety by adopting a compliant or self-effacing solution and moving *toward* people, an aggressive or expansive solution and moving *against* people, or a detached or resigned solution and moving *away from* people. Healthy people move appropriately and flexibly in all three directions, but in neurotic development these moves become compulsive and indiscriminate. Each solution involves a constellation of behavior patterns and personality traits, a conception of justice, and a set of beliefs about human nature, human values, and the human condition. Each also involves a "deal" or bargain with fate in which obedience to the dictates of that solution is supposed to be rewarded.

Horney's is above all a theory of inner conflict. In each of the interpersonal defenses, one of the elements involved in basic anxiety is overemphasized: helplessness in the compliant solution, hostility in the aggressive, and isolation in the detached. Because under pathogenic conditions all of these feelings are likely to arise, individuals will come to make all three of the defensive moves, giving rise to what Horney called the "basic conflict." To gain some sense of wholeness, they will make one of these moves predominant and repress the others. Which move they emphasize will depend upon the combination of temperamental and environmental factors at work in their situation. The other trends will continue to exist, but they will operate unconsciously and will manifest themselves in disguised, devious ways. The basic conflict is not resolved but has simply gone underground.

When submerged trends are for some reason brought closer to the surface, individuals will experience severe inner turmoil and may be paralyzed, unable to move in any direction. Under the impetus of some powerful influence or the dramatic failure of their predominant solution, they may embrace one of their repressed defensive strategies. They may experience this as conversion or education, but it will really be the substitution of one defensive strategy for another.

People in whom compliant trends are dominant try to overcome their basic anxiety by gaining affection and approval and controlling others through their dependency. Their values "lie in the direction of goodness, sympathy, love, generosity, unselfishness, humility; while egotism, ambition, callousness, unscrupulousness, wielding of power are abhorred" (1945, 54). They embrace Christian values, but in a compulsive way because they are necessary to their defense system. They must believe in turning the other cheek, and they must see the world as displaying a providential order in which virtue is rewarded. Their bargain is that if they are good, loving people who shun pride and do not seek their own gain or glory, they will be well treated by fate and other people. If their bargain is not honored, they may despair of divine justice, conclude that they are at fault, or have recourse to belief in a justice that transcends human understanding. They need to believe not only in the fairness of the world order, but also in the goodness of human nature, and here, too, they are vulnerable to disappointment. Self-effacing people must repress their expansive tendencies in order to make their bargain work, but they are frequently attracted to expansive people, through whom they can participate vicariously in the mastery of life. They often develop a "morbid dependency" on such a partner.

People in whom expansive tendencies are predominant have goals, traits, and values that are opposite to those of the self-effacing solution. What appeals to them most is not love, but mastery. They abhor helplessness, are ashamed of suffering, and need to achieve success, prestige, or recognition. In *Neurosis and Human Growth,* Horney divided the expansive solutions into three distinct kinds: narcissistic, perfectionistic, and arrogant-vindictive. There are thus five major solutions.

Narcissistic people seek to master life "by self-admiration and the exercise of charm" (1950, 212). They were often favored and admired children, gifted beyond average, and they grew up regarding the world as a fostering parent and themselves as favorites of fortune. They have an unquestioning belief in their abilities and feel there is no one they cannot win over. Their insecurity is manifested in the fact that they may speak incessantly of their exploits and wonderful qualities and need endless confirmation of their estimate of themselves in the form of admiration and devotion. Their bargain is that if they hold onto their dreams and their exaggerated claims for themselves, life is bound to give them what they want. If it does not, they may experience a psychological collapse because they are ill-equipped to cope with reality.

Perfectionistic people have extremely high moral and intellectual standards, on the basis of which they look down upon others. They take great pride in their rectitude and aim for a "flawless excellence" in the conduct of life. Because of the difficulty of living up to their standards, they tend to equate knowing about moral values with being a good person. While they deceive themselves in this way, they may insist that others live up to their standards of perfection and despise them for failing to do so, thus externalizing their self-condemnation. Perfectionists have a legalistic bargain in which being fair, just, and dutiful entitles them "to fair treatment by others and by life in general. This conviction of an infallible justice operating in life gives [them] a feeling of mastery" (1950, 197). Through the loftiness of their standards, they compel fate. Ill fortune or errors of their own making threaten their bargain and may overwhelm them with feelings of helplessness or self-hate.

Arrogant-vindictive people are motivated chiefly by a need for vindictive triumphs. Whereas narcissists received early admiration and perfectionists grew up under the pressure of rigid standards, arrogant-vindictive people were harshly treated in childhood and have a need to retaliate for the injuries they have suffered. They feel that "the world is an arena where, in the Darwinian sense, only the fittest survive and the strong annihilate the weak" (1945, 64). The only moral law inherent in the order of things is that might makes right. In their relations with others they are competitive, ruthless, and cynical. They want to be hard and tough and regard all manifestations of feeling as signs of weakness. Their bargain is essentially with themselves. They do not count on the world to give them anything but are convinced that they can reach their ambitious goals if they remain true to their vision of life as a battle and do not allow themselves to be influenced by their softer feelings or the traditional morality. If their expansive solution collapses, self-effacing trends may emerge.

Predominantly detached people pursue neither love nor mastery but rather worship freedom, peace, and self-sufficiency. They disdain the pursuit of worldly success and have a profound aversion to effort. They have a strong need for superiority and usually regard their fellows with condescension, but they realize their ambition in imagination rather than through actual accomplishments. They handle a threatening world by removing themselves from its power and shutting others out of their inner lives. In order to avoid being dependent on the environment, they try to subdue their inner cravings and to be content with little. They do not usually rail against life but resign themselves to things as they are and accept their fate with ironic humor or stoical dignity. Their bargain is that if they ask nothing of others, others will not bother them, that if they try for nothing, they will not fail; and that if they expect little of life, they will not be disappointed.

Horney's taxonomy of defenses describes a dynamic situation: solutions combine, conflict, become stronger or weaker, need to be defended, and are replaced by others when they collapse. There is always more than one solution at work, and clashes between the defenses cause oscillations, inconsistencies, and self-hate. One of the most powerful features of Horney's theory is that it makes sense of contradictory attitudes, behaviors, and beliefs by seeing them as part of a structure of inner conflicts.

While interpersonal difficulties are creating the moves toward, against, and away from others and the conflicts between the moves, concomitant intrapsychic problems are producing their own defensive strategies. To compensate for feelings of weakness, worthlessness, and inadequacy, people create, with the aid of their imagination, an "idealized image" of themselves that they endow with "unlimited powers and exalted faculties" (1950, 22). The process of self-idealization must be understood in relation to the interpersonal strategies because the idealized image is based on the individual's predominant defense and the attributes it exalts.

The idealized image does not ultimately make people feel better about themselves but rather leads to increased self-hate and inner conflict. Although the qualities with which they endow themselves are dictated by their predominant interpersonal strategy, the subordinate solutions are also represented; and because each solution glorifies a different set of traits, the idealized image has contradictory aspects, all of which they must try to actualize. Moreover, since they can feel worthwhile only if they *are* their idealized image, everything that falls short is deemed worthless, and they develop a "despised image" that becomes the focus of self-contempt. A great many people, says Horney, shuttle "between a feeling of arrogant omnipotence and of being the scum of the earth" (1950, 188).

With the formation of the idealized image, people embark on a "search for glory," the object of which is to actualize their idealized self. What is considered to be glorious will vary with each solution. The creation of the idealized image produces not only the search for glory but the whole structure of phenomena that Horney calls the pride system. This includes neurotic pride, neurotic claims, and tyrannical shoulds, all of which result in intensified self-hate. As with their idealized image, the specific nature of people's pride, shoulds, claims, and self-hate will be influenced by their predominant solution and by the conflicts between it and subordinate trends.

Neurotic pride substitutes a pride in the attributes of the idealized self for realistic self-confidence and self-esteem. Threats to pride produce anxiety and hostility; its collapse results in self-contempt and despair. On the basis of their pride, people make neurotic claims on the world in which they demand to be treated in accordance with their grandiose conception of themselves. The claims are "pervaded by expectations of magic" (1950, 62). They intensify vulnerability, for their frustration deflates neurotic pride and confronts people with the sense of powerlessness and inadequacy from which they are fleeing.

The idealized image also generates what Horney called "the tyranny of the should." The function of the shoulds is to compel individuals to live up to their grandiose conception of themselves. The shoulds are determined largely by the character traits and values associated with the predominant solution, but because the subordinate trends are also represented in the idealized image, people are often caught in a "crossfire of conflicting shoulds." As they try to obey contradictory inner dictates, they are bound to hate themselves whatever they do, and even if they do nothing at all.

The shoulds are the basis of a bargain with fate. No matter what solution people have adopted, their bargain is that their claims will be honored if they live up to their shoulds. They seek magically to control external reality by obeying their inner dictates. They do not see their claims as unreasonable, of course, but only as what they have a right to expect, given their grandiose conception of themselves, and they feel that life is unfair if their expectations are frustrated. Their sense of justice is determined by their predominant solution and the bargain associated with it. The breakdown of their bargain often results in a psychological crisis. I have argued in *Bargains with Fate* that Shakespeare dramatizes this process in his major tragedies (Paris 1991).

Self-hate is the end product of the intrapsychic strategies of defense, each of which tends to magnify peoples' feelings of inadequacy and failure. Self-hate is essentially the rage their idealized self feels toward the self they actually are for not being what it "should" be. In *Neurosis and Human Growth,* Horney saw self-hate as "perhaps the greatest tragedy of the human mind. Man in reaching out for the Infinite and Absolute also starts destroying himself. When he makes a pact with the devil, who promises him glory, he has to go to hell — to the hell within himself" (1950, 154).

Horney's mature theory provided the framework for her thinking about the therapeutic process in the last seven years of her life. *Our Inner Conflicts* concludes with a chapter called "Resolution of Neurotic Conflicts" that describes neurosis as "a protective edifice built around the basic conflict" between the moves toward, against, and away from other people and the constellations of character traits, behaviors, and beliefs to which these moves have given rise (1945, 220). Horney divided analytical work into helping patients to realize (1) the nature and consequences of their defenses, and (2) their need to resolve their inner conflicts. A knowledge of character structure such as Horney described it will help analysts to make accurate inferences about the patient's personality "from seemingly insignificant indications." It will also enable them to grasp more readily "just what the patient wants to express by his associations and hence what ought to be dealt with at the moment" (1945, 225). As before, Horney stressed the importance of patients' understanding the negative effects of their defenses and inner conflicts not just intellectually but emotionally. She again emphasized the importance of constructive forces and the role of therapy in reducing anxiety and thus enabling patients to relinquish their defenses and get in touch with their real selves.

As I have observed, Horney tended to teach courses on the topic of the book on which she was working — or to write books about what she was teaching. In 1947, 1948, and 1949, she was teaching the ideas that resulted in *Neurosis and Human Growth*. A full set of her notes has survived for "Pride and Self-Hatred in Neuroses," the course she gave at the New School for Social Research in 1947 and 1948. The course, clearly a stage in the evolution of *Neurosis and Human Growth*, consisted of fourteen lectures, the first seven of which correspond to the first six chapters of the book. These deal with the search for glory, neurotic claims, the tyranny of the should, neurotic pride, self-hate and self-contempt, and alienation from self. The lectures on human relations and work also correspond to parts of *Neurosis and Human Growth*, as do the lectures on Freud and on therapy. Important differences, of course, mark the lectures and the book. Although the titles are similar, the contents of the chapters may vary considerably from those of the lectures. The ideas in *Neurosis and Human Growth* are much more sophisticated and fully developed, and the second half of the course only faintly resembles that of the book. Here I have included lecture fourteen, on the resolution of the conflict between pride and self-hatred, which contains observations about the therapeutic process that had not appeared before in Horney's work.

Whereas *Our Inner Conflicts* had focused on conflicts between the interpersonal strategies of compliance, aggression, and detachment, Horney's lectures on pride and self-hatred in neuroses concentrated on an intrapsychic conflict that became one of the major foci of *Neurosis and Human Growth*. In lecture 6, "The Dilemma Between Pride and Self-Hatred," Horney introduced the motif of the Devil's pact, the Faustian bargain people make when they sacrifice their souls (their real selves) in an effort to actualize an idealized version of themselves that will compensate for their feelings of weakness, worthlessness, and unlovability. They try to restore their pride through self-idealization, but the strategy fails, for it is an inexorable psychological law that attempts to achieve an impossible glory result in "a feeling of worthlessness" (Lecture 6).

In lecture 14, Horney addressed the problem of how to deal with pride and self-hate and the conflict between them in therapy. She divided people who come to analysis into those who have feelings of superiority in the foreground but also underlying feelings of self-hatred, and those who have feelings of self-abasement in the foreground but also an underlying sense of superiority. She discussed the difficulties each type brings to analysis, their responses to analysis and interpretation, their attitude toward the analyst, the steps they must take in therapy, and the sequence in which these steps must be taken. She concluded by describing some curative forces.

For Horney, the therapeutic process begins with insight. Aggressive patients must see that their feelings of superiority are unrealistic and destructive and that they must be given up. Self-effacing patients must see that their self-reproaches are not "a sign of high moral standards" but rather are "cramping and futile," the product of a "sadistic hostility to self." Both kinds of patients must "see the *connection* between pride and self-hatred" and acknowledge the cost of expecting to achieve the impossible. On becoming aware of the destructive effects of their search for glory, patients will be motivated by self-interest to change.

Insight is far from sufficient, however: "awareness" is a "*first,* indispensable step, but it is like opening a door. The person may or may not go through the door." Awareness alone "may lead to a kind of intellectual ecstasy of recognition without any constructive results." An appeal to self-interest will have little effect so long as patients are in the grip of self-hatred or are profoundly alienated from their real selves. Even if they want to change, it is very difficult for people to do so because they fear that in giving up their defenses they will plunge "into the abyss of self-hatred." Mere disillusionment will not work because their feelings of superiority or self-abasement serve psychological needs, and patients will "hold on to what is indispensable" to them.

Change must be "a gradual process" in which patients acquire "some *real* strength on which to fall back." Analysts can help by making them more aware of their "real assets." Other curative forces include patients' acceptance of their problems as their own ("taking back of externalizations"), "reorientation in values," and "more realistic evaluation of [and] attitude toward self." All of these steps are "taken against great resistance" and with "silent reservations." Sometimes patients cannot bring themselves to change "unless faced with the stark necessity of seeing it as a sink or swim situation." Therapists must help them to recognize the "iron-clad psychological law" that they cannot get well unless their defensive strategies are given up. In order to relinquish their pride, their shoulds, and their claims, all of which breed self-hate, patients need the analysts' "faith in [them] and belief that [they] can come out of this Hell."

After *Self-Analysis,* Horney's fullest published account of the therapeutic process was chapter 14 of *Neurosis and Human Growth,* "The Road of Psychoanalytic Therapy." There were fuller accounts in her subsequent lectures on psychoanalytic technique (see part III of the present volume), but this chapter is important for what Horney had to say about therapy. It covered some familiar ground, but with greater sophistication than before. Moreover, Horney's thought had evolved considerably since *Self-Analysis,* and even since her lectures "Pride and Self-Hatred in Neuroses," and the chapter deals with aspects of the therapeutic process she had not discussed previously.

Horney argued that neurosis is the product of conditions in a person's environment that have resulted in a self-alienated course of development. The object of therapy is to help patients reestablish contact with themselves so that they can actualize their inherent natures. Patients resist the therapeutic process, however, because confronting their conflicts entails "the terrifying prospect of being split apart" (1950, 335), and realizing their shortcomings threatens them with overwhelming self-hate. The analyst and the patient are often pulling in opposite directions: "The analyst has in mind the growth of the real self; the patient can think only of perfecting his idealized self" (336). Patients want therapy to help them live up to their shoulds and make their solutions work.

The road of analytic therapy is the "old one, advocated time and again throughout human history" of "*reorientation through self-knowledge.*" What is new is "the method of gaining self-knowledge, which we owe to the genius of Freud" (341). For Horney, however, the kind of knowledge to be pursued differs from that of Freud in that it has little or nothing to do with instinctual drives. The patient must become aware of "his search for glory, his claims, his shoulds, his pride, his self-hate, his alienation from self, his conflicts, his particular solution — and the effect of all these factors on his human relations and his capacity for creative work" (341). The patient must recognize that "self-hate is pride's inseparable companion and that he cannot have one without the other." Individual factors must be seen in terms of "their connections and interactions" and "in the context of the whole structure" (341). Horney was at great pains to insist that the self-knowledge of which she speaks is not merely intellectual awareness, although it may begin with that, but an emotional experience; and she provided many examples of the kind of knowledge she had in mind and its therapeutic effects (342–47).

Once they have become deeply aware of their defenses, patients can engage in the gradual work of testing reality and assessing their values. They will recognize the illusory nature of their idealized images, their pride, their claims, and their bargain with fate; and they will become aware that their goals and values have been generated by their neurotic trends. This "disillusioning process" is therapeutic, but only insofar as it enables "something obstructive to be relinquished in order to give something constructive" a chance to grow (347). Horney believed that "there are healing forces operating in the patient from the very beginning" (348) and that they become stronger as the defenses are gradually relinquished and the patient's real self begins to emerge. One of the functions of the therapist is to mobilize and encourage the real self, which at first is quite weak.

Even after the real self grows stronger, it needs a great deal of support, for it engages in a ferocious battle with the neurotic drive toward self-glorification. This was a new element in Horney's understanding of the therapeutic process. In *Neurosis and Human Growth,* she described three conflicts that must be resolved in therapy: the basic conflict between the interpersonal strategies of moving toward, against, and away from other people that had been the main theme of *Our Inner Conflicts*; the intrapsychic conflict between the idealized and despised selves that had been the focus of the lectures on pride and self-hatred in neuroses; and the newly added "central inner conflict" between the patient's "pride system and his real self, between his drive to perfect his idealized self and his desire to develop his given potentialities as a human being" (356).

The central inner conflict develops in later stages of therapy, after patients have made contact with their real selves. Their growing wish to live as their real selves is opposed by their pride, for it would mean giving up their idealized image of themselves. A violent inner battle ensues, the intensity of which "is commensurate with the basic importance of the issue at stake . . . : does the patient want to keep whatever is left of the grandeur and glamor of his illusions, his claims, and his false pride or can he accept himself as a human being with all the general limitations this implies, and with his special difficulties but also with the possibility of his growth?" (356–57). This is "a most profitable but also most turbulent" phase of therapy (356) in which patients have reached a "fundamental crossroad in their lives" (357). During this phase, "constructive periods are followed by *repercussions*" in which there is a "renewed onrush of self-hate."

In the later stages of the central inner conflict, patients may idealize themselves because of their progress in therapy. They go on a "binge of health" in which they imagine themselves to be "perfectly adjusted specimen[s]." They seize on their "very improvement as the last chance to actualize [their] idealized self in the shining glory of perfect health." But their state of euphoria cannot last. Because of their heightened self-awareness, they are bound to recognize that, notwithstanding their progress, "plenty of old difficulties still persist. And, just because [they have] believed [themselves] to be on the peak, [they strike] out against [themselves] all the harder" (358). The demand that they be perfectly healthy becomes another tyrannical should, and they oscillate between pride and self-hate just as before.

If constructive forces are to triumph over pride, patients must achieve an acceptance of themselves not as they want to be or even as they could be but as they actually are (the "actual self"). They must "feel sympathetic toward [themselves] and experience [themselves] . . . as being neither particularly wonderful nor despicable but as the struggling and often harassed human being[s] which [they] really [are]." They must realize that they "need not necessarily be a unique hero or genius in order to have any self-respect" (359). Such self-acceptance is extraordinarily difficult to achieve because the demand for self-idealization is tenacious, and the idealized image can take many forms, including, as we have seen, that of perfect mental health. The central inner conflict may never be permanently resolved but may continue throughout life. Treatment can be terminated, however, when patients' constructive forces are stronger than their neurotic needs.

Horney acknowledged that "the therapeutic process is so fraught with difficulties of manifold kinds that [patients] may not attain the stage described" (364). Not only must they consent to be bereft of glory, but they must overcome their "realistic fear of not being able to cope with life without" their defensive strategies. Neurotics are after all "magician[s] living by [their] magic powers. Any step toward self-realization means relinquishing these powers and living by [their] existing resources" (363).

When the therapeutic process succeeds, patients discover that they can live even better without their illusions, and this increases their faith in themselves. Getting in touch with themselves gives them "a sense of fulfillment which is different from anything [they have] known before," and this, in turn, convinces them that they are "on the right path." It shows them "the possibility of feeling in accord with [themselves] and with life" (363). One of the things they must recognize before they are ready to proceed on their own is the necessity for never-ending self-analysis: "Having begun to accept [themselves as they are], with [their] difficulties, [they] also accept the [need to] work at [themselves] as an integral part of the process of living" (364).

"The Goals of Analytic Therapy" (1951) was the last substantial discussion of therapy that Horney published. Although the essay did not carry Horney's thinking into new territory, it treated the issue of therapeutic goals more systematically than her other writings. Written for a German audience unfamiliar with her mature work, it is, as Elissa P. Benedek has observed, "a concise reexamination of some of her most central concepts" (1991, 228).

Horney traced the shifting conception of therapeutic goals first within psychoanalysis generally and then within her own thinking. The initial aim of therapy was to remove symptoms through the recovery of an early traumatic experience. Freud gradually realized that this does not always work and that it may be necessary to "learn a great deal about the patient's life and his entire personality." "The emphasis," however, "was still on the symptom." Several progressive analysts, such as Franz Alexander and, of course, Horney herself, came to realize that "neurosis is not only a matter of symptoms but is a disorder of the personality." The goal of therapy then became the restructuring of the personality. In a passage that might have been written in the context of current debates over managed care, Horney pointed out that short-term therapies aim only at alleviating symptoms and observed that "our conception of the goals of therapy depends not only on our understanding of neurosis but also on . . . our conception of our profession."

Without overtly identifying the ideas as her own, Horney then recapitulated the evolution of her thinking about the goals of therapy. When she recognized neurosis as a disturbance in human relations, the goal became the improvement of relationships. When she became aware that disturbances in relationships are the result of inner conflicts, the goal became resolving these conflicts and achieving integration by getting in touch with the real self. Horney next became aware of the intrapsychic process of self-glorification, which leads to the creation of the pride system, and the goal of therapy became helping people surrender their illusions, which intensify their self-hate, and accept themselves as they are. Only when they have made peace with their actual selves, do they have a chance to grow.

Both in this essay and in *Neurosis and Human Growth,* Horney posited four selves: the real self, the idealized self, the despised self, and the actual self, which is a combination of weaknesses and strengths, defenses and strivings for health. If we cannot actualize our idealized self, we feel like our despised self. Coming to terms with our actual self through the therapeutic process frees us from our tyrannical shoulds and allows us to have spontaneous feelings and discover who we are. Horney described the idealized self as an "impossible self" and the real self as a "possible self." She felt that we must give up our impossible dream of glory, which gives a false meaning to life, in order to fulfill our potentialities in an intrinsically satisfying way.

7

What Does the Analyst Do? (1946)

When Horney resigned from the New York Psychoanalytic Institute in 1941, she and others who resigned with her formed the Association for the Advancement of Psychoanalysis, which then became the parent organization of the American Institute for Psychoanalysis and the American Journal of Psychoanalysis. One of the objectives of the association was community education in psychoanalysis. With that end in view, in 1942 a group of interested laypersons organized the Auxiliary Council for the Association, which sponsored lectures on various topics. In 1944–45, a course of lectures entitled "You Are Considering Analysis?" was offered. Apparently in response to the announcement, a publisher proposed issuing the lectures as a popular book, and on October 13, 1944, Horney wrote to W. W. Norton, who had published her earlier books, to say that she thought it was "only fair to tell you about it" before making any commitments. Norton replied on October 17, saying that if Horney would act as editor, he would be very much interested in publishing the book. It appeared as Are You Considering Psychoanalysis? *in November 1946.*

Horney contributed an introduction and the two essays that follow: "What does the Analyst Do?" (chap. 7) and "How Do You Progress After Analysis?" (chap. 8). The other essays included "Why Psycho-

analysis?" by Alexander Reid Martin, "What Schools of Psychoanalysis Are There?" by Valer Barbu, "What Is a Neurosis?" and "How Does Analysis Help?" by Muriel Ivimey, "What Are Your Doubts About Analysis?" and "Who Should Your Analyst Be?" by Harold Kelman, and "What Do You Do in Analysis?" by Elizabeth Kilpatrick. All of the essays reflect Horney's views about therapy. A commercial success, the book became part of the Norton Library in 1962 and is still in print.

Psychoanalytical therapy is an exquisitely co-operative enterprise. It can succeed only if both patient and analyst do their share. In the preceding chapter, how the patient contributes to the work was described. Let us now consider the various ways in which the analyst tries to help the patient.

The analyst responds to the patient's unreserved frankness with undivided attention. His attention is of a special kind. He does not merely strain to remember the exact sequence of the patient's associations or to compute the unknown quantity in the equation. He may at times make determined efforts of this kind but, if that were all, the results would be fairly barren and inconclusive. The quality of his attention must be of a more productive nature; it can be productive only if he enters into the task completely and without reservation. He responds to the patient with all his acuteness of perception, catching on spontaneously not only to the spoken words and their content but also to the emotional undertones in the associations. He listens wholeheartedly, using the knowledge he has acquired about the particular patient, drawing on his fund of experience with human beings, and letting his own emotional reactions come into play whether they be sympathy, humor, apprehensiveness, impatience, or discouragement.

While you may like the assurance that the analyst will give you his wholehearted attention, you may be disturbed by my statement regarding his emotional responses. Perhaps you feel that his mind should be as unruffled as a mirror or as a lake on a quiet summer day. But are you not asking for the impossible? If the analyst is to enter into the analytic procedure with his whole self, how can he discard his feelings — the most alive part of him? He could not possibly choke off his impatience or his discouragement without also inactivating his sympathy and blunting his sensitivity to what is going on in you.

Let us go a step further. Might not the "undesirable" emotional reactions of your analyst even have a certain value? Assume for instance that, without being in the least aware of it, you were bent on defeating your analyst. Also assume you were to proceed under so skillful a screen of zest and eagerness that for a time your analyst would fail to notice your hidden strategies, would not his feelings — more alert than his intellect — give him a signal of warning?

He would detect vague feelings of irritation or discouragement in himself. If he were to suppress these, they might imperceptibly dampen his effort. But if he is aware of such reactions he will begin to wonder whether perhaps the therapeutic progress is less satisfactory than he had thought. He will first question himself: Is his ambition driving him to effect a quicker cure than is actually possible? Is he affected by vestiges of claims for omnipotence? If your analyst does discover and analyze such traces of neurotic ambition in himself, it can only be to your advantage. He will become less concerned with his own glory and will be able to devote himself the more effectively to your problems. But he will also ask himself whether there is something in your attitude that might account for his dissatisfaction; he will no longer take your eagerness to co-operate at its face value and will thus become alert to your hidden frustrating maneuvers.

Such wholehearted attention is the condition for productive analytical work — as it is for any work that is not mere mechanical routine. It is directed toward the two available sources of information: first, what the patient tells him about his relations with others both in the past and in the present, about his disturbances and difficulties, about his attitude toward himself, about his phantasies and his dreams; second, all the peculiar drives and reactions which the patient acts out inadvertently in the analytical situation itself — his expectations for an easy solution of his problems, his claims for special attention or love, his need to triumph over the analyst, his vulnerability to what he conceives as coercion or humiliation.

It would be difficult to say which of these two sources of information is more important. Both are indispensable. However, analysis of the attitudes appearing in the analytical situation itself has the greater therapeutic value for here the patient is confronted squarely with the irrationality of his neurotic drives. The analyst may point out, for example, his compelling need to be admired, citing as evidence data the patient has given him about his life such as his feeling easily slighted, or his surrounding himself exclusively with people who admire him. The patient may remain unconvinced, arguing that his friends are people whom he happens to like, that he simply *is* superior and that his irritation at slights is absolutely justified each time. But if he is shown that in the analytical situation, too, he is merely bent on presenting himself as a superior person and that in so doing he is actually defeating his own purpose, he can hardly escape the realization that an irrational force is operating within himself.

Accordingly these very attitudes, if overlooked or insufficiently analyzed, have the greatest power to retard the analysis and may even entirely frustrate the efforts of patient and analyst both. Such feelings may appear openly in conscious claims for love or special consideration, in undisguised anger, or in attempts to berate the analyst. They may appear in disguised form in dreams or within the train of associations.

Thus one of my patients, during a period of blockage, recalled how he had to wait in a harbor for the boat that was to carry him to an island near the shore. There was no telling when the boat would leave. It might take two, three, or four hours until the freight was stored away. In the meantime he could do nothing but sit around and wait. The memory expressed most accurately what he felt at the time in reference to the analysis. He had relegated all the work and responsibility to me; he was just a passenger waiting for me, the captain, to make a move.

The patient's attitudes may, finally, determine the spirit in which he presents his associations. Thus he may say everything that comes to his mind but in a spirit of docility, defiance, bravado, or arrogant superiority to the analyst.

You may wonder how the analyst can make sense of the jumble of the patient's free associations. He proceeds on the assumption that elements appearing in sequence are connected with each other though they may seem incoherent. Instead of going into detail I shall only mention some important clues. The analyst constantly has in mind the question: why does this particular memory, thought, feeling, phantasy, or dream come up just now? Thus an embarrassing early experience may be recalled by the patient because he feels humiliated at having to face his present weakness. Snakes, witches, or gangsters may appear in his dreams because his own hidden aggressiveness is beginning to disquiet him. The analyst will often get the proper perspective on the meaning of associations by connecting them with the subject approached by the patient in the previous analytic session.

For instance, in one session a patient may have come close to seeing exploiting tendencies in himself. In the following one he dwells on incidents in which he has been cheated. He also mentions a relative who is said to have been harmed by analysis. He considers the desirability of having a thorough physical checkup. What he is actually expressing in various versions is his fear of having to face his exploiting tendencies. As he sees it he never exploits anyone but is constantly being cheated and taken advantage of by others. He voices his concern that analysis will harm him. Here again, without being aware of it, he refers to his fear that analysis will spoil his image of himself as a good, upstanding person by exposing his exploiting tendencies. When the analyst questions his desire for a physical checkup, the patient tries to brush this aside: "Oh, I've been wanting one for a long time." "Let us see, nevertheless," the analyst insists, "why this old wish of yours emerges just now." And it may then become apparent that the idea of a medical examination, rational in itself, covers up the patient's aversion to examining himself psychologically. He is unconsciously attempting to solve his real predicament by playing around with the hope that his troubles might not be psychic at all.

A clue often lies in the recurrence in variations of one and the same theme in the course of a session. Another clue can be found in the patient's involving himself in contradictions. Changes of mood occurring in or between analytical hours point to unconscious emotional reactions to matters discussed. Sometimes a clue lies not in what the patient says but rather in what he omits. He may, for instance, dwell only on the shortcomings of others and never mention his own share in difficulties that arise. Finally, the analyst may be struck by contradictions between the patient's reports about his dealings with others and the way the patient behaves toward him. In his reports he may appear as one who is unfairly treated despite his goodness and generosity; in his behavior toward the analyst he may be berating and domineering.

I have dwelt on the quality of the analyst's attention and understanding because all the help he can give the patient follows from his understanding. Allowing for some exaggeration, analysts would need no books on analytical technique if their understanding were complete. Actually, of course, it never can be complete. Each patient confronts the analyst with problems which he has not encountered before in that specific form and combination. A line of approach that was profitable with four patients may be ineffective with the fifth. There is no blueprint to guide us. We cannot hold the patient responsible for our temporary failure to understand or to help him by ascribing it to his "resistance." Such an approach would be as futile as any shifting of responsibilities. What is needed is more and more understanding.

Assuming now that the analyst has arrived at some understanding of the patient's character, how does he utilize it toward helping the patient to understand himself and to change on the basis of the insight gained? To begin with, the analyst gives interpretations — that is, suggestions as to the possible meanings — of what the patient has expressed. The aim of interpretations is to uncover unconscious processes. They may concern the patient's unconscious compulsive needs such as his neurotic need for affection, for control, or for triumph. These processes may concern an unconscious conflict between the patient's need for independence and his equally great need to shirk responsibility. They may concern his attempts at solving conflicts by creating an idealized image of himself, by keeping at a distance from people, by resigning himself to a humble place in life, by discarding reality and living in phantasy and so forth. Unconscious processes may concern the ways in which the patient's neurotic trends, conflicts, or attempts at solution operate in his life, in the analytical situation, or in his dreams. They may concern the inner needs that compel him to cling tenaciously to his particular neurotic solutions. Most important of all, they may concern the cramping influences that all neurotic formations have on the patient's life, on his self-confidence, on his happiness, on his work, on his love life, and on his social relations. They may, finally, concern the ways in which all these factors contribute to create and maintain the patient's symptoms and manifest disturbances — the bearing they have on his phobia, his insomnia, his taking to drink, his spells of migraine, or his inhibitions about work.

Despite what you have read in preceding chapters it may still strike you as incongruous that I mention, at the tail end, interpretations which provide an understanding of the manifest disturbances. You may still have the feeling that the unraveling and eventual removal of symptoms is your main reason for considering analysis. Despite better knowledge, you may still cherish the belief that if it were not for your depression or your inhibition about work you would be quite all right. But the earlier you relinquish this illusion the better it is for you. If you are organically ill it is self-evident to you that your pain, your cough, your fever *are* not your illness but are merely signs that there is some disorder in your lungs, your intestines, your joints, etc. You are also aware of the fact that the diseases to be feared most are those which, like certain forms of cancer or tuberculosis, insidiously affect bodily organs without giving you any warning signal in the form of pain or which give it only when it is too late to do anything about the disease. Exactly the same is true of your psychic disturbances. Your irritability, your fatigue, your sleeplessness *are* not the disease; they, too, are but alarm signals warning you that there is some hidden disorder in your personality. You should regard them as friends who persistently remind you that it is time to examine yourself. A young patient who was sent to me much against her will because she suffered from epileptic fits, later on almost blessed these fits because they were instrumental in making her face her conflicts and thus ultimately saved her from wasting her life.

Accordingly, try not to be impatient if your analyst does not seem to be too interested at first in your street phobia or whatever plagues you, and pries instead into all sorts of things you feel are irrelevant and none of his business. Naturally you would prefer to have your phobia removed without having to go through the painful process of changing. Perhaps you will reread the chapter What Is a Neurosis? and you will understand that it cannot be done this way. You can be reasonably sure, however, that as you understand and overcome your neurotic attitudes, the phobia, too, will gradually recede. The fact that your analyst wants you to become interested in yourself and not merely in your phobia does not mean, however, that he loses sight of it. Whenever he sees a connection between your neurotic trends or conflicts and your presenting complaints, he will point it out to you and, as the analysis progresses, you will come to see such connections of your own accord.

Since a major and chronic disturbance has several roots in your personality, the analyst will have to search for all of them and present them to you as they become accessible. Let us assume, for instance, that what disturbs you most is your inhibition toward productive and creative work. At some stage of the analysis, the analyst may realize that you behave toward it as a schoolboy behaves toward an assignment he is forced to do. He will suggest that you feel it as a coercion. At first you consider this ridiculous because you really wish to write the particular paper that is causing you difficulties. But gradually you come to understand the meaning of your reluctance on this score. Although you wish to write the paper, you did not anticipate the work it would entail. The ideas should simply flow from your pen. Maybe they do at the beginning. But then you actually have to formulate, to organize, to check whether you are really expressing what you want to say — in short, you have to work. And you rebel at just that. Your analyst may recognize at a later time that it is not only your neurotic version of freedom that makes you rebel but also that you feel it as an insult, as a positive humiliation that you, the mastermind, should have to do laborious work. Again, later he finds out that you are much more alert when you are with somebody who stimulates you or with whom you can argue and prove your superiority, that you get listless at the point when this exciting game of "who defeats whom" stops and you are left to your own resources. He may have arrived at this conclusion from observing you act similarly in the analytical situation.

In order to be effective, interpretations must not only be to the point but they must also be given at the proper time. An interpretation, however pertinent, may be meaningless to the patient if it is not correctly timed. Under the circumstances it would neither help nor harm. It may happen, though rarely, that a premature interpretation upsets the patient without benefiting him. A well-timed interpretation will set the patient thinking along constructive lines; it will help him to get out of blind alleys; and it will give him a better understanding of himself.

Sometimes the analyst can proceed only by trial and error. But the more comprehensive his knowledge of the patient's character structure, the clearer he will be in his mind about the sequence in which unconscious forces should be tackled. He cannot, for instance, tackle a patient's fear of being rejected or despised or his fear of being "phony," as long as the patient visualizes himself as a saint or as a supreme lover. The analyst will avoid pointing out to the patient his need to exploit and berate others, as long as he views himself primarily as a helpless and innocent victim.

Sometimes the analyst is not in a position to offer even a tentative inter-pretation. He may merely feel that the whole situation somehow lacks clarity, that the patient is moving in circles, or that the specific problem under discus-sion is not yet satisfactorily solved. He may have all these impressions without being able to put his finger on the source of the trouble. Under these circum-stances he can do no more than observe as accurately as possible and convey his impressions to the patient. This is by no means unimportant, because it helps the patient to become aware of the existing difficulty and elicits his incentive to look for the cause. It disturbs a spurious contentment with the progress of the analysis or with a particular solution and thereby calls upon untapped resources.

After making an interpretation, the analyst observes with utmost care how the patient responds to it. Sometimes the truth may strike immediately and forcefully. In such a case the patient will feel that the interpretation "clicks" and things will occur to him which confirm it. New avenues of investigation will open up. In other instances the patient's associations may lead to modi-fications or qualifications of what has been suggested. But his readiness to accept an interpretation may also be deceptive. He may still be too eager to please the analyst. He may accept the interpretation glibly, enjoying its intel-lectual subtlety without in the least applying it to himself. He may also be all too glad to follow the analyst's suggestion because it diverts attention from more painful and hidden subjects.

But it is not only the question of acceptance or rejection of an interpretation that counts. All kinds of emotional reactions may ensue. For instance, the patient may merely feel that it was foolish of him to have exposed himself that much and become angry at the analyst for having found him out. He may feel unjustly accused and go on the defensive immediately, bending all his energies toward disproving the suggestion. He may feel nothing but humiliation be-cause the analyst has pointed out a factor that contrasts with his idealized image of himself. Instead of testing out whatever truth there may be in the suggestion, he will become vindictive and try to frustrate the analyst or to humiliate him in turn. Such reactions often put the analyst's skill to a test because they are usually expressed indirectly. The patient may be entirely un-aware of them. He may try to consider things rationally and become blocked because the existing unconscious feelings prevent him from being productive. If the analyst recognizes emotional reactions of this kind, he usually finds them valuable for they help him determine along what lines he should proceed.

The ultimate aim of interpretations is to bring about changes in the patient. Such changes may be conspicuous or even dramatic. They are usually the result not only of one interpretation but of the preceding work as well. Anxiety may suddenly abate; a depression may lift; a headache may disappear. But there may be other changes, less obvious, yet no less important. The patient's attitude toward others or toward some particular person may change; he may take a different view of a neurotic factor in himself; he may become interested in a problem of which he had not previously been aware; he may begin to observe himself better and to catch on to a neurotic reaction of his own accord.

The analyst, hence, pays attention not only to the measure with which the patient accepts or rejects an interpretation, not only to the ensuing emotional reactions, but also to the kind of changes that take place. He will be particularly alert to the absence of any changes and, if none occur, he will point this out to the patient and search with him for the factors that are still interfering with the possibility of changes.

The analyst's task comprises more than the mere uncovering of unconscious processes. Integrated with and essential to the analytic process are two additional ways in which he helps the patient. One is a kind of philosophical help, an intellectual clarification of issues that are important for living; the other is what I shall call a general human help.

At one time or another during his analysis, the patient will become interested in questions such as these: what are ideals and what is the value of having ideals? How do they differ from compulsive neurotic standards? What exactly does it mean to assume responsibility for oneself? What *is* inner independence? Of course many patients have thought about these questions; some may even have thought about them a great deal; others have taken them for granted; again others have discarded them as meaningless. In any case the patient will become interested in them or renew his interest when he begins to find out that, without knowing it, his thinking in this regard has been muddled. It has been confused not because he lacked intelligence but because in the matter of values he was driven in opposite directions. Thus he often confounded authentic ideals with imposed duties, self-reliance with self-accusation, self-acceptance with self-indulgence, freedom with license, love with dependency, and so on.

When the patient realizes how contradictory his attitudes on this score have been and how many unconscious pretenses he has developed in order to blind himself to the existence of these contradictions, he begins to struggle for intellectual clarity. The analyst, then, will help the patient to clarify his goals in life. He will say in essence: "You speak in glowing terms of independence. Fine! but merely doing as you please, being cynical or unconventional does not make you independent. True independence entails being resourceful, assuming responsibilities, living by your convictions. Of course it is up to you to decide whether you really want independence. But if you do, you will have to examine and eventually overcome all those factors within yourself which interfere with this goal such as expecting too much of others, putting the blame on others, and so forth."

Such a discussion of values differs from the reading of books or from a talk with a friend in that it is combined with a scrutiny of the personal emotional problems involved.

When I speak of general human help I mean the way the analyst helps the patient — not through his interpretations but through his attitude toward the patient. This includes his willingness to understand, his unflagging interest in the patient's growth, his faith in the patient's existing potentialities, his firmness that permits him to view the patient's suffering with concern without letting himself be crushed by them, to remain unswayed by the patient's admiration and undaunted by the patient's aggressive demands or hostile attacks. The value of such an attitude is underrated by some and overrated by others. Freud understood the task of the analyst as primarily an intellectual one. The less the analyst's personality was involved, the more effective the therapy would be. The advice he gave on this score was in negative terms: the analyst should *not* be condemnatory; the analyst should *not* yield to the patient's neurotic demands. At the other extreme are some modern analysts who contend that the very friendship the analyst extends to the patient is essential in curing him of his disturbances in human relationships. Such notions, while flattering to the analyst and pleasing to the patient, may easily blur the fundamental issue, namely that patient and analyst come together in order to do work.

You may wonder at this point whether the relationship between patient and analyst is not a kind of friendship. In a sense, it is friendship at its very best but I always hesitate to regard it as such because it does, after all, lack the measure of spontaneity and mutuality essential to real friendship. The question was clarified for me by the distinction John Macmurray makes between personal and functional relationships:

> This is the characteristic of personal relationships. They have no ulterior motive. . . . They do not serve partial and limited ends. . . . Friendship, fellowship, communion, love are all in one way or another liable to convey a false or partial meaning. But what is common to them all is the idea of a relationship between us which has no purpose beyond itself; in which we associate because it is natural for human beings to share their experience, to understand one another, to find joy and satisfaction in living together; in expressing and revealing themselves to one another.

According to Macmurray, all relationships that have a purpose over and beyond personal friendship are functional. Thus, when you join others in a scientific or political group your association with them is determined by the purpose of discussing scientific or political matters. In this sense the relationship between patient and analyst is essentially a functional one. Your analyst and you may mutually like and respect each other. Yet you enter into the relationship for a definite purpose: to free you from your neurotic shackles and thereby create better conditions for your future growth as a human being. This definition is also satisfactory in that it leaves the emphasis where it should be, namely on the work to be done.

It remains true, however, that the human help which the analyst gives the patient is important and even indispensable within the framework of the analytic process. I am thinking here primarily of the analyst's consistent emphasis on what he believes to be the patient's best interests. In principle this is the attitude every good physician has toward his patient. But the difference lies in that the analyst's task is infinitely more comprehensive. The surgeon's job is usually circumscribed. The analyst's work on the other hand involves no less than the patient's whole future development as a human being. The questions he has in mind regarding his patient are somewhat comparable to the questions raised by a good educator: what furthers or hinders his development into a good, constructive human being? How can he best develop his potentialities, whether these be special talents or such general qualities as strength, courage, considerateness, or kindness?

You may feel unpleasantly reminded here of the "mother knows best what is good for you" attitude. There are, however, significant differences between the mother-child situation and that in analysis. The patient is no longer a child but is able to evaluate by himself where his best interest lies when he is helped to see the issues clearly. Moreover, the analyst is not authoritative but endeavors to find out together with the patient in what manner he is blocking his own way.

It is the analyst's consistent focus on the patient's best interest that eventually helps him to gain the latter's confidence. Of course, the patient would never have decided to work with the analyst if he had not had some confidence in him to begin with. But his initial confidence, though based on a good intuitive feeling, is not built on especially solid ground. After all, most of us are aware of the difference between an intuitive trusting of another person and the repeated, concrete evidence of his reliability. For the neurotic, however, this difference is considerably greater. With all his anxieties, suspicions, and defensive hostilities — conscious or unconscious — he needs proof after proof before he can dare take the risk of really trusting someone.

As for the analyst's nonauthoritative attitude, I prefer to define it in positive terms as an endeavor to place the patient under his own jurisdiction. The analyst firmly believes in the desirability of every person taking his life into his own hands, as far as possible, and assuming responsibility for himself. He respects individual differences and knows that each person can ultimately decide only in accordance with his own wishes and his own ideals. Hence he sees his main task as helping the patient to recognize his own wishes and find his own set of values.

This attitude is responsible to a large degree for the analyst's reluctance to give advice. Another perfectly good and simple reason for his reluctance on this score is that in most cases he feels incapable of giving advice. Being more aware of the complexities of the human mind than most people, he has developed an attitude of realistic humility that allows him to be fully aware of his own limitations. Naturally he will express his opinion whenever it is clear to him that the patient is about to act against his own interest. Furthermore, if certain of the patient's symptoms point to the possibility of an organic disorder, he will suggest a physical examination. He may definitely advise against a major decision if he is convinced that the patient is acting under the pressure of irrational emotional factors.

Although you will agree that such an attitude on the part of the analyst is helpful in making you more independent, you may not always like it. You may want guidance. You may expect at the beginning that the analyst will solve all your problems by making a decision for you. You may insist that he has answers for everything, but is withholding them for some mysterious reason. Try to remember, then, that he can often be more helpful to you by trying to understand the background of your question or indecision.

Another way in which the analyst helps the patient is his attitude of accepting him as he is. What does this mean and why is it important? It may mean scientific objectivity. Freud expected the analyst to look at the patient with the eyes of a scientist and to eliminate value judgments. This, however, necessarily creates an artificial situation because no one can exclude his set of values when human behavior and motivations are involved. Actually, the patient himself does not believe in such objectivity but assumes that it is adopted for the sake of therapy.

It may mean tolerance. Tolerance is, of course, important in view of the self-condemning attitude harbored by most patients. Although the patient may distrust this attitude, too, it is actually genuine by virtue of the analyst's understanding.

It means, finally, that the analyst is interested in the patient as a human being who is engaged in the process of development and that he appreciates the patient's every move ahead. In order to help you to understand the value of such an attitude I must tell you something that may surprise you. When he begins analysis, the patient as a rule is not interested in himself as he *is*. He is constantly concerned with what he *should* be and blames himself for his short-comings instead of tackling them realistically. Naturally this has to be analyzed. But it is also the analyst's consistent interest in him as he is and as he could be that helps the patient to develop a constructive interest in his real self.

The analyst can have this positive attitude because he believes in the constructive forces within the patient which will eventually enable him to resolve his neurotic conflicts. Is this a blind optimism on the part of the analyst, or is it a realistic faith in the existence of such forces or at least in existing potentialities? On the basis of our experience it is a most realistic faith. Initially, the patient's constructive, forward-moving forces may lie buried under illusions, hopelessness, *and* destructiveness. But with rare exceptions we see them come to life during analysis.

As he gains insight into the workings of his mind, the patient gradually comes to feel: "*I* can do something; *I* can have feelings other than mere irritation and fear; *I* can like somebody; *I* can enjoy things. *I* can want." And with each taste of freedom and of strength his incentive to gain more of it grows. The analyst's belief in and clear recognition of the patient's potentialities helps the patient to regain his faith in himself. This is particularly important at those periods in analysis when the patient loses faith in himself or when it dawns upon him how little of it he has ever had.

The analyst thus takes a most active part in the analytical process. He observes and examines the patient's every move, the flow of his associations, his reactions to interpretations, the variety of ever-changing attitudes toward the analyst and toward the analytical situation, the changes that take place in his relations to others and toward himself and in his set of values. But the analyst does not merely follow the patient. Through his interpretations, explanations, and questions, he influences the course of the analysis. He helps the patient out of blind alleys and suggests scrutiny along more profitable lines. He encourages the patient to persist in working at a problem even though he is caught in the clutches of some emotional reaction. By means of these activities the analyst actually conducts the analysis. And this is as it should be. For while analysis is a co-operative enterprise between patient and analyst, it is the analyst who for many reasons carries the greater responsibility.

8

How Do You Progress After Analysis? (1946)

The very suggestion that you might still have problems to cope with after your analysis is terminated may arouse protest. Many of my patients were upset when I pointed out to them that they would have to continue working with themselves. They had expected to emerge from analysis as "finished products." Theirs would be a paradise of untroubled serenity where problems and conflicts did not exist and where the power to create and enjoy was absolute.

Such expectations are illusory. It is true that analysis is a means toward outgrowing your personality difficulties and developing your potentialities. And when we speak of potentialities we have in mind not only your innate talents or gifts but even more your latent power to become more direct, more wholehearted, more alive, and more effective in your human relationships and in your work. Your growth as a human being, however, is a process that can and should go on as long as you live. Hence analysis as a means of gaining self-knowledge is intrinsically an interminable process. Analytical therapy, while it helps you to disentangle yourself from the web of conflicts and to develop on a sounder basis, only initiates this development; it does not and cannot complete it.

This raises a difficult question. If our growth as human beings is interminable, and if analytical therapy merely sets this process in motion, when does the patient reach the stage where he no longer needs treatment?

Originally, when Freud made his first discoveries concerning the unconscious factors that cause neuroses, this question was easily answered. The treatment was terminated when the symptom, on behalf of which the patient had sought help, had disappeared. This delightfully neat solution has proved to be fallacious. Even though the "symptom," for instance hysterical paralysis of an arm, is removed, the person remains hysterical in his way of dealing with life. Furthermore, a subsequent upset may cause the development of another symptom such as hysterical blindness.

Since psychotherapy as it has now developed deals with personality structure as a whole, it is more difficult to decide when treatment should be terminated. Our question would be: has the patient's personality improved to the extent that he can safely be dismissed from treatment?

We have tried in discussions to formulate basic criteria for such an improvement. Briefly, we arrived at formulations like these: before terminating an analysis the patient should become less rigid, less vulnerable, less arrogant, more assertive, more warmhearted, more cooperative, more honest, more realistic. Such improvements, however, while undoubtedly desirable are too relative to serve as the sole criteria. A patient's grandiose notions about himself may have diminished considerably in the course of the analysis but certain areas in his life may still be governed by wishful thinking rather than by realistic considerations. It would be difficult therefore to say exactly how realistic he should be before terminating his treatment.

Moreover, if we were to release our patient solely on the basis of what has been accomplished in the way of personality improvements, this might entail a certain danger for there would always remain some unsolved problem, some fears that could be diminished, some sensitivities that could be lessened, some inhibitions that are still disturbing. Thus if both patient and analyst focused their attention entirely on what remained to be done, they would be tempted to go on and on forever.

These criteria must be complemented, therefore, by another consideration: at what stage of his development is the patient ready to continue on his own? Of course, only those analysts will raise this question who trust that it is possible for a patient to proceed on his own, and who have relinquished the belief that the patient cannot overcome his difficulties without the analyst's help. Hence the broad question of termination becomes more precise: when can the patient deal constructively with his own problems? What capacities must he have acquired to be able to do so?

To begin with, he must have clarified his *goals* in life and he must have a clear recognition of his own values. It is not necessary or even feasible that he *attain* his goals during analysis—he can never do more than approximate them—but he must know in what direction he wants to develop. As long as he is still driven compulsively toward some goal which he considers the solution to all his neurotic problems, he cannot proceed by himself, for he will be interested merely in analyzing the factors which prevent him from attaining his particular neurotic goal. He will certainly not be willing to examine the goal itself.

The attempts at "self-analysis" made by Simon Fenimore in Somerset Maugham's *Christmas Holiday* exemplify this kind of approach. It is Simon's driving life ambition to attain a huge vindictive triumph over others. He analyzes and changes in himself those qualities that might deflect him from his role as the future Gestapo chief in a totalitarian state and in the same manner he singles out and develops those tendencies which will enable him to become more efficient and destructive. With such a goal in mind he could not possibly be interested in analyzing his incapacity for love, his asceticism, or his cynicism. Similarly a woman who believes in "love" as the magic solution to all her distress could not possibly touch upon her hidden aggressiveness, her morbid dependency, or her lack of resourcefulness. She would analyze in herself only those factors that render it more difficult for her to find or to attach to herself a man who would fulfill her magic expectations. In other words the patient must have abandoned his neurotic goals or at least have questioned their validity.

Secondly, the patient must have his feet sufficiently on the ground; he must be interested in seeing himself as he *is* and *could be* instead of trying to live up to a phantastic notion of what he should be or of seeing himself merely as the superior being he is in his imagination.

Finally, the patient must have gained sufficient incentive to continue working with himself; he must have overcome the pervasive feeling of hopelessness and the paralyzing inertia resulting from it, expressed by the "I can't" attitude. He must have largely overcome his tendency to make others responsible for his difficulties, and he must realize instead that heaven and hell are within himself.

Is it possible, then, to estimate in analysis when these conditions are fulfilled? I believe that one can be fairly accurate about the time when the patient is no longer obsessed by neurotic goals. The two other conditions, being more comprehensive, are more difficult to gauge. The following criteria would be important. Does the patient have a more spontaneous interest in facting his problems and working at them? Has he become more capable of observing and understanding himself outside the analytic sessions? Has he become more honest with himself? Has he become more co-operative in his relations with the analyst?

But in spite of such criteria the evaluation will remain tentative. And the analysis should be terminated with a clear understanding of the tentative nature of the step. While the patient should be prepared to work by himself and to try to find the solutions to his problems without leaning on the analyst at every opportunity, he should, nevertheless, feel secure in the knowledge that he can always discuss matters with his analyst should any problem prove too difficult for him.

How are you to proceed from here? You go on examining yourself; if a difficulty arises, you try to recognize your share in it; you learn from experience; in short you analyze yourself. I need not delve here into the polemics concerning the possibility, feasibility, and limitations of self-analysis. Though it has not yet been determined how many people can analyze themselves successfully and to what extent they can do it without previous treatment, there is no doubt whatever that self-analysis is feasible after analytical treatment.

It would not be appropriate within the framework of this book to discuss at length the procedure of self-analysis. I prefer, therefore, to present an example which will illustrate some of the most important points. My illustration will demonstrate that self-analysis, far from being superficial, can penetrate to deeply repressed neurotic drives, if we are sufficiently bent on finding the truth about ourselves. It will also show that what counts in the procedure is our attitude and the spirit in which we go about it.

The example is presented in very condensed form — it omits many minor difficulties and abortive erroneous pursuits and points out only the highlights in a piece of self-analysis extending over a period of nine months. Although I have tried to present it as simply as possible, it may be difficult for you to understand the amount of work done and to follow its sequence because it touches upon problems with which you may not be familiar. But for more than one reason it may be worth your while not only to read it but to make a thorough study of it. It constitutes a particularly successful piece of self-analysis on the part of an interior decorator, Eileen, who had gone through a short but rather successful analysis some years earlier. Certain inhibitions in her work and an overdependent attitude toward her husband had greatly diminished.

Before Eileen arrived at the stage of self-analysis presented here, she had already recognized to what an extent she was glorifying her appeasing, conciliatory attitude. Although she had known for a long time that these trends were mostly conditioned by fears, she had nevertheless registered them at their face value and unconsciously credited herself with being an unusually good person. This "halosickness" as she herself called it had been very much under cover and it had taken her a long time to unearth it.

Eileen, then, began to investigate her "putting up with too much." She found that she was tolerating fairly flagrant impositions and insults. In many instances she was not even aware of being unfairly treated or became aware of it only much later. Instead she would react to the offender with an increase of appeasing endeavor. She had noticed this weakness before, but could not approach it realistically until the analysis of her "halosickness" had dispelled much of her eagerness to appear better than she was.

She now observed many isolated instances in which she was putting up with such impositions, and this led her to the discovery that she actually reacted to such occurrences with rage. This rage had hitherto been hidden under spells of paralyzing fatigue. Her reactions still remained delayed for some time. She would wake up in the middle of the night enraged at someone by whom she had felt badly treated. She had done that before but she could now connect her anger reaction with specific situations in which she had been insulted, imposed upon, or disregarded. She also discovered that she had no such reactions whenever she had been able to assert herself.

She then discovered that her anger was directed not only against the offender but even more against herself. She arrived at a clearer understanding of the nature of her anger when she observed a change in her attitude toward "nice" people. Formerly she had tended to like them indiscriminately; now she became more and more alert to their appeasing strategies and would designate them in her mind as "doormats," thus expressing her contempt for their cringing attitude. In this roundabout way she became aware of the angry contempt she had for her own cringing.

Eileen now began to wonder why her anger reactions were so intense. She observed that their intensity was usually not warranted by the occasion. Comparatively trivial matters upset her greatly. An unappreciative or overly demanding customer, an impolite taxi driver might throw her completely out of gear. This observation was disturbing, because it undermined rationalizations and pointed to an unknown disorder within her. Was there an explosive force powerful enough to be touched off by the slightest provocation? At the same time the realization was promising because it aroused her interest to find out about the nature of these unconscious forces.

For months she tried in vain to find an answer. She asked herself whether she was not perhaps more aggressive than she believed; whether she was actually motivated by a desire to triumph over others and felt disgracefully defeated whenever she could not even defend herself. These were very sensible questions but they did not strike the right chord in her; they remained speculative and theoretical. Perhaps she tried to solve the problem too directly or too intellectually, instead of simply continuing to observe herself. To call this a period of resistance would be misleading. Actually another problem had to be tackled before this one could become accessible.

I dwell on this uneventful period because temporary impasses like this one are bound to occur in every analysis and may easily lead to feelings of discouragement unless it is kept in mind that one cannot unlock the suitcase in a closet without first unlocking the closet.

An accidental experience finally supplied the missing link. Eileen fractured her leg in an automobile accident. Since no private rooms were available in the hospital, she was placed in the general ward. At first she felt this to be quite unbearable and verged on despair. She urged her husband repeatedly to obtain a private room for her. Then the thought flashed through her mind: "Maybe some patient who has a private room will die and I can move into her room." Just for a flicker of a moment this thought startled her; for a flicker of a moment she realized dimly that she was reacting disproportionately to the situation and that there was violent anger behind her despair. Apparently she was not yet quite ready to grasp the meaning of this thought, but it showed that something was working in her and probably prepared the way for the insight she arrived at two days later.

By then she had overcome the first shock. She had grown familiar with the other patients and their suffering. It was then that she asked herself: "Why should I insist on being better off than these people?" And shortly thereafter a more precise question emerged: "Is there something in me that makes me feel entitled to special privileges?" The thought came to her with the utmost surprise because she had always considered herself the very opposite of demanding and arrogant. But now she was too keenly aware of it to push it aside. She realized, then, that she had always felt entitled to special consideration and attention and that initial despair grew not so much from the fact that she had to lie in a ward but rather from the frustration of her claims. The annoyance she had felt at first had actually had the character of indignation — indignation at being exposed to what she felt was improper treatment.

With this insight her irritation vanished; she became patient, friendly with the others, and even began to like life in the ward. The insight opened up a vast field of hidden naïve expectations. She discovered that she had always felt entitled to good luck and favorable circumstances: timetables should be convenient; her sarcastic remarks should be taken in good grace; the weather should be fair when she went on an excursion; and so forth. Furthermore, she had always harbored the secret belief that she would never age or die. Now for the first time in her life she could think calmly and realistically that some day she would die, like everybody else.

Her relief was so profound that she believed — for a while — that she had already solved the whole problem of special claims. Actually, a great deal of work remained to be done. Nevertheless this first reaction was by no means altogether unjustified. In the first place she had managed to penetrate to a problem which for her apparently was crucial and which had been deeply repressed. For in her actual behavior she had been leaning over backwards to please others, she had been overappreciative, contented with little and had seen the wishes and rights of others much more clearly than her own. In the second place she had actually dispensed with the special claims that were involved in this particular situation. The illusory part of Eileen's reaction was the belief that the whole problem was solved for good and all.

Such illusions sometimes occur in analysis. They can be tenacious and may then present an obstacle to further progress. It may possibly have delayed progress in Eileen's case, too, but the fact is that she resumed working at the problem in subsequent months. We could make light of the reaction by saying that everybody would overrate an important finding in his first joy of discovery. But the reason I make these remarks at all is to point to a more powerful factor. As so many patients do in similar situations, Eileen indulged in wishful thinking. She would have liked to be rid of her disturbing claims without having to make the necessary effort to eradicate them.

Because she was in such a hurry to settle her problem of special claims, Eileen missed out on one important detail — namely, the flash of hope that somebody would die so that she would have the benefit of privacy. This would have revealed a certain callous aspect of her personality of which she was totally unaware. It would have been of special importance in this connection if she had reconsidered this momentary hope after she had gained insight into her special claims, for it might have revealed to her the intensity of the claims and their absolute egocentricity.

Eileen's taste of freedom during this period, short-lived as it was, nevertheless had its great value. In all likelihood it gave her an additional incentive to resume work on the problem of special claims. For she knew now, with an inner certainty that only experience can provide, that her work would be rewarded.

As she resumed her ordinary routine of life in subsequent weeks, she came up against some of her old difficulties. Each time this happened, she re-examined her special claims and thus gradually gained new insights. She came to understand more about the nature of her claims. The claims she had noticed while at the hospital concerned outside circumstances. Now she discovered additional ones of a different type: she felt entitled to special consideration, to being singled out, to being exempt from criticism and from doing what others expected of her.

Since none of these claims had ever been felt consciously or asserted openly she could discover them only in indirect ways. She realized that she sometimes felt greatly abused only to find a day or two later that the situation was but half as bad. After observing this sequence several times she arrived at the only possible conclusion, namely, that her initial reactions were exaggerated. Gradually she grew skeptical toward them. Finally she was able to question the validity of her reaction in the midst of feeling profoundly abused.

This was a difficult and, if I may say so, a brave step to take. For while she was feeling abused, her reaction seemed absolutely real to her and, hence, absolutely justified and logical considering the monumental wrong done to her. To question her own reaction, despite the seemingly overwhelming evidence that she was in the right, was by no means easy but it was rewarding: she was now able to understand that her excessive reaction resulted from the frustration of her special claims.

Actually, although Eileen was not yet aware of it, this piece of analysis undermined her whole "putting up with too much" complex. She had seen before that her own compliance made her defenseless, that she hated others for being aggressive and herself for being compliant. This proved to be a true but incomplete observation. What she had not seen and actually could not see before tackling her unconscious claims for special privileges was that she overreacted to "aggression" and that the intensity of her ensuing anger was largely due to her humiliation at having her claims punctured.

Eileen also came to understand more clearly how she had rationalized her claims. These had appeared under harmless and rational screens. For instance, she had felt entitled to help from others because of her own helplessness; she had made demands on others under the guise of "love"; she had consistently dodged responsibilities toward others because she had so little time or was overworked.

A short comment on this latter piece of analysis: it was correct but it lacked depth. Only later, following the segment of analysis described here, did Eileen begin to realize the full implication of these findings. By resorting to helplessness and a lovable appearance she was persistently putting a check upon her resourcefulness and her inner independence and thereby undermining her self-confidence. Moreover, this attitude made her dependent on others and forced her into being compliant and ready to play up to others. Most important, by resorting to helplessness and lovability she actually entangled herself in an irreconcilable conflict. For although she felt entitled, unconsciously, to all

sorts of special privileges, she actually got very few of them and had to ingrati-
ate herself with people for what little she did get — thus the source of gnawing
humiliation was constantly renewed. This was really the main conflict underlying the whole complex of "putting up with too much."

Eileen herself did not see these implications at the time because the appeal
she could make to others on the basis of helplessness and "love" was too
important to her as an implement with which to assert her claims in a hidden,
indirect way. Nor was she yet ready either to relinquish her claims or to assert
them in other ways.

Also she had by now lost sight of the problem of "putting up with too
much." She did return to it, though, with her next finding which concerned
one of her main claims. Briefly, she realized that she expected others to give her
everything she felt entitled to without having to assert herself, to express a
wish or even to be clear in her own mind what she wanted. Merely by appearing "nice" or friendly she would be entitled to everything. Accommodating
and appeasing techniques had thus acquired an almost magic power. She now
saw that her lack of assertiveness had compelled her to develop this particular
claim. And she made an even more pertinent discovery, namely, that this claim,
once established, actually perpetuated her weakness. A kind of magic gesture
would make any self-assertion on her part unnecessary. It was even beneath
her dignity to assert herself or to fight for or against anything. This, by the way,
was the reason why, despite her endeavors, she had not been able to get at her
aggressive trends. As long as she felt that even the most legitimate kind of
aggression was undesirable, she could not possibly be interested in unearthing
whatever aggressive tendencies she had. She saw how her claim for special
consideration actually resulted in her "putting up with too much." She also
found a more complete explanation for the intensity of the ensuing anger. It
was not only anger at her own weakness — as she had originally assumed — but
also an expression of feeling frustrated in her special claim.

This last insight revealed her "putting up with too much" in a new light. We
can see here how, despite honest self-scrutiny, it is sometimes impossible to
give an accurate description of a particular disturbance. Hitherto, Eileen had
thought of her "putting up with too much" only in connection with instances
in which she really was taken advantage of or unduly disregarded. Now she
saw that she had not only exaggerated in her own mind the wrong done to her
but that she had often reacted similarly to situations in which she was not
wronged at all. These were situations in which people failed to live up to her
unrealistic demands.

Let me summarize the segment of analysis just reported. Essentially it concerned Eileen's unassertiveness. She had first seen how glorification of her

existing core of weakness gave her the illusion of being purely good-natured. When analysis undermined her unconscious pretenses of "goodness," she was able to face her unassertiveness directly. She reacted to this realization with violent anger at others and at herself but felt unable to change. Strangely enough she made no real efforts to become more assertive in her everyday life, although she smarted under her compliance. And here she made her crucial discovery, namely that her desire to become stronger was paralyzed by her unconscious feeling of being entitled to a soft and easy life. Others should guess her wishes, should help her, yield to her, and fight her little battles without any effort at assertion on her part. Naturally, this bit of expected magic did not work. Time and again she was merely confronted with reality. Only after she had recognized and relinquished her special claims could she feel free to make efforts in her own behalf.

Such discoveries are not arrived at easily. On the contrary, I can assure you from experience that they are extremely difficult to make even with the help of an analyst. It is true that many questions were left unanswered. Eileen had yet to discover many of the roots of her special claims on life and to find out why they had been so deeply repressed. But it is true of any piece of thorough analysis that, as some problems are satisfactorily solved, others begin to be discernible. Eileen's was a real achievement and her success has greatly strengthened my confidence in the amount of analytical work that can be done alone.

What made it possible for this patient to attain such comparatively good results? Or, in other words, how can Eileen's experiences benefit your efforts at self-analysis?

Eileen's quiet determination to recognize and go to the roots of the factors in herself that blocked her way was of paramount importance. Her determination was apparent in the consistency of her efforts. You may protest here that there was no system in her attempts, that in fact they appear to have been quite sporadic, that months passed between one trial at self-analysis and another, months in which nothing apparently happened. True enough. But I am sure that even during this time more must have gone on in Eileen's mind than she reported or was aware of.

Certainly there was no regularity of conscious effort in the sense that she set apart an hour every day in which to analyze herself. When I spoke of her consistent determination to reach a certain goal, I was not thinking of a regular working schedule. I am not in favor of such planned regularity. Self-analysis pursued in this manner can too easily become an aim in itself — art for art's sake — instead of a living struggle with concrete difficulties. Besides, the resolution to analyze oneself day by day at a fixed time cannot be carried out anyway. External matters may interfere or you may not be in the proper frame of mind. Your intentions will easily peter out or your resolution to analyze yourself will become an inner obligation which you stick to under duress. As a result your work is in danger of turning sterile because you are likely to feel it as a self-imposed yoke and revolt against it. If, on the other hand, you analyze yourself when you really feel like doing so, your incentive will be fresh and spontaneous.

If you analyze your difficulties as they arise, you will gladly turn to analysis as you might turn to a friend when you are in distress. This is exactly what Eileen did. She tackled her problems whenever she felt in need of clarification, and she pursued them as far as she could each time. Only once—when she actually reached an impasse—did she try to force a solution, but in so doing, accomplished nothing. Then her problem would seemingly lie dormant for a time. But when another difficult situation arose or when she was caught once more in the grip of neurotic disturbances, her energies were mobilized and she would make another attempt at understanding her difficulties.

Eileen's consistent determination to come to grips with herself expressed itself in another way as well: she never grew discouraged. Even when she came to an impasse while analyzing her "putting up with too much" attitude, she did not show any marked signs of despair or impatience. Rather, she let the problem lie dormant until a new approach to it opened up. She did not expect miracles; she was fully aware that analysis is a slow process. But she also knew that every finding would contribute to an eventual solution even though it might not yield immediate tangible results. Recall the time when she believed that her entire problem was now solved. Even when she understood that this belief had been partly illusory, she was not discouraged. She simply realized that more work remained to be done.

A further way in which Eileen expressed her consistent determination has already been touched on. What Eileen actually tackled from various angles throughout the whole period described was her feeling of being abused by others. You have probably experienced such a feeling and know therefore how tempting it is to immerse yourself in it and respond with self-pity or rage against others. Before her analytical treatment, Eileen, too, had had profound spells of despairing self-pity. During this period of self-analysis, however, her temptations to deal with the problem through rage or self-pity were but short-lived. Time and again we see her going straight to the point of searching for her own share in the difficulty.

You may still expect me to discuss technical details regarding self-analysis. But remember that I am not dealing here with self-analysis in general but with the more specific subject of self-analysis following analytical treatment. When you have been analyzed you will be familiar with the fundamentals of the procedure. Moreover, just as every patient behaves differently in analysis, so each one will evolve his particular ways of analyzing himself. As I gather from inquiries concerning self-analysis, many people seem to harbor the illusion that technical rules would supply them with a magic key opening the gates to self-recognition. What is of crucial importance, however, in analysis as elsewhere, is the spirit in which it is done.

What were the practical results of Eileen's self-analysis during the period outlined above? To begin with, a disturbing symptom disappeared: the spells of fatigue, which had already diminished as a result of previous analytical work, now vanished for good and all. She became less tense in her relations with others; she felt less easily abused and whenever feelings of impotent rage at being "victimized" did emerge, she was quick to detect them and could then deal with the particular situation in a more sober and matter-of-fact way. She became more discriminating toward others. Since her expectations had become less exorbitant and undercurrents of hostility had diminished, she could see other people more realistically than before. She was also able to participate more spontaneously in discussions at professional as well as social gatherings. Formerly she had felt like a bystander; her efforts to contribute her share had, at best, been strained. This latter change may seem insignificant but I regard it as an evidence that Eileen felt less apart from others. Since she felt less unique in a fictitious way she was able to enter into closer relations with others.

At the same time she felt more capable of defending herself whenever necessary, of expressing her own wishes and opinions and standing up for them. In other words, she felt less "chosen by God" and could thus be more of a real person.

I have described the results of this segment of analysis in such detail because it permits a generalization. Of course not every piece of analysis will result in the disappearance of a symptom — as in this case the remnants of neurotic fatigue. Moreover, the nature of the symptom that does diminish or disappear varies from case to case. But the more subtle character changes resulting from the thorough analysis of any problem are essentially similar. Supposing, for example, that the problem concerned a person's insatiable hunger for success and triumph, analysis of this entirely different situation would similarly result in a diminution of vulnerability and isolation.

In the light of absolute achievement, the practical results of any piece of analysis are not at all impressive. "What is the use of making all these efforts toward self-recognition," you may say, "if they result each time merely in a little less of this and a little more of that?" Is not analysis, then, an endless road toward a destination it never reaches? True. And because it is true we had better face it. But this outlook is discouraging only as long as we are captivated by the vision of absolute and ultimate attainment.

It is certainly necessary to be aware of our goals lest we flounder aimlessly. But what really matters is the actual process of living and the actual steps we take toward our goals. Whether we take these steps alone or with the help of an analyst, the result each time is a gain in inner strength and freedom.

9

Foreword to Gertrud Lederer-Eckardt, "Gymnastics and Personality" (1947)

Gertrud Lederer-Eckardt's article "Gymnastics and Personality," with a foreword by Karen Horney, was published in the American Journal of Psychoanalysis *7 (1947), 48–52. The author was identified as a teacher of gymnastics and body development who provided individual corrective work and who was formerly at the Falke-Schule, Hamburg; the Truempy-Schule, Berlin; the New School for Social Research; and the Dramatic Workshop. Gertrud Lederer-Eckardt's second husband, Emil Lederer, was an economist who left Germany to escape the Nazi regime and became the first dean of the University in Exile at the New School for Social Research. Horney met Lederer-Eckardt when her daughter Marianne became engaged to Wolfgang von Eckardt, Gertrud's son by her first marriage. Gertrud treated Karen's aching back by giving her twice weekly massage and instruction in exercise, and the two became close companions, Gertrud joining Karen on her weekends away from New York and managing her affairs. Horney agreed with Groddeck, Simmel, and Reich that "many somatic symptoms, including muscle tension," were caused by psychological conflict, and she often sent patients to a physiotherapist for concurrent exercise, dance therapy, relaxation work or massage (Rubins 1978, 196). Lederer-Eckardt's practice flourished as a result of Horney's referrals.*

Most neurotic persons have one or the other disturbance in their muscular systems — spasms, backaches, neckaches, arthritic propensities, weakness in moving this or that part of the body, poor coordination in gait and posture, shaky bodily balance.

Some of these are secondary adaptations to organic deficiencies such as deformed feet, or a curvature of the spine. But the ailments under which the patient suffers are often less due to the original deficiency than to the secondary faulty use of muscles. These can be corrected by competent gymnastics.

What is of special interest to the analyst is the fact that many muscular disorders are the expression of psychological difficulties. Thus general or localized muscular tension can be the expression of psychic tension engendered by the necessity to suppress an explosive hostility. Cramps in the neck or legs of an acute nature may indicate a spell of a destructive self-condemnation. A gait in which only the legs move forward while the trunk leans back may express a conflict between aggressiveness and self-effacement — and so on. The analyst may observe at least some of such psychosomatic parallels; or he may be aware that complaints about muscular pains occur at a time when certain conflicts become more acute in the analysis. But he tends to be over-confident. Since the faulty movements or posture are determined by psychic factors, he expects them to disappear automatically when the particular neurotic difficulties are straightened out. To some extent such changes actually do take place spontaneously. The patient's physical balance, for instance, will improve as soon as his psychic equilibrium is stabilized. But often such expectations are not borne out by facts, the reason being the same as mentioned before in the case of an originally organic defect. The faulty movements or posture, however determined, do not remain static; other muscle groups are set in motion in order to compensate for the first wrong attitude; and these adaptive changes in turn influence other parts. The secondary changes, then, are no more psychological; they are due to physical necessities. This is why they do not yield to psychotherapy.

It would be better, therefore, to encourage the patient to get expert help for his bodily difficulties. To do so will benefit him also in two other ways: To do gymnastics requires active and consistent effort on the patient's part because it means not only to take lessons but also to do regular exercises on his own. And here he runs up against frequent difficulties: knowing full well that exercises are in his own interest, he just cannot get himself to do them. He is faced, thereby, more unequivocally than in analysis with his resistance against doing something for himself constructively.

The other benefit lies in the observations of an intelligent gym-teacher. The analyst may be an astute observer; yet he would not see in handwriting what a graphologist sees. Similarly, concerning bodily movements and attitudes, he will fail to observe many peculiarities which would strike the trained gymnastic teacher. The latter's observations will frequently coincide with factors discussed in analysis. For instance, the patient may have recognized in analysis how alienated he is from himself. The gym-teacher will observe that the patient, complaining about a pain in his foot, is unable to indicate the exact spot which hurts. This means that he is not directly related to his foot and must interpolate a period of thinking before he is able to find out the source of his discomfort. If this is discussed with the patient, his alienation from self is demonstrated to him on a basis that is different from analysis. Experiences of this kind carry quite some conviction, particularly for those patients who tend to regard psychological findings as a matter of purely intellectual interest.

Finally these observations dispel an illusion which many patients cherish. Not having much real regard for themselves, they often discard their own neurotic suffering as unimportant. What counts is to maintain an impregnable facade. Their pride would be wounded if others would be cognizant of their inner difficulties. They like to believe, therefore, that their disturbances are invisible to others. Being presented with evidence to the contrary may come to them as an unpleasant surprise but also gives them an additional incentive to overcome their predicaments.

Intelligent gymnastic work, then, has psychological value. It calls the person's attention to his peculiarities in gait or posture which he has not observed on his own. It points out to him possible connections with psychic difficulties. It makes him aware that these latter are noticeable to others. It gives him, last but not least, a feeling of the unity between body and soul.

10

Pride and Self-Hatred in Neuroses
Lecture 14: Solution in Therapy (1947)

In the files of the American Institute for Psychoanalysis is a fifty-two page, single-spaced typescript entitled "Pride and Self-Hatred in Neuroses by Karen Horney, M.D.," dated 1947. The typescript consists of an elaborate set of notes for fourteen lectures that Horney gave on this topic at the New School for Social Research in 1947 and 1948. When the course was announced under the title "At War with Ourselves: Self-Contempt and Self-Acceptance," Horney immediately received an inquiry from Storer B. Lunt, then head of Norton after the death of its founder, as to whether this might be "the groundwork of another possible Karen Horney book" (Horney-Norton correspondence, October 9, 1946). Horney replied that it might, and the lectures clearly prefigure Neurosis and Human Growth, *published in 1950. The table of contents of the typescript reads as follows: "1. Search for Glory; 2. Claim for Special Prerogative; 3. Tyranny of the 'Should'; 4. Neurotic Pride; 5. Self-contempt and Self-hatred; 6. Dilemma Between Pride and Self-hatred; 7. Alienation from Self; 8. Influence on Human Relations; 9. Influence on Love-Life; 10. Influence on Work; 11. Influence on Sex-Life; 12. Pride and Self-hatred in Freud; 13. Pride and Self-hatred in Literature; 14. Solution in Therapy." The first seven lectures correspond to the first six chapters of* Neurosis and Human Growth, *and the eighth and tenth lectures to the chapters on human relations and work. The chapters "Theoretical Considerations" and "The Road of Psychoanalytic Therapy" are anticipated to some extent by lectures 12 and 14.*

The book's important chapters titled "The Expansive Solutions," "The Self-Effacing Solution," "Morbid Dependency," and "Resignation" have no counterpart in the lectures, although they do in the chapters on moving against, toward, and away from people in Our Inner Conflicts. *In the lectures, Horney was entirely focused on intrapsychic processes, whereas in* Neurosis and Human Growth *she tried to integrate the interpersonal and the intrapsychic.*

Because the lectures on love-life, sex-life, Freud, and literature contain much material that does not appear in Horney's published work, I plan to include them in a companion to this volume that will bring together the remainder of Horney's unpublished and uncollected writings.

The version of lecture 14 presented here has been lightly edited. I have changed a few words when Horney or her typist seems to have made an error. For example, the second line in the notes begins "Differences vary," but it makes more sense to say "Difficulties vary." Also, I have occasionally supplied a definite or an indefinite article, and I have changed the punctuation to make the notes more readable. Whereas Horney separated each thought with an ellipsis (. . .), I have supplied commas, semicolons, and periods.

Difficulties Carried into Analysis:

Difficulties vary with what is in the foreground: either the feeling of self-effacement or of superiority.

1. Patient comes to analysis with feeling of superiority which may be quite conscious or which may be unconscious. Superiority may rest in the intellect, in love, being moral, on aesthetic level, etc. May also be hidden by a superficial self-effacement which masks superiority.

Patient may have many disturbances: i.e., headaches, insomnia, asthmatic attacks, depression, inhibitions in work, etc. Yet he comes to the analysis with the idea that he is essentially all right and only needs a few visits to clear up the situation. This really means that he expects the analysis to make him even more perfect. This poses the question: how does he manage to have these hopes and expectations of an easy analysis when SO MUCH is the matter with him? The reason is that the patient makes a neat distinction between his idealized image and his neurosis. The neurosis has nothing to do with him and the idealized image is all right. This is the basis of the false expectations.

Also the patient may have only a vague idea of how the analyst can or should help him. Make comparison with going to a dentist. Patient sits back and puts himself in the hands of the analyst. He can't do anything, has feeling of inertia, believes he has no influence on the situation and needs only to talk and sit back and the rest is all the responsibility of the analyst. This means the patient is miles away from his real self, has no idea as to responsibility for self.

But even with expectations of a quick and painless cure the patient will still have moments of despair because the structure of self-hatred is there in the background, while the superiority is in the foreground.

2. Patient comes to analysis with feeling of self-effacement in the foreground. Feels abject, self-torturing, filled with destructive self-doubt. Such a patient feels hopeless and worthless; feels unworthy of troubling the analyst and taking time for himself. Some arrogance may be visible even with such self-effacement in the arrogant shoulds, in spite of self-belittling. Feels humiliation in accepting and needing help from analyst.

The prognosis is better if at the start the battle is out in the open. On one hand the self-hatred and self-frustration and on the other hand the fantastic claims on life. Then the analyst doesn't have to go so long a way in showing the patient that there is not *only* superiority or *only* self-hatred but *both*.

Responses to Analysis and Interpretation:

1. Direct hurt pride reaction. Turns vindictive. Resents the whole process of analysis as a constant humiliation, resents criticism, resents needing help. May begin analysis with cruel, brutal fantasies as to what they would like to do to the analyst.

2. Discards analysis. At first feels abused and then just does not take the analysis seriously at all, or feels above the analyst and discards what the analyst says as unimportant. Or thinks analyst can't understand, and so again there is the silent discarding of the analysis.

3. Wants quick results. Has analytical hour then thinks about it. Sees it all and believes now that the problem is all cleared up. Really means that it is so intolerable to the pride to see a flaw that patient strives for quick correction, only the correction is superficial and has no realistic results.

4. Patient on the defensive—i.e., not really independent but rebels against authority. Patient says it is due to his mother and it is a good thing he did rebel. Partly true, but it misses the point and means putting up defensive arguments instead of acquiring insight into the situation. Fights facing reality.

5. Seems to be interested. Questions why everything is so. This is no help. Or sees some difficulty and responds with running self down and becoming de-

pressed. Or something gets clearer and patient is enthused about it and is productive, but then, in the next hour, he has forgotten the previous hour and has lost all that he seemed to gain. This may mean that patient thinks seeing a problem once is enough and it needs no more work, or that he bends his energies into frustrating his own progress.

The patient does everything but the one thing that is helpful, which is to test out his new knowledge, see how it applies to him, what it does to him, what application it has for him.

Attitude to Analyst:

Pride and self-hatred impairs human relationships, and this impairment is carried into relationship with the analyst. Due to pride the patient feels humiliated, accused, driven. He projects inner dictates on analyst; feels unlovable so feels analyst doesn't really care about him, or feels analyst is looking down on him. This is externalization of self-contempt.

Means a precarious relationship with analyst. Needs to have a conscious confidence that analyst knows what he is doing and has a real interest in the patient and has integrity in the treatment.

Patient's reaction to getting better or worse: A. If patient is getting worse, feels it is the fault of the analyst, who has the responsibility. B. If patient is getting better, at times it may help situation but also it may frighten the patient, and he responds with the voice of self-hatred. It is only temporary, but patient feels hopeless, and this hinders the analysis.

The more the patient lives in imagination and the more he has built up the armor of self-righteousness, the harder it is to reach him in analysis.

Steps in Therapy:

One answer to what should be done is to say the patient must see the claims to superiority and must give them up along with the desire for power, pride, etc. If there are no claims for superior power, then patient will "come down to earth." If patient doesn't demand the impossible of himself, then he will have better relations with self.

This sounds plausible, and if it is a mild neurosis or with children who are treated early and put in good environment, then this would be all right. This is the main way Adler took, especially with children. But with a deep neurosis it won't work this way. It is like operating on the original cancer when there are many metastases.

We lack dialectic thinking; lack vision of seeing the self as a whole organism.

Each part acts on other parts; can't just eliminate one part. I.e., with the superior person, the feeling of superiority has its function for the person; it means a lack of self-confidence. The superiority gives the person a false self-confidence and a basis on which he can relate himself to others. If by a miracle the feeling of superiority could be eliminated in a short time, on what could the person fall back? Can't fall back on real self because that has been lost sight of. Even more, he is afraid that if he gives up the superiority, he would fall into the abyss of self-hatred.

Sometimes life may do this to a person, strip him of all his prestige. Then it kills or makes for strength, but no analyst would try this, and it wouldn't succeed anyway because the patient would hold on to what is indispensable to him.

It must be a gradual process, not only in the sense of taking place slowly but also in the work to be done — work in which the patient is given some *real* strength on which to fall back.

Sequence in Analysis:

This differs with the patient.

1. Starting with superiority. The first thing is to help the patient to see the superiority not as a fact but as a problem, that he needs to feel superior and what it means to him. He may struggle against this but then starts to see it as a problem — that there is some psychological necessity behind this need — and then becomes interested in what is behind it. Inkling of something to be re-evaluated. At the same time, analyst brings to patient's attention his real assets, to give the patient some strength to fight the need for superiority. But these are realistic assets.

Next is the realization that the patient functions well only when he is in a position of being superior to others. He realizes that this is limiting and energy consuming. Then he may start to see his huge claims on others and on life and see the waste of time and energy in feeling frustrated and indignant. Sees he can't take things in his stride. No longer has pride in his claims.

2. Starting with self-reproaches. The patient feels they are all right as they are a sign of high moral standards. When he goes deeper, he sees what he does to himself with this sadistic hostility to self. Sees these reproaches are cramping and futile, and they appear to patient in an entirely new light.

In all these steps, the patient becomes more realistic and starts to question these expansive drives and starts coming back to his real self. Has beginning interest in self. Energies redirected into constructive channels.

When patient is stronger, then he can see the whole extent of the self-hostility. Then may run into new difficulty; may react with despair. Then gradually sees self-reproaches just as unrealistic as the grandiose ideals.

Or if patient questions the grandiose pursuits and has given up the more obvious parts, may go into throes of self-hatred. But then sees this as unrealistic. Must see the *connection* between the pride and the self-hatred. It is hard to accept this connection because this means giving up the last vestiges of arrogance and pride.

In these last stages the patient most needs the support of the analyst, most needs the analyst's faith in him and belief that he can come out of this Hell.

Curative Forces:

We could say that patient must become *aware* of his difficulties and then, by seeing the consequences of the neurotic drives, he will decide to change the neurotic drives because in seeing the consequences he sees it is to his *self-interest* to change. But much has to be added to this.

Awareness is certainly necessary, but what helps is what the awareness *does to the person*. Just awareness may lead to a kind of intellectual ecstasy of recognition without any constructive results. Or may result in self-reproaches. Or sees the conflict and bends energy to getting around it. Then even if there is awareness it is unproductive of change.

Seeing the consequences is very valuable. If analyst shows the patient all the handicaps of the neurotic drives and conflicts, it may appeal to self-interest to change; but as long as the patient has little self-interest due to self-hatred, then such an appeal has limited effect. Or patient may see the consequences clearly but bends energies to outsmarting them, so again there is little effect in constructive change.

So — awareness is the *first*, indispensable step, but it is like opening a door. The person may or may not go through the door.

Following awareness there must be:

1. Taking back of externalizations. If patient realizes it is not others' claims on him but his own claims, own shoulds, etc., then he takes the problem home to himself. Must see it is his own problem before he can do anything about it. So gradually takes problems back to self. This means improvement in human relationships, but it also enlarges the territory of self: feeling of "my problem and it is up to me to do something about it." This is gaining strength.

2. Constant reevaluation in analysis and reorientation in values. To see the real values in life does away with cynicism and this goes on through the analysis. Sees claims realistically as dangerous to self and what is preventing

person from using real resources. I.e., vindictiveness no longer seen as strength but what robs person of constructive energies. Also, gradually reevaluates belief that feelings are something to be ashamed of or are dangerous and sees that without feelings we are dead. Need feelings to be a real person and have real self-confidence. Or, was proud of self-reproaches as indicating high standards. Sees they are futile and search for glory is his worst enemy. Sees outsmarting others is a debatable value. Tries to find real values in relationships with others.

This reevaluation of wrong attitudes goes slowly and very painfully, but the more it goes on the better the progress.

3. Reevaluation of assets. Sees true values in self and true strengths. Gets rid of self-hatred and has a better and more realistic evaluation of self, more constructive attitude toward self. With reorientation, the energies are bent into more constructive channels. Instead of being scattered and driven into many directions, the person acquires firmness and knows what his real goals are in life. Puts self-confidence on a much firmer ground.

4. Improvement in relations with others. This already mentioned in taking back of externalizations. Results in less hostility against others. With less arrogance, relationships are better. With less vulnerable pride, there is less withdrawal and less vindictiveness. With giving up of claims, there is feeling of belonging with others. Relationship with the analyst does its share in improving all relationships. This gives the patient experience with a good relationship, which carries over into other relationships. This gives patient more strength and feeling of belonging. No longer needs to battle everyone. Becomes more cooperative.

With all these steps, patient comes closer to what he is, what he feels, what he wants to combat and to cultivate, with feeling of real me. Starts to fight self-inflicted sufferings. Becomes free to use energies to grow constructively. Takes on responsibility for self and for overcoming his problems. Dares to hope and to aspire for something.

Last curative factor. May not operate always. All previous steps taken against great resistance and silent reservations. In face of all these difficulties, patient often doesn't make up his mind to change unless faced with stark necessity of seeing it as a sink or swim situation. Analyst works toward patient's seeing this necessity. Patient must face his own neurotic drives and see that he can't get well unless neurotic drives are given up. This is iron-clad psychological law that patient must accept if he is to get well.

With this impasse patient may feel despair. Analyst sees it as a puzzle. How can this impasse be overcome? Then next time patient starts to see some things concretely and is much more constructive. Here is a fault, but the fault is not an all-pervading poison gas. Hits depths of despair and then starts to come up out of it.

In the analysis, the constructive forces in the patient are used to get him out of his entanglement. E.g. "Pavilion of Women" [Pearl Buck] and "Left Hand Is the Dreamer" [Nancy Wilson Ross]. Shows reorientation of values.

What is most important is prevention. Knowledge of these factors in relation to self must be applied in the schools and in the home to help create true, basic confidence in children. Must try to get a new generation to be strong so it won't succumb to the struggle of the Devil's Pact. Will have real self-confidence, so won't have to go in search of glory, with resultant self-hatred.

11

Finding the Real Self
A Letter with a Foreword
by Karen Horney (1949)

In New Ways in Psychoanalysis, *Horney began to see the central feature of neurosis as the "warping" of "the spontaneous individual self" because of parental oppression. The object of therapy is "to restore the individual to himself, to help him regain his spontaneity and find his center of gravity in himself" (1939, 11). Horney introduced the term "the real self" in "Can You Take a Stand?" (1939b, 130) and used it again in* Self-Analysis *(1942, 22, 290–91), where she first spoke of "self-realization" (10). By the time she wrote* Neurosis and Human Growth, *the real self had become the basis of her conceptions of both health and neurosis.*

Although the idea of an inherent self has become unfashionable today, Horney was far from alone in positing a real self and regarding healthy growth as a process of actualizing it. Her position is akin to the developmental, self, and object-relations approach articulated by James Masterson in The Real Self, *where he observes that "in our daily toil with our patients, our work revolves around a person with a self, not a collection of objects and an ego" (1985, 5; see also Stern 1985). Horney's real self bears some resemblance to Kohut's "nuclear self" (1977, 1984) and even more to Winnicott's "true self" (1965). According to Winnicott, as a result of inadequate nurturing "something that could have become the* individual becomes hidden away[,] . . . protected from further impingement" by a "false self" that develops reactively and supersedes "the true impulsive self which might under more favorable circumstances have been gathering strength" (1987, 61). This sounds like Horney, as does much of Alice Miller's discussion of the loss of and search for the true self in childhood (1981, 1983) and R. D. Laing's account of ontological insecurity (which is comparable to basic anxiety) and the development of a false-self system in response to it (1965). Abraham Maslow (1970) adopted Horney's conception of the real self and made it the foundation of his theory of self-actualization (see Paris 1994, chap. 29).

Horney realized that her ideas about the real self were nebulous and elusive, difficult for her to formulate and for others to grasp. The real self will seem like "a phantom," she wrote, unless we are "acquainted with the later phases of analysis" (1950, 175). Although "the real or possible self" may seem like an abstraction, it is "nevertheless felt" in the course of successful therapy, and the patient's experience of it is "more real, more certain, more definite than anything else" (158).

Horney was delighted by a letter one of her patients wrote describing her discovery of her real self in analysis. The patient was Barbara Westcott, who had started reading Horney while hospitalized for depression and who later sought her out for treatment. Westcott's husband wrote that he had "no doubt that Karen Horney saved [his] wife's life" (quoted by Quinn 1987, 383). Horney wrote a foreword and published the letter anonymously in the American Journal of Psychoanalysis 9 (1949), 3–7. Since Westcott was steeped in Horney's writings, she often sounds like her mentor, but her letter helps us to grasp what Horney meant by the real self and gives us a sense of how she worked as a therapist. (For a fuller discussion of the real self, see Paris 1994, chap. 26.)

Foreword: The letter we have put at the head of this year's publication is a document of greatest value. It was written after only 38 hours of analysis by a woman patient of great integrity, a woman endowed with the faculty of concisely expressing what she feels.

Five years prior to analysis Mrs. B. had suffered a severe nervous breakdown, occasioned by difficulties with her child. To bring it down to bare essentials, it was provoked by the patient's being confronted for the first time in her life with difficulties she could not overcome by reason and will power. Previously Mrs. B. had succeeded through consistent remoteness from herself and others.

It is not necessary here to go into details of either character structure or history. It is enough to say that the five years following the breakdown were years of intense suffering; years full of emotional upsets, of depressions, of states of unreality, of periods of self-hate and despair. With considerable understanding, a psychiatrist in a sanatorium helped her through the acute stages of her anguish. This letter was written to the psychiatrist and was motivated by a spontaneous wish to tell him about what she felt — and what has proved since them — to be a turning point in her life.

A year after she had left the institution, she decided to seek analytic help. She still gave the impression of great brittleness; she was subdued, tense, and full of palpable anxiety. The main area that unfolded in the first 30 analytical sessions was the relentless system of "shoulds" which dominated her. She experienced a turning against herself whenever she could not measure up to her rigid inner standards. Toward the end of this period, however, she took a positive step of great consequence. She started to wonder how much this kind of regimen stifled her spontaneity. From this the analyst drew courage to try to penetrate to her real self at this early stage with a question: "What do you really want?"

She was able to take up the challenge. She responded by realizing her loss of self and by visualizing the possibility of finding herself. All this is expressed in the letter. The insight was not a passing elation but indeed instigated a radical change in her entire outlook on herself and on life in general. She had found a piece of firm ground upon which to stand, from which she could safely tackle her neurotic problems.

Such an experience raises many questions most relevant for therapy. If the discovery of the real self is of incisive importance for therapy, how can the analyst help the patient to find himself? At what time and under which conditions can he try to direct the patient toward himself? Are there any dangers in approaching this subject prematurely? What, exactly, are the consequences of such a step? And, since the discovery of the self is usually not as dramatic as in this instance, how can we recognize and encourage the *less* perceptible moves the patient takes toward it?

I trust that we will be able to answer these questions in the near future — provided our conviction about the importance of finding the real self proves well founded. The following letter will give us an incentive to investigate these questions.

Dear Dr. X:

You'll be happy to learn that you are the father and by now the grandfather of a small miracle — I nearly telegraphed you of it three weeks ago but thought I'd better wait and be quite sure. It is simply but definitely that I am getting well — at long last. Meaning of course "as well as the next guy," since our capacity for being human is almost never absolute. . . .

I mean just this: Until now I have known nothing, understood nothing, and perforce could love nothing, and for the simple, unbelievable reason that I wasn't here! For over forty years I have been exiled from myself without even suspecting it.

Merely to understand this, now, is tremendous. It is not only the end of all that dying, it is to begin life.

The story begins with your friendship, your generosity — when I was almost too sick to receive it. In the deepest sense that *was* my sickness. I couldn't be friends; I had never been free, humanly, nor ever wanted to be. And you did somehow get through in spite of me, although two years more were to pass before this final chapter. The end, now, the opening of the door, belongs to my present analyst, Dr. Y.

As you know, she didn't begin with me until September, and things have been moving fast, so fast that she too thinks it somewhat miraculous; but don't worry, she means to verify it before turning me loose. Now that I have both feet on the path, I don't care how rough the going may be.

It was a long journey brought me to her. Years of paralysis and depression. Then those months at the sanatorium. . . . Remember how you tenderly patched and bandaged me, and how on Easter Day you lent me the book *Our Inner Conflicts?* That day was the day I began to move. Of course I wasn't ripe for her sort of therapy yet, but I did react to that instant overwhelming recognition of myself, my neurotic self X-rayed upon the page. I did exist! Chapter Five and the end of Chapter Twelve were proof of it, illumination of it, and stirred me or the ghost of me from the limits of despair all the way to a new peak of exhilaration — on the strength of which I was able to come home, in installments. You know how difficult the next twelve months were: ceaseless effort to combat or to tolerate the days, nights, weeks, with my obsessive hallucination on the one hand and my own living "inhumanity" on the other; vain effort, punctuated only by occasional psychotic episodes. . . .

The last of these episodes, about Thanksgiving Day, was highly significant — although at the time I could see nothing in it but redoubled terror, guilt, and hopelessness. What was actually my first audible bid for life I then took to be just one more ghastly proof of madness, no more than a dim and desperate hallucination that "somewhere there must be a *meaning,* that somehow I would find mine."

By last spring a sort of cold peace had set in and I felt strong enough to begin thinking about psychoanalysis, and at last to get in touch with Dr. Y. She "would like to work with me . . . but . . . it was out of the question until next fall." I would wait. Then in May, while on a trip to Oregon, came my second overwhelming reaction to the written words — this time in *New Ways in Psychoanalysis*. I had scarcely finished the chapter on the "superego" when the very ground I stood on began to slip. Or, it was as though without warning or preparation, while I slept, my one remaining leg had been amputated at the hip. About all I could do then and during the next four months was to keep my eyes shut and try not to breathe until I could start work with Dr. Y in the fall.

Thus you might say I was "softened up" when I came to her, but I still had the disease; and she set to work ever so quietly but swiftly — *showing* me everything (myself in action), *telling* me nothing.

The first thing she tackled was that which was readiest at hand: my cast-iron "should system." My complete armor of "shoulds": duty, ideals, pride, guilt. This rigid and compulsive perfectionism was all that held me up; outside it and all around lay chaos. . . . She let me talk, fumble, stop, turn, begin again, always going in circles until at last, little by little even *I* could begin to see what sort of strait jacket held me: I existed only because I *should!* I began to mention "spontaneity" — to dare think of it, and at last to realize how I longed for it — I who had always deliberately fought it, even in childhood! And Dr. Y. pointed out that there is an inverse ratio between genuine, spontaneous feelings and the "should system."

Then, on January 10th, she played a trump card — daring to play it so early in the game. Just four words! An apparently innocent, even naive question; but it was loaded. As she put it: "Perhaps there isn't even an answer to this as yet . . . but what *do* you want, really?"

I tried to keep it from striking home and retreated any way I could to defend what was still my sole *raison d'être,* but within hours the medicine began to work way down inside me. For the first time in my life I saw that I was quite simply unable to *want* anything, not even death! And certainly not "life." Until now I had thought my trouble was just that I was unable to *do* things: unable to give up my dream, unable to gather up my own things, unable to accept or control my irritability, unable to make myself more human, whether by sheer will power, patience, or grief.

Now, for the first time I saw it — I was literally unable to *feel* anything. (Yes, for all my famous super-sensitivity!) How well I knew pain — every pore of me clogged with inward rage, self-pity, self-contempt, and despair for the last six years and over and over again and again! Yet, I saw it now — all was negative, reactive, compulsive, *all imposed from without, inside* there was absolutely nothing of mine! There just was nothing. Had I been a little less numb I suppose I'd at last have cut my throat. And Dr. Y knew it.

This was it: the crisis, the turning point.

I went home and began once more to think down to the bottom of my rootlessness. Perhaps a week or two passed.

There is only one way out of chaos; and now that I knew all the other doors were locked, I made the tremendous discovery. The miracle that Dr. Y. had forced me to make on my own, not out of books this time — at least not directly — but out of my own bowels. From ten thousand miles away I saw it as a blinding light: the importance, the necessity of a Self! One's own single self. My original life — *what had happened to it?* Chaos was here — all around and in me — that I understood in all my fragments. But was that all one could ever know? What about the perfect planets, this earth, people, objects? Didn't they exist and move? Couldn't they be known? Yes . . . but there has to be a knower, a *subject,* as well! (Meaning is a bridge between *two* things.) Beginnings, direction, movement had to be *from* a single point; and ours is where we stand, alone, our being *sui generis.*

Suddenly vistas spread out and out to the sky, and all came together at my feet. Was it possible that I had touched the key to the universe — the key which every man carries so nonchalantly in his pocket? Instantly I knew in my bones, and by grief itself, that I had discovered the very core and essence of neurosis — my neurosis and perhaps every neurosis. The secret of wretchedness was SELFLESSNESS! Deep and hidden, the fact and the fear of not having a self. Not being a self. Not-being. And at the end — actual chaos.

With this (the hallucination to end them all?) I went to Dr. Y. and talked for two hours. My own calm surprised me. She listened intently. I knew this time she was not being just a spectator. I told her that at last I had seen my true poverty. I saw now all the way down, how and why, and how completely neurotic *needs* come to replace desires . . . until you are canceled out. One couldn't ask a starved man, a dead man, if he would *prefer* oysters to caviar; cut off from desires the very concept of *choice* cannot exist. Here at the end of this thought I had seen how neurosis happens and what it's all about. Selflessness! (The lack of self, of selfhood, of entity, of integrity.)

How is it possible to lose a self? The treachery, unknown and unthinkable, begins with our secret psychic death in childhood — if and when we are not loved and are cut off from our spontaneous wishes. (Think: What is left?) But wait — it is not just this simple murder of a psyche. That might be written off, the tiny victim might even "outgrow" it — but it is a perfect double crime in which he himself also gradually and unwittingly takes part. He has not been accepted for himself, *as he is.*

Oh, they "love" him, but they want him or force him or expect him to be different! Therefore *he must be unacceptable.* He himself learns to believe it and at last even takes it for granted. He has truly given himself up. No matter now whether he obeys them, whether he clings, rebels or withdraws — his behavior, his performance is all that matters. His center of gravity is in "them," not in himself — yet if he so much as noticed it he'd think it natural enough. And the whole thing is entirely plausible; all invisible, automatic, and anonymous!

This is the perfect paradox. Everything looks normal; no crime was intended; there is no corpse, no guilt. All we can see is the sun rising and setting as usual. But what has happened? He has been rejected, not only by them, but by himself. (He is actually without a self.) What has he lost? Just the one true and vital part of himself: his own yes-feeling, which is his very capacity for growth, his root system. But alas, he is not dead. "Life" goes on, and so must he. From the moment he gives himself up, and to the extent that he does so, all unknowingly he sets about to create and maintain a pseudo-self. But this is an expediency . . . a "self" without wishes. This one shall be loved (or feared) where he is despised, strong where he is weak; it shall go through the motions (Oh, but they are caricatures!) not for fun or joy but for survival; not simply because it wants to move but because it has to obey. This necessity is not life — not his life — it is a defense mechanism against death. It is also the machine of death. From now on he will be torn apart by compulsive (unconscious) *needs* or ground by (unconscious) conflicts into paralysis, every motion and every instant canceling out his being, his integrity; and all the while he is disguised as a normal person and expected to behave like one!

In a word, I saw that we *become* neurotic seeking or defending a pseudo-self, a self-system; and we *are* neurotic to the extent that we are self-less.

Think what this 25th of January meant to me! From now on I had something to believe in, not yet in my *own* self perhaps — for to think it is not quite to be it — but at least I could believe in my *right* (innate, potential) to wish, to want, and to live for no purpose or reason other than that I do. *Sum ergo sum.* (Indeed, hadn't scientists "believed" in uranium long before they discovered it?)

I can see you smiling now as you read this because long ago you gave me the answer to this thing, though neither you nor I could correctly formulate the *question* that it answers. (Oh, the truth lies all about us like the grass.) You once told me, remember, that there were only two reasons for doing anything in life: either because it needed to be done, or because one wanted to do it. The clue is that word *want* — to wish, not to need. You know, as I do, that the neurotic, so far as he is neurotic, is no longer able simply to want or wish anything but is driven right, left, and around in circles by his compulsive needs, which can never be less than absolute starvation. He really does need everything, desperately, and therefore *cannot* give up anything; and there is no solution. He *has* no choice; alternatives he has (many, and all bad), but *who is there* to do the choosing?

And I remembered Dr. Z's neat description of the neurotic: The patient says, "I cannot"; his friends say, "He will not"; and the doctor says, "He cannot will." Now carry this one step further, and there is the reason which none suspects: He cannot will because he cannot even wish! Almost literally he is not there. He may strive desperately toward his goal and never make it (or at what a cost!), because *it isn't he* that is doing the striving. His real self is stifled by the neurosis, the Frankenstein monster originally designed for his protection. And it makes little difference whether you live in a totalitarian country or a private neurosis, either way you are apt to end up in a concentration camp where the whole point is to destroy the self as painfully as possible.

Having discovered the necessity for it, I now began to see the significance of the self. Oh, the million things you discover with the first touch of life! Almost before you've turned the key all the separate fragments of existence rush to fall into place. How can you see, think, speak, remember fast enough to keep pace? Is there nothing which doesn't fit here, even dying and terror and broken things? There is nothing of it unknown to you, and little that the average healthy man doesn't simply take for granted — but I had never before seen the sun rise. How could I have understood that the self is as significant as humanity? And this is not at all Freud's ego, but rather, as William James describes it, "what welcomes and rejects." (Freud's ego and superego, as I understand them, *are* the neurosis!)

If our human purpose is to live and grow and express ourselves, then the *chance to grow* is everything — for it takes years, even with incalculable love or luck, to walk and wind our own willingness through the whole structure of things. Yet it is this willingness we can't afford to give up. It is our sole strength, our wish to live! Who gives it up, from fear or force, has to that extent lost himself; he is emasculated (well symbolized by Freud's "castration complex") and sold into slavery and compulsion. He may look like a man, but that is only his body, which he hopes will be fed. How shall he (being less than a man) bridge the gap between discipline and the self-discipline which is choice? How shall he take one step from utter frustration (from self-pity, scorn, greed, guilt or rage) to compassion, generosity and respect? Not by remorse, nor will power, nor broken-hearted charity; not by any miracle of "brotherly love" which is not and cannot be in his heart; not by suicide, murder, or the rope trick. Babe or neurotic, he cannot make one step forward because he *cannot want* to. And why in fact should *he* want to, he who sees only the cost and not the gain? (Unwilling renunciation is a kind of suicide and breeds more monsters.) You cannot will yourself to *want* a thing! I know. I've tried for years.

One thing only separates "I should," or "I need," from the simplest "I do want" — and that is not *choice* but the *freedom to choose*. (Sheer intellect and stupendous resolution are as nothing. The emotion is all: the "attaching of values," a man's entire meaning and content.) And this is the significance of the self: that it alone *can* choose. It has this freedom because it has and *is* the emotion. It is free because it has a place to stand — its own live roots, and not the shifting ground of expediency; and because it can have no ulterior motive. It relates directly to things. (I do not mean that such a self has no problems, no defeats, but that in choosing it will be limited by perception, and not by any effort of the will; its problems may even be insoluble but they will not be overwhelming.) At the very deepest level the self knows only two words — and it *wants* to say yes, that widest of words, because its only purpose is to be! In this sense I suppose dualism is not around us but in ourselves, our multiplicity of selves, which means always the distance from our true self.

Who for that matter would not rather *be himself,* affectionate and free, if he could afford it? No other self is free to feel, to express our nature, to know another and be known. This alone is the human self, that can go out; that can love, and endure, and be loved — because it wants to live.

12

The Goals of Analytic Therapy (1951)

This essay was originally published in Psyche 7 *(1951), 463–72, as "Ziele Der Analytischen Therapie." No longer comfortable writing in German, Horney composed the essay in English and had it translated by Marianne Von Eckardt, the second wife of Gertrud Lederer-Eckardt's first husband. The original English version having been lost, the essay was translated from the German by Andrea Dlaska, University of Innsbruck, with my editorial assistance, and published in the* American Journal of Psychoanalysis 51 *(1991), 219–26. This special issue of the journal commemorated the fiftieth anniversary of the founding by Karen Horney of the Association for the Advancement of Psychoanalysis, the American Institute for Psychoanalysis, and the* American Journal of Psychoanalysis.*

Elissa P. Benedek and Paul J. Fink, both of whom had been president of the American Psychiatric Association, were invited to discuss Horney's paper. Benedek observed that "Horney's work brought new treatment techniques and helped close the distinction between analysis and therapy from which the field benefits today." She wished "that those involved in managed care . . . would read Horney's work and respond to her ideas" because she makes a good case that the goal of therapy "is not simply to remove symptoms but rather to help patients under-

stand their own neuroses so that they can reach a true understanding of
who they are and eventually solve their problems themselves" (1991,
228). Fink noted that Horney was correct in identifying "character pa-
thology as the appropriate and real province of psychoanalytic interven-
tions" (1991, 232). He saw Horney's paper as "a precursor to object
relations theory" and felt that she "anticipated the whole development
of self-psychology" (234).

The goals of psychoanalysis have changed in recent years. When Freud
made the astonishing discovery that symptoms, such as the paralysis of an arm
or anxiety, could be eliminated by calling back to mind the traumatic experience the patient had forgotten, or, as we say, had not gotten over at the time, it
was of course the aim of therapy to remove the symptoms. The next discovery
Freud made was that this simple method of removing symptoms did not always work. In some cases, no individual experience could be found that was
responsible for a specific physical disorder, and it seemed necessary to make a
long detour and learn a great deal about the patient's life and his entire personality in order to understand the symptom and help the patient to overcome it.
Freud gradually realized the fact that symptoms do not simply vanish but can
only be removed if we understand the human personality, and especially neurosis. The goal was therefore redefined as removing symptoms through an
understanding of the personality. But the emphasis was still on the symptom.

The next development was that several progressive analysts noticed with
surprise that there are neuroses without symptoms. It was Franz Alexander
who rather naively named this discovery "character neurosis," a formulation
we feel to be totally wrong today, since every neurosis is a character neurosis;
but at the time, the discovery was a considerable advance. What Alexander
was trying to say was that neurosis is not only a matter of symptoms but is a
disorder of the personality.

We have still not overcome the focus on the symptom, however. Because an
enormous number of people suffer from neuroses, it is only natural that the
doctor should look for a short way to free patients from desperate situations,
from depression, insomnia, alcoholism, or whatever the symptom may be. It
gives him the feeling, justified to a certain extent, that at least he did help. The
fact that short-term therapy plays such an enormous role is due to a genuine
need, but it reflects a widespread ignorance among both doctors and patients.

I can illustrate this with an example. A patient who started an analysis at age
forty told me that she was engaged at the age of twenty-one and had suffered
from such severe symptoms of fatigue that she was unable to do anything at
all. It was quite natural that her doctor told her that she was simply weak and

needed some rest, although this did not improve her exhaustion. Then a friend appeared who had just become acquainted with analysis, was full of enthusiasm, and said, "This is all psychological; your tiredness has to do with your doubts about your fiancé. You have some reservations with regard to marriage." Her fatigue ceased instantly, and she could climb a mountain.

This is impressive, of course, and, like short-term therapy, it helped the patient to master an obstacle. But it ignored a great many questions. Where did the ambivalent feelings toward her fiancé come from? Why was she not aware of them? Why did she never raise the question of whether she should marry that man? These would have been reasonable questions at the time. Or the question of whether her reservations only related to this specific man or would arise with every man or with every human being.

When I later analyzed this patient, deep traits of self-denial emerged behind the reservations, which appeared to have been produced by a current situation. After her marriage was dissolved, she took up a relationship of typical morbid dependence, a self-denying relationship in which she had deep feelings of being sacrificed.

This example shows that a symptom cannot be understood unless one enters more deeply into the personality. As soon as one starts asking very simple questions — Why didn't she become conscious of the conflict right away? What was the conflict? Why did she want to get married at all? Why didn't she have any doubts? — as soon as one does this one gets involved in the deep entanglements of the personality. When we understand that the hidden traits of the overall structure contribute to this patient's symptoms, we realize that symptoms are not isolated but that a neurosis is a disorder of the personality as a whole. The goal of therapy increasingly shifts to an embracing of the entire personality.

In other areas of medicine the doctor is usually not contented with the removal of a symptom. He will hardly be satisfied to get rid of a cough without trying to cure its cause. Therefore, the objection that the personality is not the concern of analysis cannot really be sustained, unless one clearly contends that the task of the doctor and of modern psychoanalytic therapy merely lies in achieving a symptomatic cure. We realize that our conception of the goals of therapy depends on our understanding not only of neurosis but also on our Weltanschauung, i.e., our conception of our profession.

When we realized that neurosis basically is a process in which human relationships are disturbed, the goal of therapy emerged as the improvement of human relationships. This was a much more complex goal than relieving symptoms, since human relationships are decidedly the most important part of life. But what does improvement of human relationships mean? We can say, for instance, that a person who is either too dependent, or too dominating, or too aggressive, or who exploits other people can be considered improved if we can help him to view relationships with others on a basis of mutual respect and to learn to give something. Similarly, a patient who is defensively aggressive toward others and to whom we open the possibility of friendly feelings and common goals can be considered improved. It would be an improvement if a person whose relationships are mainly determined by habitual intimidation of others, habitual friendliness, habitual praise, or distancing through politeness — all compulsive strategies — could be helped again to spontaneous feelings. By improvement we mean, then, turning such relationships into something more constructive.

Probing deeper, we realize that such disorders in human relationships are more or less determined by conflicts. A person feels a strong need to distance himself from others but he may also desire affection. Or, a person feels that he has to fight and subject everybody, but he also needs warmth. We see the goal of therapy as helping people to resolve conflicts of this kind and to achieve a harmony of feelings and a sense of inner integration. If we try to help a person to have direct and wholehearted feelings for others, to replace deliberate or automatic strategies with spontaneity, we say that we are helping the person to find himself.

We end up with three objectives: reorientation, constructive integration, and finding oneself. This leads to the fourth concern, which is a person's relationship with himself. In a way, of course, this was included when we talked of a person's relationships with others, since no dividing line can be drawn between a person's relationships with others and with himself. They are connected with each other and inseparable, but the emphasis may lie on the one side or the other. We are gradually beginning to examine intrapsychic processes more closely. I have to condense here considerably.

What we see on the surface are a person's feelings toward himself, which usually vary considerably. At times, someone may feel that he is the most brilliant and generous person ever, but at other times he may feel just as profoundly that he is a complete idiot. He can consider himself the most glorious lover and feel it to be the utmost cruelty to reject a woman who approaches him because it deprives her of the unique experience of himself; but he may also feel that a girl who loves him can only be despicable, or he may feel safe only with strumpets. Such waverings may be conscious with some people, hidden with others, but they are always there.

In neurosis a process sets in regularly in which a person despairs because he feels lost, divided, inferior, and takes refuge in fantasy. He begins to glorify himself and feels that, like a personified god, he is, or should be, equipped with infinite power and perfection, that he is as good as St. Francis or has absolute courage. If he does not possess absolute courage, he considers himself a downright coward. In other words, by building his pedestal so high, by idealizing himself in such a fantastic way, by raising his standard to an impossible level, he is beginning to turn against himself as he really is. He begins to hate and despise himself the way he happens to be. If this self-hate and self-contempt get the upper hand, he does indeed feel guilty, stupid, depraved, hopeless, whereas the minute the self-glorification gets the upper hand he feels on top of the world.

We can summarize this process with the titles of two books: *Man Against Himself* by Menninger, and *Man for Himself* by Fromm. Man turns against himself with the whole bitterness of his worst enemy. If I am not capable of writing a brilliant article on a subject I haven't even thought about, I am simply good for nothing. If my child is ill and I do not devote every minute to him without thinking of anything else, I am simply a miserable mother. As Rashkolnikov says, "If I am not as ruthless as Napoleon who could kill without qualms, if I cannot slay one poor pawnbroker, I am good for nothing and a damned coward."

One might expect that at this point the goals of therapy should be to help a person surrender such illusions and realize that, in reality, he is claiming to be like god, and at the same time, to make him aware of his self-hate, so that he finally can see and accept himself as the person he is. One cannot simply attack the patient's illusions, however. If one treated a patient in this way, showed him outright where his illusions lay, and told him that he had to surrender them in order to be happy, he might say, if he is the more arrogant type, "I don't know, are you crazy or am I?" There would even be some validity in this question, for if he really accepted what the doctor told him, he might break down immediately and fall into an abyss of self-contempt. If he takes the suggestions of the analyst seriously there is also the possibility that the patient will fall prey to something I call "insincere resignation." "All right, I realize I'm not exactly a genius, at least not without effort; it seems I have to accept myself on a lower level." This means, in effect, that he is settling for a "swallow the bitter pill" attitude. "Of course I would like to live these wonderful ideals, but since you tell me that they are not realistic, well, I'll simply give them up."

We should ask ourselves why a direct approach is not possible. I found an answer to this question in O'Neill's play *The Iceman Cometh,* in which a man meets some drunks in an inn and tells them, "These are all illusions, you would like to give them up yourselves; show us what you can do, lead an active life."

But they cannot do it and only feel even more miserable. For these illusions are not simply phantoms. The patient cannot give them up before he has become much stronger without doing damage to himself.

I would like to cite an old German fairytale to illustrate this process from a slightly different angle. It describes a little fir tree who wants to have golden leaves. It gets them, but in the night they are stolen by robbers. The tree thinks that his idea was no good and wishes for glass leaves. He gets them, but a storm breaks them all. This wasn't right either, says the tree, and now I wish for leaves like a maple's, but in no event my own. So he gets the green leaves, but a goat eats them all. Finally, the little tree decides that it was best to simply be a fir tree.

Here you have a glorification of the gold and glass leaves, which the tree believes he wants to have because they are something better. He wants to be something different from what he really is, for in reality he happens to be a fir tree, and only as a fir tree can he grow. Even without the robbers, the goats, the storms, a fir tree with golden leaves would perish as a fir tree. His real self would be destroyed in the process.

In our own words, this means that if we begin to idealize ourselves, if we consider ourselves outstanding, godlike, more important than befits us, if we want to be something we are not, without knowing it, we lose our own self. From the perspective of this understanding of the neurotic process, it is the goal of therapy to help a person to find his own self, to rediscover his own feelings, his wishes, what he really believes — to help him to make his own decisions; for only if he finds himself has he a chance to grow and fulfill himself.

If we suggest this to the patient in general terms, he will probably say, "Right, that's exactly what I want, to be myself." But this would again be a deception. Remember Peer Gynt who constantly talks about being "himself," while in reality he is only chasing the phantom of his self-glorification. He becomes emperor of the Sahara, where he solves the enigmas of the Sphinx, but he ends up in the madhouse, having destroyed his whole life. It is right that one should wish to be oneself, but one has to wish for the right thing. Initially no neurotic can achieve that; he mainly lives on his neurotic pride and his illusions. The way to his real self is painful, for it is not only full of obstacles and disruptions but is also full of confusing and diverting delusions.

The neurotic has to do a number of things simultaneously in order to gradually reach himself. First, he has to experience and understand all the false values on which his pride is founded. Then he has to realize what he can and cannot do. He has to understand, for instance, that he has talents for real achievements, but that he has to develop his abilities before he can do very much with them. In the past, he has neglected to recognize his real capacities and to develop them, but now their discovery and development must become genuinely desirable for him.

He must also realize through analysis that he does not recognize his own feelings and never has recognized them, that he only feels what he thinks he ought to feel, and that this has made him insecure, has deprived him of vitality, and has robbed his feelings of intensity and depth. He must come to understand that nothing in life is more desirable than genuinely experiencing his real feelings in all their intensity. He has only believed what others believed and has never asked himself, "What do I really believe?" He must discover that finding out what he really believes is an important part of his growth. He may also realize that he was too proud ever to ask for anything. He may originally have called that modesty, but he now understands that this was not a good method, since this way one never learns from one's experiences. To profit from one's experiences it is necessary to admit to one's needs and imperfections. He may have believed that he only reproached himself, condemned himself, and had guilty feelings in order to demonstrate the loftiness of his moral standards. But now he has to realize that he has not really recognized his imperfections and that he has never attempted to overcome them in a constructive way.

This process gradually undermines false pride while making clear what the self lacked so far: real emotions, real beliefs, and personal decisions. The patient recognizes that real emotions or the effort to achieve them are the really desirable thing. False positions are slowly surrendered and a genuine insight into the self takes their place; there is now strength of feeling, a knowledge of what he wants, and the ability to take responsibility. The patient no longer considers it a loss to detach himself from his illusions, for now he knows that striving to be his real self is the only productive way of living.

I would like to illuminate the same issue from another perspective. One may ask whether one should really say with Socrates that the goal of analysis is to know yourself. I would argue that this depends on what one means by self-knowledge. We can shed some light on this, if we differentiate between the actual self and what William James calls the real self. The actual self is everything I am, my aggressions, my false pride, my vindictiveness. At first, the patient cannot see this, since he will admit to certain traits he is proud of, according to his type, while he will deny others. An arrogant person will admit to his vindictiveness, which he will call a sense of justice, while he will deny his need for sympathy or affection and his great vulnerability. The dependent type will admit to self-denying traits with comparative ease, will gladly take the part of a martyr, a victim, or assume the dependent attitude in a love relationship; but he will refuse to own up to vindictiveness, pride, ambition, or competitive feelings: "Oh no, that's not like me." Some patients do this on a large scale. What they like is their self, and the rest is their neurosis. One patient said, "The idealized image is I, the rest is unconscious."

The patient must learn to recognize what he is really like, but it is *not* enough to know about oneself without taking a firm viewpoint or reorienting oneself. In reality, this never happens anyway, for the more a person knows about himself, the more he is forced to differentiate between good and evil. The more he knows, the more unconditionally he has to decide for the constructive forces of his real self. One might say in brief, "For the patient, the goal of analysis is to learn to know himself as he is (actual self) in order to reorient himself and to make finding his real self a possibility." It is difficult to describe the nature of the real self. It is something one can only describe from experience; something within us that can decide, accept, and discard, that can want something, have spontaneous feelings, and exercise willpower. We can call it constructive energy — something that holds us together.

Every neurotic is aware of certain aspects of himself and unaware of others. Because he denies certain parts of himself, according to the nature of his disease, he only lives a part of himself. One patient expressed it as follows: "I might be compared to a person whose one lung does not function at all, while three quarters of the other is ill." It is always surprising to see with how little a person can still function — but only as long as things go smoothly. Any situation that taxes the patient can lead to a severe and unexpected breakdown.

A neurotic does not perceive himself as a whole organism, as a unity, but tends to feel painfully divided. He manages, in one way or other, to create a pseudosolution in order not to feel this division constantly, a pseudofeeling of unity that allows him to live. Pseudosolutions can be of very different kinds. One solution is seclusion — I am thinking here of people who live tolerably well, who seem to lack nothing as long as they keep their distance from others and, I would like to add, from themselves. This is one of the neurotic solutions that allows a partial functioning without the person being aware of how divided he really is. Others find their neurotic solution in "love," which in this case means a dependent relationship. The person expects love to provide all the answers to his problems and worries, to provide an integration through merger with another. Others look for their solution in ambition, yet others simply in fantasy. We must not make light of these solutions, for while they lead the person deeper and deeper into neurosis, they at least allow him to function. The fact that such pseudosolutions can develop also shows that a constructive force is at work that aims at integration. It is not very useful in this form, since it leaves the neurotic divided into compulsive traits; but it is there and is a powerful drive that we can use in therapy. If we try again to define the goals of our work when we have realized that the neurotic lives only in a divided way and not with his whole self, we may say, "The goal of psychoanalysis is integration and unity."

Integration, finding oneself, and the ability for growth are constructive forces. They are extremely strong drives in our selves, maybe the strongest, the only ones that really count. Therapy depends on these strong constructive drives, and even the most skilled analyst would get nowhere without them. It is a goal and a means of therapy to mobilize and strengthen these forces, for only with their help can a person overcome the retarding forces within himself. If the analyst tries to bring the patient closer to himself, he is basically doing no more and, in a way, even less than the somatic doctor, who has the means of the clinic at his disposal, while in analysis the actual healing forces lie in the patient himself. This is a fact of which by no means every analyst is aware. I cannot bring about the growth of the patient myself, any more than he can bring about mine. The analyst can make suggestions here and there, he can make the patient aware of things, he can foster the patient's wish to be himself, but the patient must do the growing.

In conclusion, let us return to Ibsen's Peer Gynt, a man who shouts from every roof top that he is "himself," that he wants to be "himself" all his life. But Peer Gynt only wants to be self-sufficient, which, to him, implies a godlike self-sufficiency, a perfection without any needs. Ibsen shows very clearly that this is not human. Peer Gynt never was himself, for in that case he would have had another goal. "Be true to yourself" does not mean "be self-sufficient," for self-sufficiency is at once too much and too little for a human being.

13

Abstracts and Symposia

A. The Future of Psychoanalysis

In May 1946, a celebration of the fifth anniversary of the founding of the Association for the Advancement of Psychoanalysis was held in New York. Horney's address was called "The Future of Psychoanalysis," and a summary was published in the American Journal of Psychoanalysis *6 (1946), 66–67. She emphasized the difference between Freud's pessimistic view of human nature and her own belief that under favorable conditions of nurture, or as a result of therapy, human beings can become "creative and constructive." She acknowledged that many of her psychoanalytic insights were the result of her struggle with her own difficulties (see Paris 1994) and insisted that therapists have to work on themselves if they are to be effective in helping others.*

We separated from the orthodox Freudian group of psychoanalysts five years ago for carefully thought out reasons. The fact that, as a radical minority group striving for reformulations, we were suppressed, mattered but little. We were sufficiently aware of the historical process going on to be able to take the suppression in our stride. But the sterility of the scientific discussions gave us a feeling of futility because we ran up against a blank wall of petrified dogmatism. The determining factor in our decision to form a new association was the realization that what separated us from Freud was nothing more or less than a whole philosophy of life.

The basic philosophy of Freud is a pessimistic one. In a symposium at the New School for Social Research in 1944, Brill — following strict Freudian concepts — said most clearly that man is at bottom driven by elemental instincts of sex, greed, and cruelty. Freud himself has expressed the same idea in terms of men being like porcupines who are bound to hurt one another if close.

We, on the other hand, believe that man has potentialities for good and evil, and we see that he does develop into a good human being if he grows up under favorable conditions of warmth and respect for his individuality. On the other hand an individual who is thrown into insoluble inner conflicts becomes inhibited and destructive. As the analysis of such an individual progresses, we see him becoming constructive and creative. He begins to grow as a human being. This is what psychoanalysis has become for us: a means for liberation and growth as a human being.

Between these two philosophies there is no bridge. We believe in human potentialities and the possibility of bringing them out through analysis. We felt therefore that we had an obligation to the younger generation of psychiatrists — the obligation of educating them in this spirit, helping them to become more constructive themselves, and enabling them to help their patients become more constructive. Feeling that if we believe in something we must do something about it, we took upon ourselves the responsibility and hard work of building another organization and creating a new teaching institute. The name we chose was the Association for the Advancement of Psychoanalysis.

Let us examine what we have done toward the goal implied by this name. We have concentrated on the training of psychiatrists as psychoanalysts. We have made concerted efforts toward a deeper understanding of neuroses. Among the results we have achieved are: the recognition of the nature and role of inner conflicts; increased appreciation of the role of imagination in neuroses; deeper understanding of the meaning of dreams, of the traumatic syndrome, and of the curative process in psychotherapy. All of these insights have helped us gain a better grasp of the structure of neuroses, and thereby to make our therapy more effective. We considered such knowledge necessary before setting ourselves more concrete tasks such as: working out methods for group therapy, securing statistics of psychoanalytic therapy, elaborating dynamics of psychosomatic disorders, developing techniques for the treatment of the psychoses and shorter therapy for the neuroses. At the present time we are convinced that the only solid way toward a shorter therapy is a still greater understanding of the problems involved.

How can we arrive at this better understanding? I think there are two ways. One is to cultivate a spirit of scientific inquiry both in ourselves and in our students. I would not feel any better if my colleagues were to take for granted what I say than if we had taken for granted what Freud has said. A second way to gain understanding is to keep delving into our own intricacies. Our mind is the tool with which we work, and we all must strive to make that tool more and more effective and more transparent. As long as we have not found ourselves, how can we help others to find themselves? Only through finding and overcoming our own inner difficulties can we be productive, gain understanding, and really advance the science we serve.

B. Pride and Self Hate in Psychoanalytic Therapy

The American Institute for Psychoanalysis did not have a home of its own until 1947, when it established headquarters in an apartment on West 98th Street that it shared with the Association for the Advancement of Psychoanalysis. Regular "scientific meetings" of the institute were held at the New York Academy of Medicine, and in the mid-1940s so-called interval meetings, convened primarily for the benefit of candidates, were held on Sundays at Horney's apartment. The presentations at these informal meetings were then reported in the American Journal of Psychoanalysis. *A summary of one such presentation, Horney's talk on pride and self-hate in psychoanalytic therapy, was published in volume 7 (1947), 68–69. This talk was an elaboration of ideas Horney had introduced in her lectures titled "Pride and Self-Hatred in Neuroses."*

Patients in whom self hatred is in the foreground, present attitudes of self-minimizing, self-accusing and self-frustrating with a resulting low self-confidence, feelings of having no rights, being unwanted, worthless. From others they long for or demand as their right, love, support, and company, often as protection against their own vindictive self-hatred and despair. They have renounced ambition, feel pride comes before a fall, and are in terror of any competition which would make them aware of the crushing of all belief in themselves.

Other patients in whom pride is in the foreground, show a constant attitude of high pride, triumph, and lofty claims, not necessarily related to realistic achievement. Their claims are supported by arrogance, rigid rightness, the ignoring or embellishing of their own faults, and the blaming or disparaging of others, while from others they wish constant admiration and recognition.

Patients vary in willingness and ability to examine these attitudes. Early in analysis pride may be closer to the patient's awareness and therefore more accessible, or he may be wholly unaware of such feelings and only self-contempt is accessible, although occasionally both are accessible and can be tackled. However, these attitudes toward the self are basic in determining relations with others. Pride and self-hatred are never present singly but are always inseparable. The patient must be able to see both before he can see that each depends on the presence of the other, and that in both cases he fears and expects humiliation, taking only in each case a different route toward safety from it: in pride, he struggles to feel superior in order to overwhelm it; in self-hatred, he abases himself, hoping no one can be so cruel as to humiliate him further.

Only when the patient begins to see what his claims are, what he demands or expects of others and of himself, and what he feels entitled to, can it become clear to him how he actually regards himself, and can he become aware at what cost he tears himself apart with bitter vindictive attack or insatiable ambition because of his failure to live up to his enormous claims on himself.

C. Responsibility in Neurosis

On December 11, 1949, Horney gave a talk at an interval meeting of the American Institute for Psychoanalysis entitled "Responsibility — Healthy and Neurotic" (Rubins 1978, 300). An abstract was published in the American Journal of Psychoanalysis *10 (1950), 84–85, under the title "Responsibility in Neurosis." The original title gives a better idea of Horney's focus, for she argued that, because of their shoulds and claims, neurotic people hold themselves responsible for things over which they have no control and that it is the object of therapy to free people from their illusions and compulsions so that they can assume real responsibility for themselves.*

The term "responsibility" as used in psychoanalysis has several meanings. First, we see it as meaning reliability in respect to fulfilling obligations. This capacity varies widely in different neurotic structures. Secondly, it may mean assuming responsibility for others. Here there also may be wide variations, some individuals taking too much responsibility, others far too little. Those who compulsively assume responsibility in this sense feel that by this means they ought to be able to make everybody happy. A third meaning is that of moral responsibility. Am I responsible — *i.e.*, to be blamed — for whatever I am doing or thinking, whether I am conscious of it or not? It would be senseless to blame a person for something of which he is not conscious. The neurotic, however, feels otherwise. Because of his grandiose shoulds, he holds himself responsible for whatever he has felt, thought, or done, whether he could have known it or not.

This is the dictate of an overweening pride, which demands constant self-mastery. Self-hate is also a factor in this, as is the neurotic pressure toward self-blame and self-doubt. A healthy individual may regret deeply what he has been unable to do, but the neurotic feels self-condemnation — which is something quite different. Real moral responsibility exists only where there is freedom of choice, but the demands the neurotic makes upon himself are too lofty to accept this. No matter how insuperable the difficulties, he will feel he *should* have vanquished them.

On the positive side, one of the goals of analytic therapy is the development of ability to assume real responsibility for one's self. Neurotic pride gives rise to obstacles, hounding the patient to take too much blame. The healthy individual aims only at being matter-of-fact, being truthful with himself rather than blaming others. This the neurotic cannot do because he is so alienated from himself and because he is under pressure from his neurotic "should" and his self-condemnation. One of the goals of analysis is to free him from them. One can only begin to take responsibility when one is actually aware of something. Then responsibility for one's own growth can be assumed; to be healthy, one must come to the point of wanting to do so.

D. Psychotherapy

"Psychotherapy" was the concluding talk, presented on March 22, 1950, of a conference held at the Institute of Living in New York City. The abstract was prepared by someone with the initials M. B. J. and published in the Digest of Neurology and Psychiatry *18 (1950), 278. Because the language seems to be Horney's, the abstract may have been prepared from a text that she supplied. Horney was working on* Neurosis and Human Growth *at this time, and the talk reflects some of the central ideas of that book. Horney's emphasis is on the insufficiency of insight and the disillusioning process to bring about change and the importance of mobilizing the patient's constructive forces.*

There is room in psychotherapy for many aims and means. Orthodox psychoanalysis has not stated them too clearly, and has tended to overemphasize certain facets to the neglect of others. Thus in any psychoanalysis, major stress is placed upon bringing unconscious factors to awareness. The questions arise whether more knowledge about oneself necessarily changes anything; whether the positive transference invariably operates as an incentive to change; whether realization by the patient that his emotional drives are irrational actually enables him to change.

Reason is not an effective agent for combating emotional forces. Self-knowledge per se is not enough. The disillusioning process of analysis is important, to be sure. Every neurotic, whether he be on the expansive side, or the self-abnegating side, is shot through with all kinds of illusions as to how he is, could or should be. Every neurotic has his inner dictates which drive him toward attaining the absolute of knowledge, of fearlessness, of considerateness, of unselfishness, or whatever his ideals of perfection may be. He has all kinds of unconscious pretenses, with a disdain for reality. He has self-hate if he fails to achieve his strivings; false pride, not in his real assets, but in those he does not have. However the neurotic is approached analytically, it is largely a disillusioning process, but the therapeutic effect of this is generally overrated. Undermining the artificial structure will have no therapeutic effect unless, at the same time, with or without the analyst's doing much about it, something constructive in the patient starts to grow.

Just as there are curative forces in the body helping a patient recover from a somatic disorder, there are curative psychic forces. Given favorable conditions, a human being has the natural urge to develop his human potentialities and to realize himself. It is the aim of character analysis to help people achieve a greater inner freedom so that they may grow as human beings. Self-realization is of great importance — realization on the part of the patient of what he really feels and wants, rather than what he thinks he should feel and want; realization also of the ability to tap his own resources, gradually to assume responsibility for himself, to develop constructive relations with others, to do productive and meaningful work, to develop whatever special gifts he may have. Self-realization implies the ability to assume his place in the world, and to do his constructive share. These are all constructive forces in the human being, to be elicited and mobilized with the help of the therapist, and the task of doing so is as important as the disillusioning task. Mobilization can be done in dream analysis, for in dreams we are closer to the reality of ourselves. It can also be done in a great variety of other ways, depending on the character type of the patient and the function being served by his neurotic symptoms. The aim of all analysis should be to help a person, through self-knowledge, to a reorientation in life, with a shift from self-idealization to self-realization. This concept provides a useful criterion for terminating analysis.

E. The Individual and Therapy

On April 4, 1951, the Auxiliary Council to the Association for the Advancement of Psychoanalysis sponsored a symposium entitled "Psychoanalysis and the Constructive Forces in Man" in New York. Moderated by Harold Kelman, the symposium featured talks by Karen Horney, Paul Lussheimer, Alexander Reid Martin, and Frederick A. Weiss. Horney spoke on "The Individual and Therapy," Lussheimer on "The Family," Martin on "The Community," and Weiss on "The World." Perhaps in response to criticism of her theory as too optimistic, Horney asked "whether it is Pollyanna-ish for us to believe in, and to base our therapy on, the concept of constructive forces." She reiterated her belief that destructiveness is reactive rather than innate, that it can be diminished in therapy by undoing the damaging effects of pathogenic experiences, and that constructive forces will then emerge.

We believe in the inner dignity and freedom of man and in the constructiveness of the evolutionary forces inherent in man. The main question I am raising is, "How do we, as psychoanalysts, come to work with the concept of constructive inner forces moving us towards self-realization?" We presuppose the existence of these forces in every human being, although they may not be visible and although there exist elsewhere many beliefs concerning the destructiveness of man. There are not only wars, but the process of the dehumanization of man, such as exists in a police state where a human being is a number and not an individual. The subordination of the individual man and his dignity to an abstract idea, whether this goes on in a police state or elsewhere in the world, is a real danger.

In view of all the destructive greed and corruption going on around us, we have to ask ourselves whether it is Pollyanna-ish for us to believe in, and to base our therapy on, the concept of constructive inner forces. Is the individual inherently destructive, as the Freudians claim?

We are not denying the existence of destructive trends in patients as evidenced in hostility, vindictiveness and selfishness. But we deny that their presence means that man is innately destructive. They are reactions to distress beginning in childhood. Observation and study of the growth of children gives us plenty of evidence that children brought up in a favorable environment grow in a wholesome way to become responsible, mature adults whereas those raised in an unfavorable milieu show describable developmental patterns of hostility, suspiciousness, isolation, pessimism and illusions.

Observation of our own therapeutic work reveals that even in individuals with no overt evidence of obstructive or destructive tendencies, we, as analysts, can see these trends showing through the veneer of friendliness. Though we may see in some patients open suspiciousness, hostility, greed, abused feelings and egocentric demands on others, we know these are not the basic problems. If we come to understand how such a person experiences life we would say that any person like that would have to be destructive. We, therefore, try in our therapy to change the way he experiences other people and life itself, and we are able to effect such a change. Now we see his hostility and suspiciousness disappear, according to the extent that experience is not distorted neurotically. Constructive forces, such as a real wish to develop one's real potentialities, to do creative work, to develop good human relationships and to be considerate of oneself and others, are then free to express themselves.

The individual who has lost contact with himself has to prove he is something he is not. If he no longer has to prove this because we have undermined his illusions during successful therapy, then he eventually asks, "Who am I?" He becomes interested in his growth and actively wants to be himself. This desire does not stem from our suggestion. We see it arise earlier, before he has expressed it consciously, when he relates his dreams. The desire to be himself grows within him now that it has a chance to grow.

There are many people who share these beliefs such as the educators who have learned that it is not enough to give children education; they must be helped to become constructive human beings. The Eastern philosophers, who have always believed in the spiritual powers of man, have seen these powers develop as man stops violating his nature.

Psychoanalytically, we can trace step by step the process of becoming destructive or constructive. Evidence is present in our work, as well as in general observations made on the lives of individuals not being analyzed, that bitter, pessimistic and destructive people can and do again turn towards life. In psychoanalytic therapy, however, we can observe this process in greater detail and can distinguish between what is genuine and what is spurious. This process bears fruit in the individuals arriving at a healthier and better way of living.

F. Values and Problems of Group Analysis

On October 7, 1951, a symposium was held in New York on "Group Analysis — Some Problems and Promises" on the occasion of a reception for Karen Horney sponsored by the Association for the Advancement of Psychoanalysis, the American Institute for Psychoanalysis, and the Auxiliary Council. Horney spoke on "Values and Problems," Sidney Rose on "Some Advantages of Group Analysis," and Benjamin Wassell on

"Group Composition and Patient Selection." Harold Kelman provided an introduction. Excerpts from the symposium were published in the American Journal of Psychoanalysis, *12 (1952), 78–81.*

Although Horney had not written about group analysis, she had had some experience with it. Jack Rubins tells us that when one of her supervisees, Alexander Wolf, was drafted in 1943, he needed colleagues to take over his groups. Horney obliged and found the experience so challenging that she had "to telephone for help from several junior colleagues who had more experience with groups" (Rubins 1978, 274). After six months, she discontinued the group, but she remained impressed by the possibilities of the technique and helped set up a research study project in group psychoanalysis at the American Institute in 1945. In her symposium remarks, she observed that the primary advantages of group work are that it "enhances the incentive to come to grips with oneself" and does so "in an atmosphere of feeling 'I'm not the only one.'" One of her chief concerns was that although "emotional awareness may come quickly," there is a question as to "how far it will be worked through." She encouraged self-analysis in conjunction with work in the group.

*The members of Horney's circle who wrote about group work were Harold Kelman (1948) and Sidney Rose (1953, 1956). There was a second symposium on group analysis in 1953, with contributions by Frederick Weiss, Louis Landman, Sidney Rose, and Louis DeRosis (*American Journal of Psychoanalysis *15 [1955], 32–44). More recently, Horneyan theory has been actively applied to group work by members of the Society for Interpersonal and Group Analysis (SPIGA) in Rome: see Lapponi (1996), Maiello (1996), and Garofalo (1996).*

Group analysis is valuable not only socially but also for the promise it holds out as a short therapy. It is not only a way of reaching more people but it is a peculiar kind of therapy with problems of its own. These problems are of three kinds: advantages, difficulties and dangers, and limitations.

The advantages one sees most clearly. The group spirit encourages and enhances the incentive to come to grips with oneself. Irrational drives are exposed more readily and quickly. Two illusions are quickly laid open — that the neurotic member is easy to get along with, and that the others don't see in him, or that there do not exist in him, any difficulties. Furthermore, the individual may quickly see that his reactions are determined not by the others, but by what is happening in him. All of this goes on in an atmosphere of feeling

"I'm not the only one." The illusion of being the exceptionally troubled person goes by the board.

There are also difficulties and dangers. New technical problems arise, *e.g.,* the composition of the group. There is the difficulty of evaluating results, of what trends to take up in a varied group. How much is lost? How preserve the continuity? How get everybody participating in the group and prevent some from imposing on the group? What part does the group pressure play on each member? There is the danger merely of behavioristic changes, which may be picked up but not easily contended with. There is the danger of arousing too much anxiety prematurely, with which the person concerned may not be able to cope and may be swept away by it. This also exists in individual therapy, but here the danger is greater.

The limitations will take a much longer time and experience to learn. According to Dr. Wassell, not everybody is suitable for work in a group: for instance, persons with too little incentive, too much self-effacement or with too much alienation. How far group analysis can help, one cannot tell as yet. Emotional awareness may come quickly, but the question is how far it will be worked through. This is a matter for more experience. Personal interviews with the members of the group is one way of getting closer to some answers as to how far and how much group analysis can help.

Two factors are important. The more the individuals can analyze themselves, the faster and the more effective will the group analysis be. Also, the more the analyst is capable of maintaining a constructive spirit in the group, the better are the chances for success. Not only uncovering neurotic drives but finding the core of themselves, the real self, is the problem.

It is apparent that group analysis is of great value; how great remains to be seen. It is of such high promise that it should be continued, not only for adults but also for younger people, such as adolescents.

PART **III**

Lectures on Technique

Introduction

As analyst, supervisor, and teacher at various institutes, Horney had pondered the therapeutic process for many decades, and, as we have seen, she included discussions of it in four of her books. Had she lived, her next book would have been on technique. As a preliminary to writing this book, she taught courses on technique after the completion of *Neurosis and Human Growth*. She had also taught on the topic after the completion of *Our Inner Conflicts*. Her last course was recorded, and transcripts have been published in *Final Lectures* (1987), but the course was interrupted by her final illness in November 1952, well before the end of the first term.

Fortunately, after Horney's death reconstructions of her lectures were compiled by colleagues and candidates who had taken her courses. Between 1956 and 1967, eleven such lectures were published in the *American Journal of Psychoanalysis* under the heading "Karen Horney on Psychoanalytic Technique." All were described as having been compiled from notes from courses she gave at the American Institute for Psychoanalysis in 1946, 1950, 1951, and 1952, but some of the compilers had attended only one or two of these courses.

There is some overlap between *Final Lectures* and the reconstructions collected here, since Horney spoke on similar topics from year to year, and some of the compilers had attended the 1952 course. Even when the topics are similar, however, the reconstructed lectures tend to be more comprehensive and detailed, perhaps because many were composites based on notes from more than one course. Moreover, most of them deal with subjects not covered in *Final Lectures* or anywhere else in Horney's works. The eleven reconstructed lectures address almost all of the topics Horney had planned to address in her 1952 course. The topics were:

1. Free associations and the use of the couch
2. The quality of the analyst's attention
3. Specific psychoanalytic means of understanding the patient
4. Interpretations: meaning and aims
5. Timing of interpretations
6. Consistency of interpretations
7. Form and spirit of interpretations
8. The patient's reactions to interpretations: validity
9. Intellectual process or emotional experience
10. Retarding forces: blockages
11. Dealing with blockages
12, 13. Mobilizing forces toward self-realization
14. The patient's attitude toward the analyst
15, 16. The personal equation of the analyst
17. Dealing with conflicts
18. Dealing with central inner conflicts
19. Critical situations: giving advice
20. Evaluating the patient's progress: termination. (Horney 1987, 117–18)

Horney scheduled two sessions for some topics and subdivided others. The reconstructed lecture "Interpretations" deals with all the aspects of that topic that were to have been covered in sessions 4, 5, 6, 7, and 8. "The Initial Interview" and "Dreams," topics included in the present collection, were not listed in the announcement for the 1952 course, although Horney lectured on these subjects in earlier courses. Horney spoke on "Intellectual Process or Emotional Experience" earlier than planned, and a transcription can be found in *Final Lectures*. Between *Final Lectures* and the present collection, we have a record of most of Horney's teachings on the therapeutic process. We do not have accounts of her lectures on transference and termination.

I have compared the reconstructed lectures with the notes from which Horney lectured (now in the Karen Horney papers at Yale) and find them to be faithful accounts of her teachings, but they are not to be taken for Horney's own writings, of course. Furthermore, I have edited all of the reconstructed lectures for clarity, coherence, usage, and syntax. Thus, in the versions published here some of the language is mine. I have retained the use of the pronoun "he," since that was the practice of the day and to have changed it would have required extensive rewriting. I have also edited the reconstructed lectures for consistency in style and point of view. Although most were written as though Horney were speaking, some referred to her in the third person and included material from her publications. I have maintained the first person perspective throughout and have deleted quotations from Horney's works and passages that I found digressive or confusing. In general, I have tried to preserve Horney's ideas while making the lectures more readable.

We must remember that even if these lectures were entirely in Horney's words, they would still be but the raw material from which she would have shaped a finished account of her thinking. They might have stood to her proposed book on technique as her lectures on "Pride and Self-Hatred in Neuroses" stand to *Neurosis and Human Growth*.

In arranging the lectures, I have been guided to some extent by the order Horney followed in her courses, but my main concern has been to present them in a sequence that would make sense to the reader. It seemed logical, for example, to put "Interpretations" after the lecture entitled "Understanding" because Horney defined interpretation as the process whereby the analyst "tries to convey his understanding . . . to the patient" ("Interpretations"). And I have placed "Blockages in Therapy" immediately after "Interpretations" because Horney taught that when offering interpretations, the rule is always "blockages first." I have arranged the lectures so that they move from the general to the particular, from a focus on the analyst to a focus on the patient, and from issues that arise in the earlier stages of therapy to those that arise later.

Despite the fact that the language of these lectures is not entirely Horney's and that their ideas are not developed as they would have been had she lived to write her book, I believe they constitute an important addition to Horney's corpus and are very much worth our attention. In addition to containing much practical wisdom about how to help patients, they apply her mature theory to the therapeutic process in more detail than elsewhere, they contain an antitheoretical strain and an emphasis on intuition and emotion that are somewhat surprising in view of her penchant for systematic thought, and they show her developing a model of the therapist-patient relationship that is mutual, cooperative, and democratic. It is the last two aspects of the lectures on which I shall concentrate here since the introduction to part II provides an account of Horney's mature theory that will enable the reader to follow its applications to clinical issues.

From reading her books, one might develop an impression of Horney as a cerebral therapist who relied heavily on rigorous analysis of her patients in terms of an elaborate taxonomy of defenses. A different picture emerges from her lectures. Although she continued to employ her theoretical framework, she taught that intellectual insight is only one aspect of understanding and not the most significant. Indeed, she feared that theory might obstruct an awareness of the patient's individuality, that "a detached, purely intellectual attitude" would lead not "to understanding but to a mechanical classification of the patient's personality according to our preexisting ideas" ("Understanding"). Therapists should not subsume patients into categories in an effort to understand them but should try to get a feeling for their "uniqueness, so that [their] differentness no longer feels strange" ("Quality"). After having "become attuned" to their patients' "individual ways of experiencing and relating, [therapists] will no longer think in technical terms but will form and convey . . . interpretations tentatively" ("Understanding").

Horney felt that therapists must be able to attend to everything at once, not just to a limited set of factors and that "approaching the patient with preconceived ideas" restricts such "comprehensiveness" ("Quality"). She liked Freud's idea of "free-floating attention" but observed that "for him much of this was an intellectual floating concerned with fitting what he observed clinically into the theories he was formulating." She warned that "this may be done with anyone's theoretical formulations," including, presumably, her own. For her, the object of listening "idly" was to arrive at "a truly holistic view of the patient." She insisted that "theory should serve only as a general framework and should never be more important than the patient." Theory should not be used to pigeonhole the patient, and the patient should not be used to confirm the preconceived ideas of the analyst.

Horney taught that therapists should attend to everything in the patient with "all [their] capacities and faculties." In addition to employing their "reason" and "specialized knowledge" ("Quality"), which will be influenced by theory, they should respond with their intuition, a faculty that operates unconsciously and represents "the sum total of all the analyst's past experiences, emotional and intellectual" ("Initial"). It is "not a mystical quality but an understanding on a deeper level" that taps therapists' "great store of inner experience" and generates insights that arise without their having an "immediate awareness" of where they have come from ("Understanding"). When determining what to tell the patient and when, therapists "must be guided by [their] intuitive understanding of [his] capacity to take in that which may still be too upsetting to his shaky equilibrium." For example, "something in ourselves may warn us that he is not ready to confront the meaning of his dreams, and if we ignore such an inner warning and interpret prematurely, he may either stop dreaming or stop telling us about his dreams." Such decisions cannot be reached by logical thought or the application of theory.

Horney believed that therapists should open themselves not only to intuition but also to their emotions — "to all the feelings that can exist between two people: liking and disliking, dismay, disappointment, humor, hopefulness, anger, sympathy, and so forth" ("Quality"). Understanding is "a process of moving toward another person's position while still maintaining our own," and therapists do this very largely through their emotions, which enable them to feel their way into the patient's situation, to "enter into his feelings and live through them with him" ("Understanding"). Understanding "is a movement of emotional as well as of intellectual energies": "We must know what the patient is experiencing and not simply know about it." We gain such knowledge through compassion and by drawing on our own experience. We remember from our own analysis, for example, how frightening it is to be confronted with truths about ourselves that we do not want to know and how desperately we cling to our threatened defenses. This helps us to "lay ourselves open to the anxiety which may engulf . . . a new traveler on the road toward self-awareness." Such emotional knowledge is relatively independent of theoretical preconceptions: "It leads to more and more comprehension of an individual patient with his distinct personality and problems."

Therapists can use their emotions not only to help them gain empathic understanding but also to assist them in evaluating the patient properly. Sometimes their emotional responses can alert them to things they might otherwise miss, such as the patient's excessive adulation, covert hostility, or ways of subverting the therapeutic process. Their emotions can also help them assess the genuineness of what the patient says, does, and feels and of the changes that appear to be taking place. They should pay attention to such reactions as boredom, uneasiness, frustration, and anger, sometimes communicating these reactions to the patient.

Horney felt that analysts should focus as fully as possible "on all the patient's communications, verbal and non-verbal," and that they should respond with all their "capacities," such as listening, seeing, and feeling, and "faculties," such as reason and intuition ("Quality"). In order to do this, they must be open both to the patient and to themselves: "The closer the analyst is to his totality of experiencing, the more available will he be for understanding the patient" ("Initial"). Analysts should direct their whole being to the whole being of the patient. They should try to put aside problems and needs of their own and to approach the patient with something comparable to what Ernest Schachtel described as "allocentric perception" (1959) or Abraham Maslow as "Being-cognition" (1970). Horney characterized the analyst's proper attitude as one of "undivided" and "wholehearted" attention:

> In order to approach the ideal of wholeheartedness, we [analysts] must be able to surrender to the work, letting all our faculties operate while nearly forgetting about ourselves. This is like surrendering ourselves to music or a work of art. As our knowledge and experience become an integral part of ourselves, we are barely conscious of all that we are while at the same time *being* all that we are. We can extend the boundaries of ourselves and be more open to the being of others" ("Quality").

Analysts must not relinquish themselves, however, for "if we lose our own stand altogether, we will not have understanding but blind surrender" ("Understanding"). If "[we can] lay ourselves open without losing ourselves, we can listen wholeheartedly while simultaneously becoming aware of our own reactions to the patient and his problems."

Horney felt that therapists' capacity to understand the patient "is a function of [their] relationship to [them]selves" ("Understanding"). The freer they are of compulsive needs and defenses, for example, the more capable they will be of giving patients wholehearted attention. Horney recognized that wholeheartedness is a state that can only be approached or attained sporadically at best, and she readily acknowledged that "there is no ideal analyst, just as there is no perfect human being" ("Equation"). She insisted, however, that "this should not be used as an excuse to curtail our efforts to improve ourselves." Since it is not only their minds but their whole personalities that are their analytic tools, therapists have an obligation to keep themselves in the best psychological shape possible. In her lectures, Horney frequently referred to ways in which analysts' "neurotic remnants" affect the reliability of their feelings and intuitions, the quality of their attention, and the effectiveness of their therapeutic efforts. She felt that although they may not be able to free themselves of their problems, they can at least try to take them into account when assessing their responses to their patients.

Horney addressed countertransferential problems most fully in "The Analyst's Personal Equation." She began by pointing out that some of the difficulties inherent in analytic work will be exacerbated by the therapist's unresolved difficulties, each of which "will make itself felt in the analytic situation." For example, it is challenging enough to evaluate results, but "the situation may be further complicated by the analyst's unconscious needs to see himself and his work in a favorable light" or by his tendency toward self-deprecation, which will lead him to underestimate the patient's progress. Patients tend either to overrate or undervalue their analyst, and narcissistic or insecure analysts will be unduly influenced by such judgments and fail to understand and interpret them.

In "The Analyst's Personal Equation," Horney discussed the impact of neurotic remnants in analysts of each of her psychological types: self-effacing, narcissistic, perfectionistic, arrogant-vindictive, and detached. Her idea, presumably, was that if analysts are aware of themselves, they can be on guard against the problems to which their particular defenses dispose them. A brief account of her discussions of therapists with self-effacing and detached neurotic remnants will give the flavor of this important lecture.

Self-effacing analysts are afraid of antagonizing their patients. They exaggerate their patients' assets, ignore their aggressive tendencies, and shy away from bringing out their hostility and tackling their idealized images. Their need to be liked results in a lack of firmness and tempts them to relate to patients in a personal rather than a functional manner. Their interpretations are too tentative, and they relinquish them too easily. Because they tend to see things from their patients' perspective, they fail to grasp the whole personality structure and to exercise leadership. They have too much sympathy with neurotic suffering, which they fail to distinguish from that which is reality-based, and they can be too helpful and reassuring.

Detached analysts are good observers who have fewer blind spots than others, but they observe from too great a distance. Afraid of becoming involved, they avoid stirring up affection or hostility, and their patients feel themselves to be "in an emotional vacuum." Whereas self-effacing analysts may have too much feeling for their patients, detached analysts have too little. Their hatred of coercion and intrusion leads them to adopt an excessively passive, hands-off policy. Because of their own resignation and disbelief in the possibility of change, they fail to encourage their patients' growth and are prone to share their feelings of hopelessness.

Horney urged therapists not to overestimate their own mental health, to have a proper humility. They should constantly analyze themselves, paying attention to their feelings and trying to determine how reliable they are as guides to understanding the patient. By analyzing their responses, they "can determine which are appropriate to the situation and which may be the result of [their] own neurotic remnants" ("Equation"). If they have sufficient self-awareness, their own difficulties can be a source of insight into their patients. The analyst's "having become cognizant of previously unconscious aspects of his personality in his own analysis permits him to recognize trends and drives of which the patient is unaware" ("Understanding"). The analyst must constantly examine his "reactions and even his associations" if he is "to help the patient toward self-realization and to keep growing himself."

This brings us to Horney's model of the therapist-patient relationship, which she saw as mutual, cooperative, and democratic. Ideally, it is not only the patient who is associating, being analyzed, and growing but the therapist as well. "How much can have happened with the patient in analysis," Horney asked, "if nothing happened to the analyst while working with him? In a successful analysis, something happens to both people. If the analyst is merely a catalytic agent and nothing has changed in him, how much really could have gone on within the patient?" ("Quality"). In her books, Horney seems to be the all-wise, all-knowing analyst who is no longer troubled by difficulties of her own and who serenely considers the problems that plague the rest of us with compassionate understanding. The Horney of the lectures is closer to the person I discovered in my biographical research, an embattled human being who never stopped struggling with her own unresolved difficulties (see Paris 1994).

Horney's model is not one in which therapists and patients analyze each other but rather one in which therapists continually analyze themselves while helping their patients toward self-understanding and growth. Their self-analysis benefits their patients as well as themselves because it helps mitigate countertransferential problems and makes them better therapists in a variety of ways.

Although Horney did not advocate involving patients in their therapists' efforts at psychological growth, she did advocate emotional honesty. In "The Analyst's Personal Equation," she warned that "the fear that neurotic remnants may be exposed will make some analysts unduly cautious, thereby depriving the patient of the opportunity to experience his analyst as a human being with both shortcomings and assets." The analyst is not to be a remote authority figure but a real person with strengths and weaknesses, just like the patient. In "The Quality of the Analyst's Attention," Horney cautioned analysts to "be careful not to let the intensity of [their] attention convert a mutual analytic situation into one where the patient is in the brilliant spotlight on a clinical stage while [they] are in the darkened audience. With both [patient and therapist] sharing more subdued light in the same room, [they] can become more open and real to one another."

Horney felt it was important for analysts to explain to their patients that "analysis is a cooperative undertaking" ("Association"). Patient and analyst must "work together in searching for the truth and fostering the patient's growth toward self-realization." Although the analyst has training and experience, he or she "is an outsider to the patient, who has all the raw data."

Analysts can help their patients "formulate and clarify the data," but the patients must supply it by revealing themselves. Perhaps the most important ways of doing this are free association and the sharing of dreams — activities Horney emphasized more in her lectures than in her books. Self-revelation is difficult and must be facilitated by the analyst's having a genuine respect for the patient, a sincere desire for the patient's well-being, and a wholehearted "interest in everything the patient thinks and feels." This will create a feeling of trust that will make it easier for the patient "to tell the analyst everything that comes to him without selecting."

Horney rejected the then-prevailing authoritarian model of the therapist-patient relationship and proposed a democratic one instead. The therapist must display a democratic spirit, "not just talk about it": "He must strive to eliminate grandiosity in himself and all need to show off his superior knowledge and ethics — no corner on intelligence or morals — no acting like a schoolmaster or judge or talking down" ("Interpretations"). It will help therapists to attain a democratic spirit if they remember that, however experienced they are, they are "dealing with a particular patient and [their] knowledge of this patient is limited." They should regard all interpretations as "more or less tentative" and should "be truthful about the degree of certainty" they feel. Their truthfulness has two advantages: their "groping will stimulate the patient to be active, to wonder, to search," and it will have more meaning for the patient when they feel confident.

For Horney, the object of therapy is to help patients relinquish their defenses, accept themselves as they are, and replace their search for glory with a striving for self-realization. Insight is useful in leading patients to see that their defenses are self-defeating and cannot possibly work, but they must experience as well as understand the destructiveness of their solutions if their disillusionment is to lead to change. As they become less defensive in the course of therapy, their constructive forces grow stronger, and the central inner conflict emerges. The art of the therapist lies not only in helping patients to perceive, experience, and work through their neurotic solutions by interpreting their behavior, their associations, and their dreams, but also in helping them to mobilize their constructive forces and supporting them in their struggle to find and actualize their real selves.

In her lectures, Horney urged analysts to be sensitive, compassionate, understanding, and supportive at every stage of the therapeutic process. If, in the initial interview, they address the reasonable fear that "upsetting changes" will occur as a result of being in analysis, this "understanding attitude may help the patient come to a positive decision" about entering therapy ("Initial"). As therapy proceeds, their empathic understanding will enable them to be tolerant of the patient's resistance to self-awareness and change: "When we [therapists] have become familiar with the patient's plight, we may have a new understanding of his need to keep its deeper meanings out of awareness. . . . We may understand his need to perpetuate the status quo when we realize how much energy he has spent in allaying anxiety, in erecting a facade, in avoiding a fight. The better we become acquainted with the patient, the more we will be able to appreciate his inner suffering" ("Understanding"). Therapists must understand that there is a constant battle in patients between their desire to change and their fear of letting go of the strategies that have enabled them to survive in what they feel is a dangerous, frustrating, unsympathetic world. They are motivated to change by both a desire to relieve their suffering and the constructive forces that are still alive within them, but they can relinquish their defenses only if the therapist makes them feel safe enough to do so. Otherwise, their anxiety will be too great.

Analysts must determine how much anxiety patients are able to endure so that they know when to back off and when to provide encouragement and support. Whereas "detached analyst[s] will be at a loss" when confronting anxiety, "warm human being[s]" will "give just as much help as a panicky patient can benefit from" ("Understanding"). "Feeling [themselves] into [the patient's] situation" will prevent them from "giving a false reassurance" that "may be dangerous. Yet [they] can encourage him by letting him know that [they] are 'standing by' him, even when he turns against [them]." The analyst's unfailing support "gives the patient the strength to make repeated efforts to take a stand against the forces that obstruct his healthy development." It may make it possible for him "to accept his actual self and try to comprehend how he became the person he is."

Throughout the therapeutic process "sensitive and understanding" analysts "will try unflaggingly to awaken the patient's numbed confidence in his own creative abilities until he is strong enough to mobilize them for self-realization" ("Understanding"). They will realize that "a war" is going on from the beginning between the patient's constructive and obstructive forces and that the therapeutic process will make the conflict more intense ("Mobilizing"). When patients begin "to relinquish [their] defenses, there is the terrible realistic fear of not being able to cope with life without all the neurotic props which have seemingly stood [them] in good stead and have given [them] a sense of integrity and identity. To give up this familiar known for a mysterious, emerging unknown is frightening, yet the healthy drives within [them] keep urging [them] ahead." The analysts' role is to assuage their patients' anxiety, reinforce their healthy drives, and encourage them "to continue in [their] struggle to change." As the central inner conflict rages, patients will oscillate between health and neurosis, but analysts must not "become bewildered" by these swings. If they have "a clear vision based on [their] own constructiveness" and are "unambiguous all[ies] of the endangered self, [they] will be able to support [their] patient[s] at this most trying time."

The conflict between healthy and neurotic forces may never be finally resolved, but there may be a decisive shift in the balance of power. As the prospect of "changing and growing becomes a tangible possibility," "the new sense of his own authentic direction gives" the patient "a feeling of strength and unity": "Any move he makes toward being himself gives him a sense of fulfillment different from anything he has known before. Seeing himself live better without pretense and the illusion of magical powers gives him more faith in himself and his genuine resources. Beginning to feel at one with himself and with life gives the patient the greatest incentive to continue to work at his growth" ("Mobilizing"). The topic of termination is not dealt with in this set of lectures, but Horney had addressed it in earlier courses and discussed it briefly in "How Do You Progress After Analysis?" Analysis does not turn out a finished product; the struggle against obstructive forces and the process of self-realization are life-long affairs. Horney observed that if "both patient and analyst focused their attention entirely on what remained to be done, they would be tempted to go on forever" ("Progress"). Therapy can be terminated when the balance of power has shifted decisively to the side of the strivings for growth, and patients are ready to deal with their problems themselves through continuing self-analysis.

Aims of Psychoanalytic Therapy

This lecture as reconstructed by Ralph Slater was published in the American Journal of Psychoanalysis *16 (1956), 24–25. Although much of it is a recapitulation of ideas developed at length in* Our Inner Conflicts *and* Neurosis and Human Growth, *the discussion of the four categories of self-realization with which it concludes does not occur elsewhere.*

Since the beginning of the psychoanalytic movement with Freud, the aims of therapy have undergone considerable change and development. The first goal was symptom removal. Thus, in the treatment of a phobic patient, the analyst's object was the removal of the phobia. Subsequently, Freud added as a goal of therapy helping the patient attain a greater capacity for enjoyment and work. These aims were developed within the framework of the libido theory. Subsequently, H. S. Sullivan emphasized that the object of analytic treatment was to help the patient establish good human relationships. *Our* aim is to help a patient improve in his relationships with others and with himself. This means helping him to move in the direction of greater freedom, inner independence and inner strength — in short, of self-realization.

The human individual needs favorable environmental conditions if he is to grow up to be himself, to actualize his potentialities, and to have healthy relationships with other people. If a child's environment provides genuine love and affection and healthy friction, discipline, and guidance, he will grow according to his own inner laws.

A disturbed, unhealthy environment makes the child basically anxious rather than basically secure. In these circumstances he cannot grow in accordance with his nature; instead, he moves compulsively toward, against, and away from people. These moves are unconscious strategic devices by which he attempts to deal with dangerous adults without being too frightened. When a child adopts these strategies, he puts a check on spontaneous thoughts, wishes, and feelings, which become unimportant and indistinct. It is as though the child said to himself: "It doesn't matter how I really feel and what I really want, as long as I can cope with these people around me without being too frightened." The three compulsive interpersonal moves are incompatible with each other, and the child usually resolves this basic conflict by submerging two of the three and making one predominant.

Since this method of resolving his conflicts does not really work, the individual strives for a more comprehensive solution through the creation of an idealized image of himself. The needs which lead to the creation of the idealized image are the following:

1. The need for a firmer and more comprehensive integration. The first neurotic step has led to a precarious state of being in which the individual is threatened not only from without by the original dangerous environment, but also from within, through the impairment of inner strength and unity.

2. The need for a substitute for genuine self-confidence which has had no chance to develop. The use of one predominant approach to people leaves large areas of the personality undeveloped and impairs self-confidence.

3. The need to lift himself above others. This is the outcome of his feeling less substantial, less well-equipped than others, particularly his contemporaries.

4. Because of his alienation from himself, there is a need for a feeling of identity that will give the person a feeling of importance, power and significance.

To fulfill all his needs at one stroke, the person creates in his imagination an idealized image of himself. There is a general self-glorification, which is built up from the material of his early experiences and special faculties. He also idealizes the qualities required by his interpersonal strategies of defense — aggression, detachment, and compliance. Eventually he comes to identify himself with his idealized image, which becomes an idealized self that is more real to him than his real self. This is an unconscious process that is made possible by the indistinctness of the real self.

Self-idealization is a comprehensive solution, not for one particular conflict, but for all. Because it has a mysterious, magical quality, and promises the individual an ultimate fulfillment, it becomes essential to him and cannot be abandoned. It is the logical outcome of the early neurotic development, and the beginning of a new development. The individual embarks upon a search for glory in which the energies driving toward self-realization are shifted toward actualizing the idealized self. This leads to a shift in the entire course of his life.

The aim of psychoanalytic therapy is to help a person abandon his drive to actualize the idealized self and move towards self-realization. There are four categories of self-realization:

1. Self-realization with regard to oneself. This means realization of one's feelings, wishes, and beliefs (realization here means "becoming real"). A neurotic person may experience feelings, but they are determined by pride or hurt, or by the fulfillment or frustration of neurotic attempts at conflict solution. Self-realization means developing a capacity to tap one's resources and use one's energies. It also means having a sense of direction from within, the freedom to choose and an ability to make decisions, the capacity to assume responsibility for oneself, and a feeling of true unity.

2. Self-realization with regard to others. Human relations are an integral part of our lives. Self-realization means acquiring the capacity to see and relate to other human beings as they are, and not to distort them by externalizations and to use them as objects for the fulfillment of neurotic needs.

3. Self-realization with regard to work. This means relating oneself more directly to one's work. The neurotic "I should do a perfect job" becomes "I wish to do a job well." There is a greater capacity to enjoy work for its own sake and not as a means to glory. The result of this change is greater enjoyment of work. The self-realizing person makes a more realistic appraisal of the values and difficulties of his work and of his own abilities. He becomes more productive and develops his actual talents and special gifts.

4. Self-realization with regard to assuming one's place in the world. This means that the person accepts his place in the world, with its attendant responsibility, and is aware of the broader issues.

Lecture 2

The Initial Interview

This lecture as reconstructed by Morton B. Cantor was first published in the American Journal of Psychoanalysis 17 (1957), 39–44. It was designated as part I, but a second part was never published. According to a note at the end, the second part was to have focused on "the practical aspects of dealing with the patient's initial contact with the analyst," and a sentence I have deleted from this edited version of the Cantor reconstruction referred to an upcoming "section on the therapeutic value of the initial interview." Dr. Cantor has informed me that he attended Horney's 1951 course "Psychoanalytic Technique," and Horney's notes for that course indicate that she lectured on the diagnostic, therapeutic, and prognostic values of the preliminary interview, the patient's attitude toward psychoanalysis, the means of psychoanalytic therapy, and the practical arrangements between patient and analyst.

The first two lectures in Horney's 1946 course were called "Preliminary Interviews": (1) "Diagnosis and prognosis," and (2) "The patient's fears and expectations concerning analysis. Preliminary interviews as a therapeutic situation." Although the following lecture is entitled "The Initial Interview," Horney's notes are headed "Preliminary Interviews," and it seems clear that she was talking about the first several sessions.

The initial contact between patient and analyst is much more than an introduction to analysis, much more than the moment for making practical arrangements or obtaining clinical data and past history. The initial interview can be analysis as much as any other analytical hour.

Diagnostic and Prognostic Value of the Initial Interview

When we talk about diagnostic values, we are not just concerned with the severity and extent of illness, but with what kind of human being the patient is. We must determine what he is out for, what he wants from the analyst and what is the status and availability of his constructive resources. It would be too ambitious to expect that we can get the whole diagnostic picture right away; however, it is necessary and possible to get some feeling of the patient and of the distribution of forces within him.

Intuition. Our first impressions are most important because in sizing up the patient we usually can start without prejudice. Therefore, our unbiased impressions during the initial interview may be more valid than we at first realize. We are dealing here largely with intuition, the perception and evaluation of objective reality operating unconsciously and representing the sum total of all the analyst's past experiences, emotional and intellectual. The closer the analyst is to his totality of experiencing, the more available will he be for understanding the patient. Even with our first impressions, diagnosing and prognosing cannot be done with complete scientific objectivity, for the analyst's relatedness to the patient must constantly be taken into account. It is a good idea to file away the notes from the initial interview and to review them from time to time during the analysis.

First General Observations. The analyst's first impressions of the patient may begin with a telephone call or letter. How the patient introduces himself may indicate much about his general attitude toward himself and his relations with others. What is his tone of voice, quality of interest, amount of ego-centricity? Does he come alone to the first interview? Just how does he present himself? We may learn about his hostile attitudes, his present status, and how readily he is distracted. How rigid, brittle, sick is he? How much are his feet on the ground? Is he psychotic? How resigned, domineering or dependent does he seem? Is his pride so great that he is practically unproductive? His difficulties may be so pervasive that he is inhibited in his relations with people and blocked intellectually. What can he talk about? Is he apologizing for living? How likeable, self-righteous or curious is he? Does the analyst get a picture of honesty and sincerity, or one of a series of pretenses? Does the patient mention suffering? How generally aware of himself is he, and of what is he or isn't he aware at the beginning of analysis?

Instead of leading the patient in a specific direction at the very beginning, we should wait patiently to allow him to evolve one thought from another in the way he wants to go about it. We should follow the patient as he elaborates his symptoms, steering him only occasionally to discover what he supposes to be the genesis of his difficulties. Details that he omits may be especially significant, but should not necessarily be tackled during the first hour.

Prognosis. As we make observations, we are both diagnosing and prognosing. It is not sufficient to say that prognosis depends on the severity of the neurotic process. Freud focused on the issue of severity and considered that a factor such as too much narcissism indicated a poor prognosis. According to our view, this does not take into account the totality of the picture. We must consider which type of solution the patient is using and how rigidly he is using it. The external situation is also important. How is the patient functioning and how many satisfactions does he have? Instead of thinking in pessimistic absolutes, we focus on the distribution of constructive and obstructive forces and on the possibility of mobilizing the patient's constructiveness.

FACTORS IN EVALUATING FUTURE EFFECTIVENESS OF THERAPY.

1. When we look at where the greatest difficulties in therapy lie, we are not dealing merely with the intensity of specific trends. That a patient may show particularly marked resignation or may be extensively and morbidly dependent does not in itself necessarily indicate that he is less likely to improve in therapy. The amount of personality impoverishment, waste of human energies, and impairment of moral integrity can indicate to us more specifically just how therapy may be affected by the patient's specific trend.

2. How much aliveness or deadness is there within the patient? Is there an alertness, brightness, and color in his eyes? What about his clothing, posture, or tone of voice? What may appear to be aliveness may be a covering-up of real emotional deadness.

3. How open or closed is the patient, how accessible? How easily can we reach him when talking about his problems — at least intellectually? Is he aware of psychology and psychic processes? Is he able to see cause-and-effect relationships? Can he articulate his thoughts?

4. How much constructive striving and searching is there in the patient? What looks like "constructive discontentment" may be self-righteousness, a know-it-all attitude, flippancy, or cynicism. How much healthy curiosity is present? There may be some essential honesty despite unconscious pretenses which the analyst may sense.

5. The degree of the patient's alienation from self is of great importance here. How willing or able is he to experience his feelings? He may externalize them by focusing primarily on physical symptoms or reporting what others say about him. He may have an observer attitude with very little spontaneity.

6. Almost as important as self-alienation is the patient's attitude toward his own suffering. How aware is he of it? Is it real suffering that he can learn something from or neurotic suffering that he uses to disguise vindictiveness, to provide alibis, or to serve as a basis for claims? Is there pride in endurance (which can be quite obstructive)? Is there ability to stand some suspense or anxiety and conflict? Does the patient consider suffering disgraceful and therefore disregard it? The patient may come into therapy with divided goals. On the one hand, he wants to alleviate his suffering, but on the other he may "need" it as a temporary means of easing inner tension. His attitude toward suffering can either spur the patient on to constructive efforts or keep him in a state of inertia.

7. What are the patient's expectations from analysis? Will he put forth efforts to work at himself to change, or does he wait for a magical transformation? Where is his incentive? The mere fact that he is seeking therapy is not enough in itself, but it shows some constructive elements.

MORE SPECIFIC PROGNOSTIC FACTORS

1. The first place to look for specific prognostic factors is *the patient's history*. During the preliminary interview, we try to get a bird's-eye view. Have there been great ups and downs in the patient's life? What constructive and destructive forces have been at work, and how are they presented?

In terms of human relationships, it is the quality that is most important. Whether the patient is married or divorced is not relevant in and of itself. Facts alone are not very informative unless they are manifestations of something else. We are less concerned with the patient's virginity or sexual promiscuity than how he feels about his sexual life. Does he enjoy it, does he feel it necessary for his prestige, does he feel contempt for physical enjoyment? In terms of prognosis, his attitude toward sex may be very telling. An almost complete absence of sexual feelings is very much of a negative. If detached persons are able to have and enjoy a sexual relationship and have a decent attitude toward it, the situation is much more favorable. Sexual relations may be without any human contact, with a callousness about the people concerned. A disordered sex life and random relationships are on the negative side. We are most interested in what a person's sexual behavior reveals about his total character structure.

In his human relations, what are the patient's attitudes and what does he expect? Have there been constructive forces in his relationships with others? In spite of the lack of close friends, some detached persons may have some permanent, distant relationships. This can indicate that the real self, although suppressed, still has sufficient energy to come through and make itself felt in the midst of all the wasted human energies and distortions of the actual self. Where there may have been some warm and helpful people in the patient's past, the concept of human help may not be completely foreign to him, and this may help diminish some of his suspiciousness and enable him to engage in the cooperative venture of analysis. Also, the capacity of a person to do something constructive for others is important, even if he has been unable to do anything for himself.

What has the patient done in his work life? Has he ever shown initiative or been creative? Have there been continuity, depth, and variety in his interests? What is his capacity for work, his ambitiousness, his relatedness to work? Has he drifted, been opportunistic? Is his energy predominantly in service of neurotic aims? The person who has faced many adverse situations in life without falling apart or who has shown some tenacity and accomplishment in his pursuits has a better prognosis.

In terms of specific disturbances, did the patient ever function fairly well? If there have been sudden breakdowns, was there a disproportion between cause and effect that indicates a disturbed equilibrium? Were there ever suicide attempts or alcoholism, and what was their severity and duration? Has there been a tendency to rush away from anxiety that may recur later in therapy?

2. A second major place to look for specific prognostic factors is *the present life situation*. How hemmed in is the patient? What are the possibilities of changing external conditions? Are there people in the environment who may be sources of warmth, encouragement, companionship, and support during analysis? Is the patient so dependent on family, job, or daily routine that he cannot make changes without sacrificing the necessities of life? The issue of dependency is especially important if it relates to the source of payment for therapy. This may be more important for the patients under eighteen or over sixty-five than the factor of age *per se*.

3. Perhaps the most important source of information about how the patient is likely to do in therapy is *his behavior in the office*. How does he present data? Is it all very confusing? Is he only intellectualizing? Is he terribly systematic? Is there any sense for essentials? How rigid, lucid, or sober is he? If he is highly circumstantial, that is a bad sign. How much insight has he gained on his own or through previous analysis? We cannot obtain answers to these questions directly, but we can infer them from the way in which the patient talks about himself. That may help us to gauge the available constructive

forces and how much self-analysis he can do. If previous therapy led to a massive feeling of being abused and nothing more, the prognosis is poor. Has the patient been able to see something positive in himself? How the patient reacts to some of the first interpretations is a very important factor. Does he examine them? Do they set something going? This may show the degree of his accessibility.

How much of what we observe do we tell the patient? We can tell him a lot. We can tell him, "It may be difficult because. . ." and then add that on the basis of constructive resources shown, such as energy, initiative, or honesty, we feel that something can be done. When the patient asks how long therapy will take, we can tell him it depends on him, on his energy, honesty, and ability to reveal himself. We should tell the patient all this at the beginning, even if it does not seem to sink in.

In our prognosis, we must also consider the patient's attitude toward analysis — which will be discussed next. If we focus on only one of the factors I have mentioned, we may not get an adequate prognostic picture. If we take them all into consideration, we shall be in a better position to determine what the indications are for analysis, whether the patient is ready for it, and whether he has sufficient inner strength.

The Patient's Attitude Toward Analysis

In evaluating the patient's attitude toward analysis, we must look at both his incentive and his reservations. All patients who come for therapy have some incentive, so the question is whether it is strong enough to overcome their doubts.

Incentive. We must distinguish between healthy and unhealthy motivations. Is the patient oriented toward overcoming his neurosis or making it function more effectively? When attempting to determine this, we must keep in mind that at the beginning of analysis no patient can be truly honest about revealing himself.

1. *What are the patient's ends?* What is he out for — freedom *from* something or the more positive freedom *for* something? The desire to get rid of something — e.g., symptoms like insomnia, stage-fright, or fears of being alone — has sufficient carrying power in itself. Freud wondered what would happen if this incentive were removed too rapidly. It is always to be remembered that the symptom may be part of a life-saving mechanism and that removing it too quickly may lead to an acute psychotic episode or attempt at suicide. A well-known example of this phenomenon is the frequency of suicide attempts following surgically successful rhinoplasties.

We can try to deepen the patient's incentive by showing him that he has more troubles than just one symptom or the particular "situational problem" for which he may have sought help. This can be done if he does not have too much hopelessness. Also to be considered is whether the patient's real self is suffering or merely his proud self. Incentive for seeking relief from a sexual difficulty is much greater if the patient feels that something is really missing in his life, rather than if he is merely reacting to hurt pride.

How healthy or neurotic are the patient's goals? Is he seeking therapy because he wants to marry for the sake of a closer relationship with a desired person, or is he merely afraid of being alone? When a patient states that he wants "to be more serene," what does he really mean by that? Does he seek real inner peace to help him fulfill himself, or does he merely want to get more automatic control, "poise," or non-attachment — a more effective untouchability?

2. *By what means does the patient expect to achieve his ends?* What are his emotional attitudes about how he will do it? We can ask the patient, "How do you really think analysis might help you?" Does he expect magic or something mysterious, or is he ready for real work? Does he have any feeling that his progress is up to him, or does he come with many claims on the analyst? How able is he to be frank and productive? Will direct questions help him? If he inquires about drugs, shock therapies, and hypnosis, this indicates that he is looking for someone or something else to do his work. More subtle is the patient who expects rational explanations to produce automatic improvement through the magic of the intellect.

Reservations. All patients have doubts about analysis, expressed or sensed. If there is hemming and hawing, discussion of these doubts may be saved for a later hour when there is more time and the patient has had an opportunity for further thought. We can encourage him to ventilate his doubts and look for their origin. For example, the question "Will analysis spoil my creativity?" calls for information, preferably based on the analyst's experience, which shows that creativity can be enhanced. Also, the patient's interpretation of "creativity" may be quite different from the therapist's.

In response to the question, "Do I really need analysis?" the therapist can point out the problems which, without analysis, will probably continue or get worse in the future. The meaning of this question may depend on the patient's predominant trends. For example, the self-effacing person may be saying, "I can't do anything," while the expansive person may be saying, "I can tackle these problems by myself without help because I *should* be able to." When the therapist is asked, "How long will analysis take?" he can emphasize how much it really depends on the patient. This question may hide doubts about whether analysis is really worth the time and expense. The question "Who shall my analyst be?" may derive from the patient's belief that since the analyst has powerful magic tools, he must be careful to choose the right artisan. Emphasizing the person of the analyst may also be a prestige factor for the patient.

A patient's reservations about analysis can tell us a lot about pertinent dynamics as well as difficulties that will be encountered in therapy. There may be a strong fear of becoming dependent on anybody. The self-effacing person may show the greatest willingness to enter analysis because of his self-doubts, guilt-feelings, and needs for a dependent relationship; but he may be limited by wanting nothing for himself and by doubting that anything can be done for or by him. The expansive type hates to admit faults, has a front of self-righteousness, and is limited by feeling that there is nothing he should not be able to master. The resigned person puts a premium on maintaining the status quo and not wanting anything. He feels that people do not change, is sensitive to coercion, and is averse to communication. A person like this, or a shallow living person who needs the ultimate of freedom and license, can only be brought into analysis by acute difficulties. He may be able to attempt it only if he feels that there are many doors through which he can depart.

There are numerous other difficulties that create obstacles to analysis. The rebellious person is inclined to say, "You can all go to hell, I'll do what I damned please." When a patient cannot make up his mind about analysis, he may cover this indecisiveness by insisting on unfulfillable conditions. The person who persistently damages his position in life, like the diabetic who does not keep to his diet, may not be ready for therapy. A very detached patient may also not yet be ready because any kind of closeness, connectedness, and continuity is a great threat to him. Fear of upsets in work and marriage may be given as a reason for hesitating to enter analysis. Knowing that upsetting changes in the external environment may occur, the therapist can address the patient's fear of them. Such an understanding attitude may help the patient come to a positive decision about entering analysis.

The Quality of the Analyst's Attention

This lecture as reconstructed by Morton B. Cantor was first published in the American Journal of Psychoanalysis *19 (1959), 28–32. It is based on Dr. Cantor's notes from Horney's 1951 course "Psychoanalytic Technique." Horney included this topic in every one of her courses of which there is a record. She began her last course with a lecture on this topic, perhaps because she was ill and wanted to be sure that it was covered. A transcription was published in* Final Lectures *(1987). I recommend that the reader consult both the 1951 and 1952 lectures. The lecture published here contains material not to be found in the 1952 version, while the 1952 version reflects the interest in Zen that led Horney to visit Japan in the summer of that year. When discussing wholehearted attention, Horney observed that "this is a faculty for which the Orientals have a much deeper feeling than we do. Also, they have a much better training in it than we. We, as a rule, are not trained in concentrating per se. They must so often concentrate in their exercises, postures, breathing, meditation, and Yoga" (1987, 18). She also drew on the Zen notion of nonattachment, applying it to her topic by observing that "in doing analysis one has no personal axe to grind, no neurotic craving" (1987, 31). She emphasized, however, that for a therapist "it is not enough to be a cold observer."*

The analyst's attention includes understanding and the taking in of observations. This is to be differentiated from the application of intellectual energy or the passive receiving of impressions. The analyst directs his attention to the whole being of the patient, with a view toward therapeutic action. He focuses on getting a feeling for the patient, for his uniqueness, so that his differentness no longer feels strange to him. This is of fundamental importance. There are three aspects to the quality of the analyst's attention: wholeheartedness, comprehensiveness, and productiveness.

Wholeheartedness

Wholeheartedness involves observing with all our capacities and faculties. We listen, see, and feel with our intuition, undivided interest, reason, curiosity, and specialized knowledge. This involves awareness of our own selves, general professional knowledge and experience, and all that we are aware of in the particular patient. We focus ourselves as fully as we can on all the patient's communications, verbal and non-verbal.

In an ideal state of wholeheartedness, we are not distracted by our own deeper problems or by situations which have upset us acutely. The mind is our analytic tool, as is our total personality, and we have an obligation to keep this tool in good shape if we are to do such concentrated work with it.

Once I felt myself yawning and being terribly tired while seeing a patient upon returning from vacation. Doing some quick self-analysis, I thought of a letter I had received from an old friend reminiscing about the wonderful time we had enjoyed together. I became aware of the conflict between my recent life of full ease and my present return to concentrating on other people. The patient had been talking about the movie "Treasure Island." In it the cook, who had been a compliant person, became captain. When I realized that it was having to resume responsibility that had triggered my fatigue, I felt alert again and was no longer tired.

Detached, alienated analysts who are living through their intellect may be good observers and acute listeners, and they may be able to concentrate better because they are disturbed very little by their own feelings. They have an interest in their patient's problems, but they are more interested in the structure of the personality than in the human being. Not only must our intellect and stored-up knowledge come into play in analytic work, but also our emotions. We must lay ourselves open to all the feelings that can exist between two people: liking and disliking, dismay, disappointment, humor, hopefulness, anger, sympathy, and so forth. This may be disturbing at first, but in time the analyst's feelings will be geared more to the patient than to himself. The central issue is that the patient make progress.

In order to approach the ideal of wholeheartedness, we must be able to surrender to the work, letting all our faculties operate while nearly forgetting about ourselves. This is like surrendering ourselves to music or a work of art. As our knowledge and experience become an integral part of ourselves, we are barely conscious of all that we are while at the same time *being* all that we are. We can extend the boundaries of ourselves and be more open to the beings of others.

Comprehensiveness

Comprehensiveness involves taking in everything without focusing exclusively on a limited set of factors. We must be like the driver of an automobile who has to be aware of the condition of his car, the roads, the weather, other cars, etc., all at the same time. Gradually the ability to attend to everything at once becomes automatic and permits us to function effectively. If we can be fully available to ourselves and to the patient, a pattern may unconsciously form, not necessarily during the session but perhaps the next day or even much later.

There are many things to which we must pay attention. We should observe the patient's tempo in therapy and how it changes, the pauses, pressures, and rhythm of what is going on. What is the quality of the patient's eagerness to learn about himself? Eagerness may be deceptive. Glib interpretations without interest in the analyst's opinion may arise from the patient's need to show how much he knows. Is the eagerness only intellectual or perhaps an eagerness to confess? Does the patient give the results of his self-analysis or does he engage in self-exploration during the hour, letting the analyst participate?

It is important to observe what is changing in the patient's attitude. Is he now productive outside of the analytic hour also? Is what he says pertinent, or is he floundering and scattered? Does he focus on the intrapsychic or the interpersonal features of his problems? Does he have a tendency to deal with concrete things or theoretical considerations? What is his reaction to what the analyst is saying?

How is the patient presenting himself? Is he merely complaining, feeling victimized, apologetic, or demanding? Does he talk about himself primarily in terms of how others see him? Is he critical, grateful, overly grateful, defensive, or self-glorifying? Does he give very complex accounts? What does he omit? Does he really want to change or just to show what he has learned?

Does the patient only report his feelings or does he experience them in the hour? Is the patient just telling us about a sorry state of affairs or really experiencing suffering? When he feels anger or relief or complains of head-aches or dizziness, this often indicates that something significant is going on, and we must look for a deeper meaning.

With one patient who showed no outward manifestations of anxiety and had a desperate need not to experience it, the only way I could sense his anxiety was by the change in the tempo and spirit of the hour. Suddenly he would mention ten or fifteen different problems in passing, and I felt myself becoming slightly dizzy and breathless, as if I had been trying to catch a butterfly. It was only by paying attention to my own emerging feelings that I could get a picture of what was going on.

To approach the goal of comprehensiveness in our attention, we need to be flexible enough to take in all these various elements as they come up. We must listen idly, avoiding a pin-point concentration which can close us off from a truly holistic view of the patient. We must be careful not to let the intensity of our attention convert a mutual analytic situation into one where the patient is in the brilliant spotlight on a clinical stage while we are in the darkened audience. With both of us sharing more subdued light in the same room, we can become more open and real to one another.

Productiveness

In order to be productive, therapy must start something going. We must try to assess what is really changing and what has to be tackled further. Are trends and solutions less compulsive and feelings more alive? Is the patient more aware of his own drives and desires? Is he more confident of the analyst, more independent, more accepting of responsibility? Are there fewer neurotic symptoms and fears of conflicts? Perhaps there are more somatic symptoms in the patient who has heretofore not been close enough to his physical being to be aware of bodily participation in emotional conflict.

A woman began analysis with a vague feeling that something must be wrong. After two years she was still denying any deeper conflicts, resisting the idea that her dreams or slips of the tongue had any meaning. Analysis seemed to be at a standstill. There was no evidence of psychosomatic symptomatol-ogy; nothing could be specifically pointed out to her that she could accept as an indication of anxiety. I confessed a concern about a "stalemate" in the analytic situation and said, "We'll have to light a fire under you if we're going to get anywhere." That night she developed her first psychosomatic symptom, a painful burning and itching around her anus. For the first time she began seriously to consider that there was a connection between physical and emotional processes, that there were unconscious forces operating within her, and that perhaps a person was something more than a rational being who was simply reacting to his environment.

The ever-present question is: "Is what is going on now leading to self-awareness and bringing the patient closer to self-realization?" This applies to the patient's description of an event or feeling, to free association, to the discussion of a dream or an interpretation, and to what is going on in the patient's life outside of analysis. It also applies to the doctor-patient relationship and to what is going on within the analyst himself. How much can have happened with the patient in analysis if nothing happened to the analyst while working with him? In a successful analysis, something happens to both people. If the analyst is merely a catalytic agent and nothing has changed in him, how much really could have gone on within the patient?

Attitudes Interfering with the Quality of Attention

There are many things that can diminish the quality of the analyst's attention. The analyst who is trying to get places in a hurry, who is rushing toward an understanding, will be impaired in terms of wholeheartedness, comprehensiveness, and productiveness. This may result from his own "shoulds," from his pride in omniscience and intolerance of being confused, or from his avoidance of anxiety and conflict in himself. His own egocentricity will interfere with his wholeheartedness. A one-sided view of what is going on within the patient may reflect where the analyst is in terms of his own self-analysis. For example, he may be focusing on self-effacement and minimizing expansiveness.

Approaching the patient with preconceived ideas restricts comprehensiveness. Freud coined the term "free-floating attention," but for him much of this was an intellectual floating concerned with fitting what he observed clinically into the theories he was formulating. This may be done with anyone's theoretical formulations. Theory should serve only as a general framework and should never be more important than the patient.

The Analyst's Personal Equation

This lecture as reconstructed by Louis A. Azorin was first published in the American Journal of Psychoanalysis *17 (1957), 34–38. It was probably delivered in the course "Psychoanalytic Technique" that Horney began in September 1950, in which lectures 6 and 7 were devoted to this topic. The topic does not appear in the syllabus for the 1946 course. It was to have been included in the 1952 course, but Horney did not get that far before her death. There are undated lecture notes headed "Self-Psychoanalysis of Analyst" that are probably from the course Horney gave in 1951.*

I should like to discuss first those qualities that characterize a good therapist and then some of the difficulties inherent in the analytic situation. Finally, I shall consider how the analyst's work is affected by neurotic remnants in his own personality and what he can do about it.

Desirable Qualities in an Analyst

Ideally, an analyst should possess maturity, directness, discernment, and objectivity. He should have a real interest in his patients, in their practical as well as psychological problems. It is important that he be striving toward self-realization himself and that he have an honest wish to help patients toward their self-realization. He should have a capacity for healthy emotional involvement with the patient and a searching mind with untiring curiosity about challenging problems.

To illustrate the last point, there is the case of a patient who had been working quite seriously on his power drive and who had tackled its pervasiveness, its consequences, etc., but who still found the pursuit of power very attractive. His analyst was not content with, "You're on the right track, but it takes time," and sundry other semi-rationalizations which a less curious analyst might have offered. Instead, he thought intently about the problem and came to the realization that the patient was not fully aware of the *intensity* of his drive toward glory. When the patient was able to *feel* its intensity, he began to make progress.

Intellectually we all are convinced that self-realization is a desirable goal. However, if the striving for it is not a living experience in the analyst's daily life, he cannot do justice to his patient's efforts, nor can he serve as a healthy model. Certainly no analyst is ideal or perfect, but a continual evaluation of his own progress in a spirit of ruthless honesty will help him to approach the goal of complete integration.

Difficulties Inherent in Analytic Work

1. *The difficulty of evaluating the results in therapy*. It is always beneficial to ask ourselves, "Has change really taken place, and if so, how much? Also, how lasting is the change? Could it have been accomplished more quickly?" But it is difficult to answer these questions. Comparisons with other patients are not always illuminating because we are working with a unique person who is similar to and yet different from every other human being. Then too the therapeutic process differs from case to case, making comparisons of dubious value. The situation may be further complicated by the analyst's unconscious needs to see himself and his work in a favorable light. Hence the importance of self-awareness and a constant critical evaluation of our efforts.

2. *The patient's tendency to overrate his analyst's importance*. This is most often seen in the self-effacing patient, who may employ this tactic in an effort to get the analyst to do more work and to avoid his own participation. The tactic is not difficult to discern in such a patient, but it can have many subtle aspects when employed by an arrogant-vindictive patient, who may use it to flatter, to cajole, or to ridicule. This stratagem, whether consciously or unconsciously employed, can have a distorting effect on the analyst's self-evaluation.

Naturally the more aware the analyst is of his own personality, the less apt he is to be influenced by a patient's evaluation of him.

The opposite tendency, namely, the patient's need to *undervalue* his analyst, can have an equally deleterious effect unless the trend is seen for what it is and tackled as a problem. The analyst will react to such belittling in accordance with what remains of his own neurotic needs. For example, the more aggressive analyst may react with hurt pride and be tempted to argue rather than to analyze, whereas the detached analyst may tend to protect himself by being uninvolved, by minimizing or intellectualizing his patient's dissatisfactions. The self-effacing analyst will be too ready to accept the patient's low estimate of him.

3. *The analyst's overrating of his own mental health.* Because the emphasis is on the patient's problems, not only the patient but the analyst himself may assume that he is better integrated than he really is.

4. *The factor of payment to the analyst for his efforts.* The analyst's evaluation of himself will be one factor in the determination of his fees. For example, the analyst with remnants of self-effacement will tend to charge too little, while his expansive colleague will tend to charge too much.

Given the psychological difficulties inherent in the nature of therapy, it follows that the better integrated the analyst, the more readily he will be able to tackle these problems in a realistic, compassionate manner. The analyst with residuals of neurotic traits will add to the difficulties in accordance with his particular character traits.

General Comments on the Analyst's Own Personality Problems

There is no question that every unsolved problem of ours will make itself felt in the analytic situation, as well as in every other area of life, reducing our effectiveness. The fear that neurotic remnants may be exposed will make some analysts unduly cautious, thereby depriving the patient of the opportunity to experience his analyst as a human being with both shortcomings and assets. It is imperative to realize that there is no ideal analyst, just as there is no perfect human being, but this should not be used as an excuse to curtail our efforts to improve ourselves.

There are certain measures analysts can take to enhance their self-realization. These include the completion of their own formal analysis, continuing self-analysis and occasional return to therapy, supervision by their more experienced colleagues, attendance at seminars, scientific meetings, etc.

Up to this point I have talked about the ways in which general neurotic remnants affect the analyst's work. I shall now consider how the remnants of specific defensive strategies operate in therapy. It is important to appreciate that every analyst with remaining neurotic trends has his assets as well as his liabilities.

Residuals of Compliancy or Self-effacement

Having residuals of compliancy helps the analyst to establish contact with the patient. However, his compulsive need to be liked causes him to over-emphasize the patient's assets and to minimize or ignore his hostile, aggressive tendencies. A compliant analyst I know had a stuttering patient who presented himself in a Christ-like manner. This facade was so appealing to the analyst that he overlooked the patient's veiled aggression and his proclivity toward prevarication. These tendencies could not be worked through until the analyst became aware of them and searched for their underlying causes, but he could do neither until he had made more progress with his own compliancy.

The compliant analyst is afraid of antagonizing his patients. He may consider himself merely as cautious in having regard for the patient's inability to "take it." He also tends to shy away from bringing out hostility or from tackling the patient's idealized image. He might overlook the patient's frustrating tendencies or be too generous about time or money. His inordinate need to be liked and concomitant fear of antagonizing the patient result in a *lack of firmness*. His interpretations are too tentative and too easily given up. He is too inclined to blame himself if the patient does not immediately seize upon a valid interpretation. He may allow the analytic relationship to take on too personal a character instead of maintaining its functional nature. He may tend to make the patient dependent on him. His attitude toward the neurotic suffering of his patients is one of indiscriminate sympathy; as a consequence he has too little feeling for their *real* suffering. Because of his inability to tolerate suffering, he tends to be compulsively helpful, much too reassuring, and not clear enough about the necessity for analyzing the patient's feelings of helplessness. Because of his tendency to belittle his own judgment and overvalue that of his patient, he tends to see things from the patient's perspective. As a result, he does not have a grasp of the whole structure and shows insufficient leadership.

Analysts with Remnants of Aggressive Trends

As I have said, every analyst with remaining neurotic trends has his assets as well as his liabilities. The aggressive analyst will not overlook the patient's hidden aggression, nor will he be afraid to tackle problems or to be direct in his approach. He has his drawbacks, however. He has a compulsive need to run the analysis rather than to make it a cooperative enterprise. He tends to have too little sensitivity and is likely to hurt the patient's tender feelings.

In one instance, a patient had finally accepted himself enough to express a feeling of appreciation for his analyst's efforts. His expression was a mixture of genuine warmth and neurotic sentimentality, but his aggressive analyst focused exclusively on the latter component and told him that he doubted the sincerity of his feelings. Understandably, the patient felt rejected by this one-sided and unsympathetic interpretation. Fortunately, the analyst was able to work through his own end of the problem and to admit his error.

The aggressive analyst feels that the patient should be able to "take" every-thing. Therefore, he might interpret prematurely and cause unnecessary pain. He tends to be dominating and intimidating, too self-assured, and inclined toward giving dogmatic interpretations. His need to show that he knows it all beforehand might prevent him from listening carefully.

The Narcissistic Analyst

His patients often fall in love with him because of his warmth, charm, and vivacity. He may be particularly helpful in the beginning because he makes his patients feel accepted. Also he tends to think in terms of big trends, which helps his patients gain perspective. However, because of his need for quick understanding, he tends to generalize too much and to categorize his patients rather than seeing them as unique and complicated human beings. When a patient does not accept his interpretations, he tends to feel impatient and/or hopeless. Because of his self-absorption, he becomes distracted, and his sensitivity to his patients diminishes. He often feels that he and he alone can help his patients and that if he cannot, then no one else can either. This is in contrast to the self-effacing analyst who may feel that every other analyst might do a better job with his patients.

The Perfectionistic Analyst

He shows marked tenacity and an appreciation for detail but is inclined to be didactic. He focuses more on explaining than on analyzing. When he does analyze, he may lose sight of the forest for the trees. He plans the sessions carefully and is quite dismayed when the patient insists on going his own way. Because of his overemphasis on intellect, he tends to be less interested in the patient's feelings. As his drive toward perfection indicates, he is still under the influence of powerful *shoulds*. Therefore, he may go from overcautiousness to the reverse. He *should* be able to answer all questions, *should* be able to predict, and when he cannot, he suffers. There is a marked tendency toward intense self-blame and self-belittling. This lowers his self-respect and leads to a feeling of uncertainty. He becomes too vague, too tentative, and his fear of committing himself makes it difficult for the patient to do so.

The Arrogant-Vindictive Analyst

There is an overlap here with my earlier description of the aggressive analyst. His assets are his incisiveness, his not being afraid to hurt, and his ability to conduct the analysis. His liabilities are that he has too little feeling for the patient's suffering, that he is likely to generalize unnecessarily, and that he is inclined to use patients' problems to gain knowledge and money. He will tend to make the patient dependent on him. Unlike the self-effacing analyst, he will be righteous and will be encouraged by the expression of hostility on the part of his patients. His attitude toward hostility, however, makes it difficult for him to analyze it. He may not have much of a life outside of his work, which is not good because he will expect all his satisfactions from his patients. His private life is often quite empty, his capacity for enjoyment limited, and his personal relationships troubled. Because of his competitiveness, he may unconsciously obstruct the growth of his patients, feeling "Why should anyone be better off than I?"

The Detached or Resigned Analyst

This analyst has no axe to grind. He will be a good observer and will have fewer blind spots than others. He may be very helpful to patients who belong to the compliant group because he tries to make them independent and resourceful. He is, however, *too much* of an observer. He hates coercion and intrusion, so he will tend toward passivity and be reluctant to take a stand with his patients. His fear of becoming involved leads him to avoid stirring up affection or hostility. Because the analyst tends to be impersonal, distant, and cool, the patient feels himself to be in an emotional vacuum.

The detached analyst has too little special feeling for the patient and may easily become bored. He tends to adhere too rigidly to theories and to apply them to the individual patient in too literal a manner. There is more of a tendency toward hopelessness in this analyst than with the other types because of an unconscious disbelief in the possibility of real change. He may have overcome many difficulties in his own life and then settled down at a certain juncture. His hopelessness may lead him to take nearly hopeless cases (for example, he may prefer psychotics), or he might go to the other extreme and refuse to accept anything challenging. Then too, he may consider a patient not amenable to analysis if he does not see quick results. His incentive to encourage basic change is very low.

What Can Analysts Do About Their Liabilities?

All analysts have a good opportunity to analyze themselves. We can try to be wholeheartedly aware of all our feelings and reactions, regardless of their nature. These would include, to mention a few, hopefulness, hopelessness, annoyance, irritability, boredom. If we do not experience the whole variety of human feelings, at least to some degree, something is amiss.

If the feeling of boredom arises, do not rationalize it, but rather try to feel *what* is boring. At what point did these reactions occur? What might they mean? You might feel bored because of your own reluctance to make a sufficient effort or because the patient did not follow your marvelous suggestions (dictatorial attitude). Perhaps you are reluctant to make an effort because of a defiant attitude: "Why should I?"

If a feeling of irritation arises, do not try to push it aside. Ask yourself, "Where did it occur?" Did it arise as a result of the patient having a disparaging attitude toward you? Was it the result of a feeling that the patient should have understood your interpretation right away? Did the patient say or imply that he wasn't feeling any better?

We must engage in the same kind of self-perusal with all our reactions, especially those which are different from what we might have anticipated. By being constantly aware of our reactions, we can determine which are appropriate to the situation and which may be the result of our own neurotic remnants. Obviously, we cannot work on everything we feel as we feel it. Some of our reactions are best filed away for reflection at a later time; after all, we still have to be attentive to what the patient is saying and what he may be feeling as he says it.

A constant effort to examine our reactions and even our associations and to relate them to what is going on in the patient is essential if we are to help the patient toward self-realization and to keep growing ourselves.

Understanding the Patient as the
Basis of All Technique

This lecture as reconstructed by Emy A. Metzger was originally published in the American Journal of Psychoanalysis *16 (1956), 26–31. Horney always included lectures on understanding the patient in her courses on psychoanalytic technique, but the only place I could find this specific title — "Understanding the Patient as the Basis of All Technique" — was in the syllabus for the 1946 course. Many of the ideas in this lecture also appear in Horney's notes for her later courses, so the reconstruction may have been based on notes from several courses. There is some overlap between this lecture and "Specific Psychoanalytic Means of Understanding the Patient" in* Final Lectures, *but not very much. Rather, the lectures complement each other.*

Analysis is a cooperative enterprise; it is a process going on between two persons for the purpose of helping the partner who is sick. Yet though both partners have this common purpose, their goals may differ. The patient is divided. Consciously he wants to understand himself, his compulsiveness, his fears; but he also has an inner need to maintain the status quo, to actualize his neurotic fantasies, to live without limitations according to the dictates of his idealized image. He expects magic help and demands it. The analyst is undivided. He strives for truth, for an understanding of the patient and his difficulties, their development and their present manifestations. He sees the patient as he is today and is interested in his growth and in those factors which have impeded healthy development. His focus is on the patient's self-realization and on the forces which obstruct this process. The analyst brings to this task his interest, his professional training, his experience, his feelings, his wish to understand. Yet he is an outsider from the start.

The patient is involved; he has the raw data, but is interested only in some of them and may even be driven to hide or distort vital parts of them. Living in fantasies, he is often unaware of this distortion of reality. When the analyst tries to understand the patient's difficulties, this effort will help to interest the patient again in those aspects of himself which he may have suppressed, effaced, or thwarted.

The Process of Understanding

Understanding is a process of moving toward another person's position while still maintaining our own. We can never be completely sure where the other person stands, but by repeatedly moving back and forth between his position and our own, we can grasp his position and compare it with ours. Each new movement may reveal a new aspect of his personality and enable us to grasp it at a deeper level. However, such a process is possible only if we are tolerant of the other person's position, even if it does not coincide with our own. Since our feelings of compassion help us to see more and more clearly where the other stands, understanding is a movement of emotional as well as of intellectual energies. If we lose our own stand altogether, we will not have understanding but blind surrender. A detached, purely intellectual attitude toward the patient will not lead to understanding but to a mechanical classification of the patient's personality according to our preexisting ideas. Real understanding requires a wholehearted and receptive observing and "feeling into" the other person with all of one's self. It leads to more and more comprehension of an individual patient with his distinct personality and problems.

Knowledge of one's self, which Socrates thought important for healthy living, is a basic prerequisite for the analyst. His having become cognizant of previously unconscious aspects of his personality in his own analysis permits him to recognize trends and drives of which the patient is unaware. Remembering his own need to allay rising anxiety when his defenses were endangered, he will become aware of the patient's blockages, his efforts to procrastinate, to become evasive, or to ward off premature insights. He will register such strategic maneuvers, try to comprehend them, and keep them in mind so that they can be tackled when the patient is ready. The analyst may not be ready to tackle them himself, for he may not yet have a clear enough understanding of their significance in the patient's specific neurotic structure.

In analysis, the process of understanding moves from a dawning awareness of seemingly disconnected factors toward a grasp of the whole. At first we may see only general outlines, but gradually we can differentiate details and begin to perceive links between them. New information or a change of perspective may explain things that were previously incomprehensible. Rational and irrational forces become clearer, and we learn to appreciate the intensity of neurotic solutions. The discrete particulars that we could not connect at first become parts of an intelligible system.

With each new problem, the process of understanding moves from the general to the particular, then from the particular to the general. We may first become aware of the pervading influence of "pride" in a person's life and then of specific kinds of pride. Later we recognize their ramifications, connections, and growth-inhibiting qualities. Or, a general recognition of righteousness may lead to the spotting of militant righteousness in one person and defensive righteousness in another. Needless to say, a similar process occurs in the recognition of "shoulds." When we become aware that a person is driven by shoulds, we must ask, "What particular things is this person demanding of himself?" Or, if we find *lebensneid,* "What particular things is he grudging to other people?" Such questions may sharpen and refine our understanding.

We must be sensitive to the existence of apparently disconnected or contradictory trends and try to grasp their relationship to each other. A patient who expresses a hostile attitude toward others may then exhibit self-hatred or begin to feel abused by others. In a person who seemed friendly and kind, we may suddenly spot callousness. Later the need to depreciate others may become overt, even though it is hidden under a surface attitude of admiration. In a still later hour, we may become aware of the patient's tendency to be begrudging toward those who seem better off than he. We may discover, upon closer study, that his conflicting tendencies all stem from the same root. In one hour a patient may shun pride, in another he may display a craving for affection, and in a third he may reproach himself for certain unimportant matters. These at first apparently disconnected trends will finally make sense when we recognize them as aspects of a self-effacing personality.

In the course of analysis, then, seemingly disparate character traits will be seen as belonging together in the patient's character structure. Sometimes the contradictory manifestations are the product of inner conflicts, and sometimes they are different aspects of a single solution. For example, a self-effacing person may try to dominate others by being helpless. We may be surprised at first by the aggressiveness of a person who believes herself to be saintly. As deeply hidden inner conflicts become more distinct, we can sense their intricacies and experience their impact.

Our understanding of a patient will be incomplete if we do not enter into his feelings and live through them with him. We must become aware of his anxiety when he feels torn apart by his inner conflicts. We must feel both his neurotic and his realistic suffering and experience the impact of his compulsive drivenness. We must enter into his self-idealization and the irrational pride, shoulds, claims, and self-hatred that it generates. And unless we live through his central conflict, the final battle between healthy and neurotic forces, we cannot fully experience the intensity of this struggle. As Rank and Ferenczi recognized, we must know what the patient is experiencing and not simply know about it. It is like the difference between being in jail and reading about being in jail.

It goes without saying that understanding the patient is a function of our relationship to ourselves. If we lay ourselves open without losing ourselves, we can listen wholeheartedly while simultaneously becoming aware of our own reactions to the patient and his problems. If we become unusually tired or bored during an analytical hour, we should try to understand the meaning of our reactions in relation to our own specific problems. Still-persisting remnants of our own neurotic solutions may have been stirred up by the patient's associations and by his acting out.

We must be sensitive to the patient's conscious or unconscious techniques of irritating us, of trying to distract us from the topic under discussion, or of making a desperate nonverbal attempt to draw our attention to something that has previously escaped us. Without either the patient or the analyst being aware of it, the patient may respond to the analyst's imperfections by vindictively exploiting them. Our own inner self is an instrument which often can register such behaviors and their meanings more quickly and precisely than our intellect.

We may have difficulties in understanding because we may be too focused on content or on making sense of things logically. But gradually we can learn how to use our intuition, which is not a mystical quality but an understanding on a deeper level, and which observes more than we realize. While listening we may be tapping our great store of inner experience. Suddenly something may come up in our mind without our immediate awareness of why it comes up at this particular point. I recall a patient who spent an hour talking about her grief at the death of a relative. While listening to her, I recalled a line from Ibsen's *The Wild Duck*: "In a year, her death will be for him a source of beautiful recitals." I could not verify the correctness of my association at that time, but later it proved to be accurate. This patient had a personality structure similar to that of Ibsen's sentimental photographer, who prostituted his own true feelings and was equally self-destructive and helpless.

Needless to say our understanding does not limit itself to the patient's verbal communications. Every move, beginning with the first letter or phone call, every individual nuance in appearance, posture, clothing, tone of voice, or gesture may reveal something important. His changes in facial expression, his mood swings, his rate of breathing, his blushing and coughing may be important clues to his emotional state and may awaken in us significant feelings, memories, and associations. The degree to which we are interested or distracted may become a clue to our reactions to the patient's moral qualities, his pain, his anxiety, his efforts to communicate. His attention to our interpretations and his reactions to them will also be revealing.

When we have become familiar with the patient's plight, we may have a new understanding of his need to keep its deeper meanings out of awareness. We may see superficial issues, complaints, or repetitive themes dominating his mind, while more significant but vaguely experienced problems are kept in the background. His unrealistic attitude toward vital problems may startle us at first, but later we may comprehend his need to keep them at a distance, despite his urgent request for help. We may understand his need to perpetuate the status quo when we realize how much energy he has spent in allaying anxiety, in erecting a facade, in avoiding a fight. The better we become acquainted with the patient, the more we will be able to appreciate his inner suffering, which may be obscured by his compulsive need to please, to impress, to retaliate.

After we become attuned to the patient's individual ways of experiencing and relating, we will no longer think in technical terms but will form and convey our interpretations tentatively. We will be able to interest him in the meaning of his associations by using his own language. We may be able to select whatever is most important to him and suggest the most feasible interpretations. Understanding their plight will make us tolerant of one patient's purely impersonal intellectual curiosity or another's need to confuse the issue or a third's attempt to show that he knows more than we do. We may be able to tackle the patient's specific ways of blocking his own progress at the right time if we are able to sense when he will be able to rebound from such a blow to his pride.

Understanding Changes

Participating with all our faculties in the analytical process will enable us to be more astute in comprehending and assessing the changes that occur in our patients. Knowing that symptomatic changes may have only limited value or may even reinforce pride in magical solutions, we will try to evaluate their significance in the light of our growing understanding of this specific human being. We will not become overly optimistic because of an unexpected improvement, nor will we become exasperated by a sudden recurrence of previously relinquished symptoms. We can understand how after making progress some patients may suddenly be frightened and experience a renewed onslaught of self-contempt. We must lay ourselves open to the anxiety which may engulf such a new traveler on the road toward self-awareness. Sympathizing with his despair, we will have compassion for his sudden powerless rage. Feeling ourselves into his situation will prevent us from giving a false reassurance, which may be dangerous. Yet we can encourage him by letting him know that we are "standing by" him, even when he turns against us. We may see this as an acting out of his pride, which has turned violently against his constructive forces.

Understanding Dreams

Deeply hidden neurotic solutions may become quite overt in the patient's dream material. Equally important are the emotions that are expressed in dreams and evoked when the patient tells us about them. A dream may not only help us to understand a person by its content, or its appearance at a particular time, or its relevance to the present situation, but also by its feeling qualities. For example, it may reveal a startling emotional intensity in an otherwise cold, detached person. The patient may have exhibited a lack of emotions or have ridiculed them, yet in dreams he may still be able to experience them in their true intensity. Often such an upsurge in a dream may be the precursor of a release of affect at the conscious level. We must rely on the understanding of the patient which we obtain by feeling ourselves into his situation to determine whether or not we should communicate what his dreams reveal. Something in ourselves may warn us that he is not ready to confront the meaning of his dreams, and if we ignore such an inner warning and interpret prematurely, he may either stop dreaming or stop telling us about his dreams.

Here, as in all other analytical communications, we must be guided by our intuitive understanding of the patient's capacity to take in that which may still be too upsetting to his shaky equilibrium. In some instances our spontaneous reaction to an emotional reawakening conveyed by his dreams may be transmitted to the patient, verbally or nonverbally, directly or indirectly. His reaction to our understanding and interest may set something going. This may become evident immediately, in the following hour, in a subsequent dream, or at a much later date. To register such an experience with all our being may fortify the analytical relationship.

Understanding in the Struggle toward Self-realization

If we are wholeheartedly interested, the patient may intuitively become aware of our respect for him, our sincere wish to understand him, and our sense of what would be involved in his growth. His feeling that he and the analyst share a common understanding of previously unrealized or distorted aspects of himself may give him the courage to move closer to his own constructive forces. He may be able to accept his actual self and try to comprehend how he became the person he is. He may even become more active in examining his inner reality. But such a frank acceptance of his own imperfection may arouse anxiety, and neurotic defenses may interfere with his wish to become emotionally alive. If anxiety becomes paramount, he may relinquish his efforts to achieve a constructive reorientation.

The analyst will now have to try to understand the degree of the patient's self-alienation, the relative strength or weakness of his aliveness, the intensity of his still-persisting adherence to narcissistic goals, and the obstacles to his emerging spontaneity. He must evaluate the intensity of the patient's anxiety in comparison to his capacity to endure its torture. Such a difficult weighing is possible only if the analyst's own feelings are wholeheartedly involved in his understanding. Here, a detached analyst will be at a loss, whereas a warm human being will stand by with all his faculties and give just as much help as a panicky patient can benefit from. Depending on the patient, overdoing the help might lead to a renewal of dependency or to a complete withdrawal. But if the analyst has a wholehearted understanding of the therapeutic relationship and its intricacies, the patient can emerge successfully from this stressful period of struggle between his anxiety and his constructive forces. The analyst's support gives the patient the strength to make repeated efforts to take a stand against the forces that obstruct his healthy development.

As his self-contempt diminishes, the patient will gain respect for the struggling human being he is. Gradually his claims will become less, and finally he will be able to relinquish them. Then he will be less egocentric and more self-aware. As he frees himself from the prison of his neurosis, previously obscured emotions will be liberated. At first he may experience them only as a fleeting, abortive feeling or as a sense of physical well-being or warmth. But with the analyst's steady encouragement to live with his feelings, he may deepen such an experience. However, we will have to be patient with his persisting need to condemn such feelings or to take pride in embellishing them. Even if he is still inclined to rationalize, we must try to understand this as part of his struggle to find his way to freedom after having been in prison too long. Our own emotional participation will prevent a judgmental attitude.

Much work must be done until the patient has overcome the experience of emptiness which usually arises when he gives up neurotic solutions dictated by pride and self-contempt and has only incompletely reoriented himself as to his assets. The sensitive and understanding analyst will try unflaggingly to awaken the patient's numbed confidence in his own creative abilities until he is strong enough to mobilize them for self-realization.

Lecture 6

Interpretations

This lecture as reconstructed by Ralph Slater was first published in the American Journal of Psychoanalysis *16 (1956), 118–24. It is impossible to say which course or courses it was based on, since this topic was always included in Horney's syllabus. As I pointed out in the introduction, Horney had intended to spend five sessions of her 1952–53 course on various aspects of interpretation, most of which are covered in this lecture.*

What is an interpretation? It is a suggestion by the analyst to the patient as to the possible meaning of what the patient says and does. The analyst derives his understanding from his observations of his patient, his reactions to what is being communicated, and the inferences he draws from his observations and reactions. When he tries to convey his understanding, or some part of it, to the patient, he is making an interpretation. All interpretations are more or less tentative; there is always a possibility of error. The analyst is well-advised to be truthful about the degree of certainty he feels. He may say, "I feel quite certain that. . . ." Or he may say, less positively, "I have the impression that . . ." or "I sense this might be . . . ." The advantages of such truthfulness are twofold. First, the analyst's groping will stimulate the patient to be active, to wonder, to search. Second, when the therapist expresses himself more positively, it will have more meaning for the patient.

There are various kinds of interpretations. Some are essentially uncovering and revealing in character; they call the patient's attention to some aspect of himself and his functioning of which he has been more or less unaware. The timing and form of such interpretations are very important. However not all of a therapist's comments are uncovering in nature. They may simply direct a patient's attention to the existence of a problem. For example, the analyst may point out a contradiction, an inconsistency, an overreaction, or a forgetting. Such interpretations may be called stimulating. There is no sharp line of demarcation between stimulating and revealing interpretations; the former merge gradually into the latter. There are also interpretations that point out some kind of blockage and those that alert the patient to the problems he has not yet resolved. Not all of the analyst's comments are interpretations. Some summarize or repeat, some express an appreciative understanding, and some present a healthy perspective with which the patient can contrast his neurotic belief. The analyst may ask for details or encourage the patient to produce more associations.

The essential aim of all interpretations is to activate a constructive move, to stimulate forward motion. An interpretation may be considered successful if the patient responds to it with both his mind and his feelings. The feelings may be "good" (hope, relief) or "bad" (anxiety), but they are all good, whether pleasant or not, if something is moving ahead. If an interpretation provokes an upset without activating a constructive move, it must be considered unsuccessful. We are not out to provoke upsets for the sake of upset.

Before offering an interpretation to a patient, the analyst must consider a number of things. He must appraise both the productive value and the upsetting power of a particular interpretation at this time in the analytic process. Can the patient use the interpretation? Will it help? Will it foster or disrupt the continuity of the therapy? The analyst must evaluate the pertinence, the accuracy, and the form and spirit of his comments. And he must follow up his interpretations, one with another.

Usually the analyst has a choice of topics on which he may offer interpretations. He must focus on what is most pertinent at the time and not comment on side issues. He must try to select what is most meaningful to the patient and will initiate greatest forward movement. Blockages always have priority because they prevent the patient from progressing. The motto is, "blockages first." Acute blockages, such as forgetting, wanting to quit, etc., are expressions of all the retarding forces operating in the patient. These must be analyzed first or there will be no forward movement.

The Form and Spirit of Interpretations

In what form and spirit is an interpretation to be given? This is always an important question. First, the analyst should strive for a democratic spirit. Analysis is a cooperative enterprise, but the analyst cannot get cooperation just by talking about it or asking for it. If he has a cooperative, democratic spirit himself, his example will speak louder than his words. He must strive to eliminate grandiosity in himself and all need to show off his superior knowledge and ethics. The therapist must realize that he has no corner on intelligence or morals; acting like a schoolmaster or a judge, talking down, preaching are neither democratic nor realistic behaviors. It is well for the therapist always to remember that he is dealing with a particular patient and that his knowledge of this patient is limited. A genuine realization of this fact will help him attain a democratic spirit which, together with an alive curiosity and eagerness (not overeagerness!) will stimulate the patient and help him move in the direction of greater cooperativeness and searching in the therapeutic work.

Second, the analyst should strive for clarity and precision, for greater and greater lucidity. Although he may not be active verbally, he must always be active mentally and emotionally. If he feels vague about something, he should admit that he is groping. Thus, he can say, "I have a vague sense of this possibility."

Third, the analyst should strive to become more and more sensitive to what the patient feels at the time. A greater sensitivity to the patient's feelings will have a positive effect on the lucidity of the analyst's interpretations. Also, it will automatically help him to know whether to present something sympathetically, or seriously, or with humor. Sometimes even the analyst's anger may be helpful, if it is in the real interest of the patient. However, anger which comes from the analyst's neurotic residuals — for example, anger arising from hurt pride or a frustrated neurotic claim — is not helpful, and the analyst must watch out for such reactions in himself. It is important that the analyst understand with ever increasing thoroughness how the patient experiences himself, his life, and other people.

Timing of Interpretations

Here the relevant question is, when does the analyst say what he wants to say to his patient? This question is particularly important with respect to revealing interpretations — that is, interpretations that reveal something which is unknown to the patient and which the patient has an interest in not knowing. Such an interpretation is bound to evoke a defensive reaction. If it does sink in, the patient will experience an emotional response of some kind. The important consideration here is, whether or not the interpretation sets something going in the patient and leads to forward movement. Inevitably, if there is progress, there also will be suffering; our goal is not to prevent or avoid the suffering but to keep it to the minimum consistent with progress.

What are the essential considerations which the analyst must keep in mind when opening up a problem? They include the present condition of the patient, his character structure, the continuity of the analytic work, the order in which problems should be tackled, and the spirit in which the interpretation is offered.

The analyst should be sensitive to how the patient is feeling at the time. Is he feeling abused, hopeless, despairing, contemptuous of himself? At such vulnerable times he cannot handle very much, and the analyst must be cautious in offering interpretations. If there is an upset, however, it should be analyzed, not ignored. The analyst will also assess two other factors in considering the patient's present condition. The first is, what is going on in the analytic relationship? Is the patient being cooperative with the therapist, or does he feel accused and vindictive? The second factor is, are there any circumstances that might affect the patient's ability to utilize an interpretation or the analyst's ability to follow up on it? It is not a good idea to open up a problem, for example, if the analyst is about to go on vacation.

The analyst must try to determine whether or not the patient can do something with a problem in view of his character structure. Can he take back an externalization of self-contempt? Is his present structure strong enough so that he can experience his self-hate as his own? A useful example is that of a patient who expressed angry, hostile feelings toward everyone. The analyst told him that his indiscriminate anger was based on false premises and that not everybody was hostile to him. The patient reacted with skepticism and anxiety. On reflection, the analyst saw that this patient had always assumed that the world was hostile and that he lived in accordance with this belief. He felt that he was being realistic and was proud of his realism, his strength, and his invulnerability. This pride was what had been attacked by the interpretation. The analyst then proceeded with the work by opening up the problem of the patient's need always to be vigilant, and this proved to be acceptable.

Premature interpretations are those which are given before the patient is able to make constructive use of them. Such interpretations are usually the result of the analyst's failure to be clear as to what he is tackling. He does not know what his comment really means to the patient at this time. The analyst with remaining unresolved expansive trends is prone to make premature interpretations. By and large we tend to be overly concerned about premature interpretations; we tend to focus too much on whether or not the patient will get upset, too little on whether or not it will be profitable. Many upsets are unnecessary but most pass by. Most premature interpretations slide off and do not upset the patient — something self-protective operates automatically. It is also true that the patient can usually take more than we think.

There are certain dangers both of premature interpretations and of excessive anxiety about them. In the early stage of analysis, before the patient has developed a fairly good relationship with the therapist, upsetting premature interpretations may cause him to discontinue treatment. Also, caution is necessary in borderline cases. An anxious overconcern about possible prematurity of interpretations has its disadvantages, however. It tends to cramp the analyst's spontaneity and makes for excessive cautiousness. The result often is delayed interpretation. If the analyst is in doubt as to the advisability of tackling a certain problem at a particular time, it is better to postpone the matter and to think it over. If he is still in doubt, consultation with a colleague may help.

What is the analyst to do if he realizes that he has made an interpretation before his patient can utilize it constructively? First, he should think about it afterward and try to learn from it. Secondly, he should drop the matter rather than repeat it futilely and should file it for future reference. Finally, he should try to improve the situation, not by empty reassurance, but by analytic work.

Delayed interpretations are those given to the patient some time after he is ready to use them productively. The usual cause of an unwarranted delay in making an interpretation is the analyst's failure to see something in time. The consequence is an unnecessary loss of time. However, not all delays in making interpretations are inadvertent. Some interpretations are deliberately delayed by the analyst, often because he believes that it is more valuable for the patient to discover something for himself than to have it pointed out to him.

Whether or not this is so depends on the particular patient. When a predominantly self-effacing person discovers something for himself, the result is often not worth much. Therefore, the interpretation is more effective when it comes from the analyst or when he at least echoes the patient's findings. The predominantly expansive person, however, has a need to find out for himself, and by himself. With such a patient the analyst often will find it helpful to put his interpretation in the form of a question. With patients in whom inertia is marked, the analyst may have to be particularly active at times. At other times, however, he may find it more important to encourage the patient to do his own interpreting, pointing out that "my interpretation may mislead you." Sooner or later, this issue may become a problem: why must the patient do it all himself and not let the analyst in on it, and why must a patient have the analyst do it all for him and feel unable to do it himself?

Sometimes a patient will react to a delayed interpretation with the question, "Why didn't you tell me that before?" It is a good idea to answer this question directly. For example, the analyst may say that he did not feel the patient was really ready for it before. But the question itself should be analyzed, particularly if it is repeated often. Such analysis may bring into the open the patient's belief that he should have had the insight himself a long time ago and his self-reproaches for not being as astute as he should be.

Ordinarily we might think that premature interpretations are made by active analysts and that delayed ones occur with passive therapists. This is not necessarily true. There is a long tradition of the analyst as passive observer. This tradition has its good points in that the analyst becomes an astute observer and learns the art of listening. Nowadays, analysts are more active, and actually there is much more to be observed and listened to as a result of this activity. More important than the issue of the analyst's activity or passivity is the question of how successful he has been in helping the patient to change in a positive way.

A feeling for the continuity of the analytic process is essential for the analyst who is interested in the timing of his interpretations. The analyst's task is to try not to disturb the continuity if it is present and to attempt to establish it if it is not. An effort should be made to analyze that part of the neurotic character structure which will open up new areas for investigation, which will produce a minimum of blockages, and which will maintain forward movement and productivity. Failures in the area of continuity lead to scattered interpretations. The analyst should not pick up every point the patient makes, or nearly every point, for this is bewildering.

It is easy to overwhelm a patient by talking about his compulsive self-effacement, his pride, his claims, and perhaps his detachment, all in one hour. Although the observations may be accurate, they lose their effectiveness because of their lack of focus and their multiplicity. The patient has a rhythm of his own of which the therapist should try to become aware, for then he will be able to select for interpretation whatever it is best to tackle at the time.

If interpretations are to be productive, they must be made in the proper order. Since it is the analyst's job to see to it that the work progresses, he must be alert to interferences with forward movement. To repeat what I said before, the motto is "blockages first." Therapists have to be attentive to the patient's secret or open interest in pursuing or not pursuing a problem. We cannot shove something down a patient's throat; his interest is crucial. In the beginning, a patient is not motivated very much by genuine self-interest. He is mainly concerned with preventing interference with his neurotic goals, getting rid of disturbances which hurt his pride, and maintaining the status quo. If a patient has an interest in maintaining claims, he will not be interested in tackling them. Blockages are an alarm signal pointing to a clash between the patient's goals and the analyst's. The patient may have too much at stake, and the analyst may be attacking too vigorously. The patient acts in what, consciously or unconsciously, he believes to be his best interest, which is to prevent himself from feeling torn apart. If what the therapist wants him to examine threatens his defenses too much, he will block. The analyst must realize that some aspects of the patient's defense system are more accessible than others and must offer his interpretations accordingly.

Reactions to Interpretations

It is important for the therapist to analyze and evaluate his patient's reactions to interpretations, for an understanding of these reactions helps him decide how to proceed. He may decide to drop a problem for the time being; he may pursue it further; or he may choose to tackle the attitudes which block productive work on it. The last choice involves determining what the patient is defending and what he is warding off.

There are many possible responses to interpretations. In an ideal response, the patient would take the interpretation seriously, explore it intellectually and emotionally, become convinced that it was right, and test it. This would lead to change. But the patient may have a negative reaction in which the interpretation means nothing to him and he does not respond, or it threatens him and he strikes back blindly. In the face of such reactions, the analyst might make another attempt or two, but not too many. If the response is persistently negative, it might be better for him to drop the matter and think it over.

Most responses to interpretations are neither ideal nor entirely negative. Some typical responses are anxiety, hostility, pseudo-acceptance, temporary interest, and relief.

Anxiety. As I have said before, a revealing interpretation — that is, one which uncovers something of which the patient has had to be unaware — will cause an upset. It will lead to a disturbance of the patient's precarious equilibrium, with resulting anxiety. For example, an interpretation pointing to the existence of exploitive or manipulative tendencies will cause anxiety in a predominantly self-effacing person who is proud of his goodness and unselfishness. Let me emphasize that the significant question is not, is a reaction of anxiety "good" or "bad"? What counts is whether the interpretation stimulates a forward move.

Hostility and an attack against the analyst. Such a response is most likely to occur in predominantly expansive persons whose philosophy is that a good offense is the best defense. What are they defending? All aspects of their neurotic structure, the status quo, comparative freedom from experiencing intense conflict and anxiety. One reason for a hostile reaction to an interpretation may be that it has hurt the patient's pride. This, for example, may be the reaction of a patient proud of his absolute independence and self-sufficiency when the analyst points out the existence of a need for other people. An expression of sympathy may lead to a hostile response because the patient may experience it as humiliation and ridicule, even though the analyst is sincere. A patient may become irritable because he feels that he was a fool to have exposed himself. Or he may react with anger to what he experiences as unfair accusation or condemnation. Often this reaction indicates that he has externalized his self-contempt and is experiencing it as coming from the therapist. A patient may experience an interpretation as wanton cruelty because he feels hopeless about changing, and he reacts with hostility which he may or may not express openly. Dynamically, this reaction is a manifestation of the sensitivity of his neurotic pride and the cruelty of his self-hate. Finally, a patient may resent an interpretation because it frustrates his neurotic claims, which he experiences as legitimate expectations. When the therapist analyzes these claims rather than fulfilling them, the patient may react with hostility. Among the many claims which may be made on the analyst are demands for love, sex, special attention, extra time, immediate relief, quick solutions, painless progress, etc.

Pseudo-acceptance. The patient may react with neither anxiety nor hostility but may listen with apparent seriousness and seem to accept and evaluate the interpretations. But nothing productive follows. Some reactions of this type are based on unconscious expectations of magic. There is the magic of willpower. The patient feels he ought to change something as soon as he becomes aware of it by sheer determination to do so. There is also the unconscious belief in the magic of knowledge. When a patient appears to be enthusiastically interested but nothing happens, he may be indulging in an intellectual orgy, and the analyst must drop the problem at hand and analyze this defense. Or a patient may respond to an interpretation by saying, "I know that already." The function of such a response is to safeguard the patient's pride in his intellectual brilliance; the analyst should never know more than he does. The desire to get by without effort or pain also leads to pseudo-acceptance. Or the patient may take in what is said but with silent reservations, and nothing happens.

There are yet other factors making for pseudo-acceptance of interpretations. There is the glib acceptance of extremely self-alienated patients, who can talk with conviction about anything because nothing really has any meaning for them. There is the dutiful acceptance of the patient who tells himself, "I should accept, and think, and feel, and test." Finally there is the pseudo-acceptance of the self-effacer who is motivated by the need to avoid friction. In such a person, an apparently genuine self-scrutiny may have self-destructive elements in it.

Temporarily aroused interest. Sometimes the patient seems interested, and it appears that the interpretation has started something going, but soon, perhaps in the same hour, or the next, the patient's interest peters out. Such reactions occur in people who respond in the same way in life, with easily aroused enthusiasms which flag if love or success are not obtained quickly.

Relief. Although the experience of relief after an interpretation is not in itself a proof of the productivity of that interpretation, it is often evidence that the analyst is on solid ground and that he can push ahead. The patient may feel relief from the rage of frustration when he sees a claim and the implications thereof, or relief from helplessness and fear of the unknown when he faces a conflict. These are constructive forms of relief. Less constructive is relief from feeling abused in predominantly self-effacing persons who feel safer when they can accuse themselves and avoid friction. In most reactions of relief two factors are involved. First, a concrete problem is substituted for an intangible, mysterious something. Second, the interpretation shows a patient a way out, and gives him some hope. Whenever a patient reacts to an interpretation with relief, the analyst must ask, relief from what?

Blockages in Therapy

This lecture as reconstructed by Joseph Zimmerman was first published in the American Journal of Psychoanalysis *16 (1956), 112–17. The topic of blockages was not listed in the syllabus of Horney's 1946 course, but it appeared in the courses she gave in the early 1950s. This lecture overlaps slightly with "Difficulties and Defenses" in* Final Lectures, *but it is remarkably different given the similarity of topic. Dr. Zimmerman does not seem to have drawn on the 1952 course.*

A patient in analysis wants to change but there are many factors that hinder him. I call these factors "blockages," a term that I prefer to "resistances." Blockages are all the forces that retard the analysis, all the patient's neurotic difficulties and defenses.

Although the patient's defenses produce blockages, they are not altogether obstructive to his growth or his human relationships. For example, the compulsively helpful person may be a good friend. A patient whose major defense is mastery may have a strong impetus to tackle his difficulties. A patient's pursuit of neurotic goals may lead him to seek therapy.

A patient who comes to a physician to obtain treatment for a fractured leg comes in not only with a fracture but also with his attitude toward it. We see something similar in therapy. We must distinguish between the problems for which the patient seeks help and his attitude toward those problems. What a patient withholds or avoids is an expression not only of his difficulties but also of his anxiety about them. It is the ideal patient who, when his pride is pointed out, is eager to examine it. A patient has both difficulties and defenses against recognizing them.

What does the patient defend? He does not defend his whole neurosis, for he is very much interested in getting rid of his symptoms, his inhibitions, his inability to stand up for his beliefs, his shyness, and so on. However, his neurotic strategies have served a purpose and he will defend the values he experiences as "precious" to him. Since he must expose his strategies in the analytic situation, it is not surprising that he will feel attacked and attempt to protect them.

Kinds of Defenses

There are two main kinds of defenses, those having to do with the patient's attitude toward the analyst and those having to do with his attitude toward himself. His defensiveness toward the analyst may be personal or impersonal in nature. On a personal level, he may be hostile or appeasing. He may be defending himself in an impersonal way when over a long period of time nothing seems to happen during the analytic sessions.

This reminds me of a patient whose analysis was stagnant for over six months. She just didn't budge. The defensive passivity she displayed in therapy seemed to pervade her whole life. After a while, I asked her, "Are you not defending something?" In response to this she began to associate about a friend who had died a year-and-a-half previously. She felt that something had been wrong since her friend's death and that it was not grief but "something else," something she had been avoiding. When I asked her whether it was the fact that she could do nothing about her friend's death, she denied this at first; but then the flood of associations that followed clearly indicated that this was the case. She gained a new understanding of her "need for control" and became aware that she had been disturbed by her inability to prevent the death of someone close to her. She then began to associate to the rage she experienced when the analyst missed an appointment. This was followed by anger about the use of anesthetics, her lack of control of her emotions, and her inability to avoid suffering. What started the analytic process moving was her response to the question, "Are you not defending something?" This led to her awareness of her irrational need for control.

In relation to himself, the patient may employ defenses against particular insights and also defenses of a more general kind. For example, the patient may defend himself against a recognition of his "claims." He may feel entitled to his claims and refuse to discuss them. As the analysis progresses, an over-all defense may be uncovered, such as belief in the power of will, which the patient has used to protect himself against an emerging anxiety. He believes that he can make himself into what he wants to be "by an order from his brains." It is always helpful first to find out about a particular defense and then to ask if it is part of a more pervasive defensive strategy.

Patients' defensive maneuvers in therapy will vary depending on their predominant solution. For the detached patient who has a great need for distance, becoming involved is a frightening experience. He has to make himself inaccessible to the analyst's efforts. He maintains an observer attitude and takes up everything the analyst offers with impenetrable politeness. He may also defend himself by forgetting or omitting important information or by withdrawing his interest. He may say "that's enough" or "I haven't enough money to continue," or he may always be on a "running board," ready to jump off at any moment.

The aggressive patient who has a need to fight may use argumentative, assaultive, or defeating tactics, either overtly or covertly. He may express resentment of his analyst for his shortcomings, which he manages to exaggerate. This occurs especially when he experiences his own imperfections. Unconsciously, he desperately attempts to undo whatever progress has been made in analysis.

The self-effacing patient must defend his secret belief that by loving and being lovable he can solve all his problems. He tries to make the analyst less threatening by being disarming or appeasing. Closely allied to this is the maneuver of suffering in which his self-pity is a subtle accusation against the analyst's method of helping him.

Another way of looking at defenses is to divide them into those that affirm positive values and those that have been adopted as a protection against something. For the patient, the values affirmed by his main solution are indispensable to him. They give him a zest for living; a feeling of worth, satisfaction, and strength; and a sense of his rights. He may pursue these values with the vigor and passion of a demon because they give meaning to his life. If he is an aggressive person, he may be obsessed by ambition, power, the need for vindictive triumph. He may delight in tearing others down and ask, "If I am miserable, why should anyone else be happy?" He seeks to attain a feeling of worth through mastery or omnipotence. In contrast, a self-effacing person may be relentlessly driven toward love and feel empty without it. He needs to be accepted by others and to feel useful to them. His value to others gives him a feeling of meaning and worth and is the basis of his claim that he should be well treated by them. The detached person's values will lie in the direction of freedom, independence, and imperviousness to frustration or disappointment.

Protective defenses are also indispensable, but they are not "precious" to the patient. They are essentially defenses of his predominant solution, which can be threatened by therapy, by reality, or by his inner conflicts. Protective defenses include:

a) Distracting or narcotizing maneuvers, such as excessive use of alcohol, drugs, sleep, sex, etc.

b) Warding off the destructive effects of conflicts through "streamlining" and such rationalizations as "Isn't it normal?" or "Isn't it human?" to think, feel and act the way I do. The effects of conflicts can also be warded off through psychic fragmentation (compartmentalizing) and cynicism.

c) Defenses against criticism through guilt and self-contempt ("If I blame myself so much, how can you blame me?") and through arbitrary rightness, pretenses, and belief in the power of will ("I can change any time I choose").

d) Defenses against hurts and disappointments through the adoption of a cavalier attitude.

e) Defenses against awareness of unconscious anxiety through feelings of despair, optimism, hopelessness, and emptiness, and through increased work activities.

f) Defenses against succumbing to "feelings," a sense of being lost, and inertia by holding on tenaciously to rigid "shoulds" and "claims."

g) Overall defenses such as externalization, self-righteousness, and the conviction that one will somehow get by.

How Blockages Manifest Themselves in Therapy

In the analytic relationship, the patient is protecting his vital subjective values, which are being attacked. He has to ward off "finding out," for he experiences this as a threat. There are a number of ways in which his defense of his neurotic solutions produce blockages in therapy.

Obstacles appear from the very beginning of therapy. The patient's motivations are mixed; his constructive wish for health is in conflict with his need to maintain the status quo. His need to be self-righteous or self-sufficient, indeed his whole pride system, stands in his way. His expectations may be either too high or too low. He may just want to tackle one area — perhaps his marriage, his sex life, or problems at work. Such limited expectations reduce his motivation for change. If his expectations are too high, he may feel cheated when he realizes that he cannot attain perfection. An even greater obstacle to successful analysis is a patient's belief that the analyst is a magician and that his problems will be solved without much effort on his own part. Some patients feel that they should be able to solve all their problems through the magic of intellect, "will power," or love. Patients do not enter therapy with reasonable expectations, nor, given their neuroses, should we expect them to.

During the analytic relationship, the patient may unconsciously resort to "blockages" of an acute or a chronic variety. Acute blockages may manifest themselves in the patient's resorting to frequent sexual affairs, alcoholic bouts, or excessive use of drugs. Chronic blockages may be seen in patients who show a marked resistance to change. One manifestation of this is the "negative therapeutic reaction," which occurs when a patient who is beginning to make progress regresses and complains that he is "feeling worse."

There may be blockages in the patient's productivity and ability to associate. He may become silent, listless, or forgetful, or he may show little continuity in his associations. He may lose his eagerness to talk about himself or may complain of "feeling stupid" or being "unable to understand." He may be too dutiful or polite in accepting whatever interpretation the analyst offers, or he may feign reservation of judgment by saying, "Let me think about it." There may be sterile "reports" of what is going on, in the office, outside of it, and in the patient's inner life. If he should talk about what disturbs him, he may make no real attempt to ask why he was irritated or what made him feel better. He may talk primarily of what others think, say, or feel about him.

The very detached patient may omit references to interpersonal relations and only ruminate about his inner experiences. He may have no drive to get to the real significance of what is going on, or he may want to be an "onlooker" and yet want to "find out." He may spend hours describing events and manage to be a "reporter" even in talking about his dreams. He does not want to recognize the significance of his problems and may resort to "sliding off the track" or "figuring out" if the analyst tries to get him to confront them. If you bring up "feelings," he will talk about them or think about them but will look at you blankly when you suggest "feeling them." When he does "feel them," he will call them "silly" or "not important" and refuse to deal with them.

A patient's capacity for being honest with himself may be blocked. He may have no vivid interest in the truth about himself but may produce vagueness, confusion, or an abundance of imagery. He may present the most blatant contradictions without being struck by them. To avoid being aware of his conflicts, he may resort to a great deal of compartmentalization. As a consequence of all this, he is not alert to his pretenses (nor can he be) and is unable to be straightforward about himself. He may omit pertinent material or embellish it so as to obscure the issue being examined. He may minimize a great deal, may be self-recriminatory, or may present everything with militant rightness. Patients may be blocked in their spontaneity, their capacity to "let go." In such cases, they show very little feeling and are quite remote from what they tell you. Consciously or unconsciously, they are unable to let something emerge.

Some patients contribute loads of associations but are passive about putting things together. They say to the analyst, "Here you have it. See what you can do with it." There are others, however, who must be the analyst, who must show what their associations mean. Then there are the patients who can associate better outside the hour than in it. Some patients are naturally slow in their productions, and this should not be confused with blockage.

Blockages may occur in response to the analyst's interpretations. The interpretation may not set anything going, or the patient may react with open denial or disapproval, in which case we at least know where we stand with him. Whatever he may be doing may seem quite reasonable to him. He may say, "Of course, my behavior is somewhat irrational, but by and large it's rational." He will argue that it is natural to want love or to be ambitious. His own attitude is realistic and desirable and everything short of it is unacceptable or downright dangerous. He may justify rigid suspiciousness by affirming that "In the world we live in, it is appropriate." When he becomes aware that he has little feeling for others, he may say, "It is much more desirable to have no feelings than to be hurt." He may defend his defiance by pointing out that in childhood it was life-saving. The patient is protecting the subjective values that belong to his predominant solution.

The patient may show a tendency to jump to extremes. If you call attention to sexual desires, the response may be, "Do you want to make a whore out of me?" If the patient recognizes his callousness, he may say, "If I were not so callous, others would run all over me." If he recognizes his "shoulds," he may say, "But if I didn't have any 'shoulds,' everything would be chaotic." The patient thinks in extreme terms because he is so remote from himself.

Another response to interpretations may be a kind of indirect disproving. The patient may befog or minimize the analyst's observations by saying, "It's all so complicated." He may discard what the analyst says by simply looking blank, not feeling well, or saying that he does not understand or feels confused. Some patients display a seeming acceptance of the analyst's interpretations but make silent reservations. Perhaps unconsciously, they may be telling themselves, "You say I can't get away with things, but I'll show you I can."

Finally, there is the patient who declines responsibility for his own behavior. He will frequently say, "But that's unconscious" or "That's neurotic" — which is a way of denying that the unconscious or neurotic is truly a part of himself. He may feel unfairly accused because he can't help behaving as he does. He may counterattack or use self-pity, self-accusations, or anxiety to deflect what he feels to be the analyst's efforts to blame him.

Blockages often show up in analysis when a patient considers taking a stand or changing an attitude. He may unrealistically demand that he should change immediately and then lament his lack of progress. He will complain: "Analysis makes me worse" or "nothing helps." The patient's resistance to change may take a more subtle form. He may be quite unconcerned about change and insist that he is primarily "concerned with analysis." "Change is another matter." The patient may say that he is actually changing, but the changes may be peripheral rather than essential, or they may not be commensurate with the work done. In such cases, we must try to identify the obstructive forces. Perhaps the patient has not taken his findings seriously or gone through conflict. To what extent has he actually experienced the difficulties he has "talked about"? Is his apparent lack of progress in part determined by his aversion to change itself, the thought of which fills him with anxiety?

In conclusion, in dealing with blockages in therapy we must have a constantly growing awareness of their subtle manifestations. We must attempt to understand them by asking what the patient is trying to defend.

Lecture 8

Dreams

This lecture as reconstructed by Wanda Willig was first published in the American Journal of Psychoanalysis *18 (1958), 127–37. Although the topic of dreams was not in the syllabus for Horney's last course, she lectured on it in 1950 and 1951. In her writings, Horney referred to her theory of dreams but did not develop it in any detail. She thought dreams were very important, however, as "the royal way to the truth of ourselves," and she felt their analysis to be a crucial component of the therapeutic process. In 1945–46, Horney offered a course entitled "The Meaning of Dreams" at the New School for Social Research, in conjunction with Harold Kelman, and she no doubt offered other courses of which no record has survived. The course consisted of fifteen lectures and was described as follows: "Since time immemorial man has searched for the meaning of dreams. The interpretation of dreams offers one of the significant avenues of approach to an understanding of unconscious processes. The first systematic attempt at their interpretation was made by Freud. In this course the discussion of dreams will be based on Horney's theory of neurosis. The basic contention is that dreams represent attempts at solution of conflict." Although the examples could use more development, this lecture is a good introduction to Horney's approach to dreams and makes clear her differences from Freud. The fullest dis-*

cussion of dreams from a Horneyan perspective can be found in Harold Kelman, Helping People: Karen Horney's Psychoanalytic Approach *(1971), chapters 15-20.*

Part I. Theoretical Considerations

In his study of dreams, Freud opened up a vast new territory, too large for any one person to explore. He saw dreams as "the royal road to the unconscious." According to him, dreams aim at wish fulfillment, at the release of sexual tension and the fulfillment of instinctual drives. They are censored by the super-ego, and their content is disguised in symbolic form. Freud conceived of symbols as universal and mainly as expressions of the libido: all elongated objects symbolize the penis, all vaults the vagina, etc. The function of dreams is to release tension and secure continuation of sleep.

Freud saw dreams too exclusively as an attempt at libidinal satisfaction on an infantile level. It was Jung who opened the way to a more fruitful approach to the understanding of dreams. In contrast to Freud, he — and Bjerre — stressed the constructive forces in dreams. In *Das Träumen als Heilungsweg der Seele* [Dreaming as a healing process of the mind] (Rascher Verlag, Zurich, 1936), Bjerre saw dreams as organizing processes with inherent healing tendencies and maintained that the awareness of neurotic patterns we can gain through dreams is in itself liberating and often sets constructive forces in motion. The constructive aspect of dreams is also emphasized by a representative of the Jungian School, Ernst Aeppli, in *Der Traum und seine Deutung* [The dream and its interpretation] (Rentsch Verlag, Zurich, 1943).

Dream symbols are a condensed but accurate expression of processes that are going on in the dreamer, processes that are not necessarily sexual in nature. For example, there are many symbols for the analytic situation that reveal the way in which the patient experiences it — e.g., as digging a tunnel, fishing, washing linen, painting a house, etc. Various objects and people in the dream may be symbols for the dreamer himself. Consequently, the analyst must have a flexible approach to the interpretation of symbols.

MEANING OF DREAMS

In dreams our ideas and feelings may become clarified. For instance, a mathematical problem may be solved, our attitude toward certain difficulties may change, or anger or anxiety may become more apparent. During sleep we are removed from immediate worries, or at least they become submerged, and we are nearer to ourselves and to the problems that really concern us. The sleeping state can be compared to the meditation or retreat of a monk in which the externals of life are put aside and essential issues emerge. Because analysis touches upon essential issues, they frequently appear in the dreams of patients.

Example: In his waking life a patient felt anger toward a taxi driver. He had dreamed the night before that a wild horse was galloping on a beach on which there was a jellyfish. Actually, the patient's anger was directed against himself. The jellyfish in the dream represented himself, and the horse was a symbol of his rage. In dreams one may have a clearer vision of what is really going on in oneself. One may perceive anxiety or conflict or destructiveness of which one is not aware in waking life.

Example: A patient dreamed that she had to give a lesson to a woman at the woman's house. Arriving for the appointment, she told her chauffeur to leave the car since she could drive home by herself. Nevertheless, he drove off. She then turned to the house, which was brilliantly illuminated. A party was going on. She felt excluded, crushed, because she has not been invited, and to her an invitation was a "social must." She would not go any place without being invited. The hostess came out and wanted to discuss matters with her. The patient awoke with a feeling of revelation, for until then she had not been aware how much she felt excluded from everything good in life and how she excluded herself from it.

When we dream we are closer to the reality of ourselves. The great need to play a role is lessened, and hence there is more freedom to express our feelings, conflicts, and drives, which we do in an artistic form. Whereas Freud called the dream the royal road to the unconscious, I see it as the royal way to the truth of ourselves.

Dreams are attempts to solve our problems, usually in a neurotic way but sometimes constructively. One patient dreamed of "a beautiful, pure, white bird," which symbolized her idealized self. She saw herself as a superior being who had attained what she always wanted: beauty, purity, freedom. Another patient who was very dependent on a friend to drive her around dreamt that they were on a motor tour and that she thought: "I could get a driver's license too!" This expressed her desire to become independent and to do things on her own. Dreams that express neurotic fantasies may also contain constructive elements. Thus, in the dream about the beautiful white bird the dreamer found herself up a tree, in a precarious position. When she touched the ground, she felt terrific relief.

It is important for the analyst to be aware of the constructive forces in dreams and to convey this awareness to the patient. In some dreams — such as finding an identification card, finding a way home, being on a mountain road under construction, or dreaming about pregnancy — the constructive element may be obvious. In others, it may be difficult to see. For example, a patient dreamed that he was in a restaurant and that across the table from him was an ugly, repulsive drunk. Then he saw that there was a worm under his skin. He was disgusted and went to a doctor to have it cut out. He wondered why he went to this doctor who had given up practice because his hands were unsteady. This looked like a self-destructive dream, but there were constructive forces in evidence. The patient tried to do something about his problem. Upon analysis, we discovered that the doctor was a friend and a good person and that the dreamer felt that if he were as good, he would get rid of the "wormy" part of himself.

There are constructive meanings in many dreams of death. For example, a patient dreamed that he was in a room with a schoolmate who wanted to jump out of the window. The patient tried to hold him back, but the friend jumped. The patient called for an ambulance. Analysis revealed that the patient wanted to get rid of the sadistic trends that were symbolized by his friend. This could not be done by throwing them out of the window, however, but only by accepting help, which was symbolized by calling the ambulance.

Sometimes we are in doubt as to a correct interpretation of a dream. One patient constantly dreamed about being executed, and her mother always appeared in these dreams. The patient was rather unconcerned about her executions, which were expressions of her total self-condemnation. She had contempt for her mother, who had actually strangled her life, but she had internalized too many of her mother's views, such as the belief that it was her duty to sacrifice her life for her parent. She believed that she understood this demand "rationally," but she could not free herself from it. Since she suffered from self-condemnation, she was also punishing herself for being neurotic. When her self-condemnation was tackled, the character of her dreams changed, and she began to rebel against being executed.

While working on her dreams, this patient more fully experienced the futility of her life with her mother, who was a silly woman and a strangling octopus. The mother had contributed to the formation of the patient's idealized image by her insistence that a good daughter should sacrifice her life for her mother. The daughter had adopted her mother's values, but she nevertheless condemned herself for submitting to them. When she began to rebel, she started having dreams that revealed her mother as she actually was.

ESSENTIAL CHARACTERISTICS OF DREAMS

Jung claims that dreams present the inner truth of the dreamer, the inner reality as it is, not as we suppose it to be. I believe that dreams are visions (*Wesenschau*) of our essential being, intuitive insights into our inner processes, experiences of what is going on in ourselves. Anxiety, anger, feeling lost, feeling elated — all these are experienced more deeply and more clearly in our dreams. Since feelings in dreams are of paramount importance, it is essential to ask the patient, "What were your feelings in this or that part of the dream?" If there seems to be a discrepancy between the feeling and the situation in the dream, either we have not understood the situation correctly or the dreamer cannot respond to it emotionally. For instance, if a patient dreams of a dangerous situation without feeling anxiety, it may mean that there is no danger or that he is so self-alienated that he cannot yet experience an appropriate anxiety.

Dreams concern what we like, what we dislike, what disturbs us, our conflicts, our pride, our subconscious, and our relationship to other people. They almost always express an aspect of the dreamer himself. Jung speaks of two levels in dreams: the subjective (all I) and the objective (I and others). But the objective is also subjective, since dreams in which others appear tell us what we see in them, what we feel about them, what we want them to do or want to do to them. Other persons in dreams are often aspects of ourselves. For instance, in the execution dreams of the patient previously mentioned, the mother's callous unconcern about the daughter's fate expressed the dreamer's acceptance of her fate and lack of concern for herself.

Dreams are dramatic expressions of mainly unconscious processes which we do not recognize, or are averse to recognizing, or have a special interest in not knowing about. The degree of unconsciousness may vary immensely. Dreams may be so far removed from real life that we can do nothing with them in analysis. Other dreams, close to awareness, are immediately clear.

There is increased self-awareness in dreams. In waking life we are busy rationalizing, maintaining illusions, making compromises, etc. All these processes recede during sleep. Our highways and byways of defensive reasoning are gone and now we can look inward. A vision of the character structure and of unconscious factors emerges.

FUNCTIONS OF DREAMS

Freud asserted that we are driven by unconscious instincts which press for release and seek to find it in dreams. Even in dreams, our instincts have to be disguised because of the prohibitive forces of the super-ego. Jung feels that many dreams rectify a life situation and have a compensatory function. In *Das Traümen als Heilungsweg der Seele,* Bjerre speaks of the spontaneous healing function of dreams, comparing them to such physiological processes as white blood-cells gathering in an abscess.

I feel that dreams may be part of a healing process in which the undermining of neurotic positions and the emergence of self-realizing tendencies occur simultaneously. We can interpret many dreams as though the real self of the dreamer were saying to him: "Look how you despise yourself! Look what you are doing to yourself, how you are divided, what phantoms you are chasing, what a crooked path you are following, what a foul compromise you are trying to make!"

Although some dreams are directed toward self-realization, the neurotic drive toward self-idealization is expressed in them also. In most of us, both drives are active, one more, the other less. A dream can be in the service of self-idealization and the need to chase after phantoms. In dreams of self-loathing, the idealized self may be looking at the real self with contempt. In dreams of getting by, the patient may be very proud that he was able to do it.

Dreams are often attempts to resolve conflicts and to achieve inner unity. Dreams usually arise from some disquieting pressure, whether it be of conflicting drives, fear, vindictiveness, a desire to free oneself from shackles, etc. Under this pressure, a search goes on to solve one's particular problem. We should try to determine what the disquieting factor is from which the dream arises and how the dream deals with it. In order to make a valid interpretation of a patient's dreams, the analyst's understanding must include his whole character structure, including both constructive and neurotic elements.

Part II. Dream Interpretation

The language of dreams is symbolic. It is an attempt to express something in pictures, as in a work of art. It would require a great many words to express what is said in the simple, condensed story of a dream, with its well-chosen symbols. The following dream may serve as an example. A patient goes with someone to buy a secondhand submarine in order to dive down into the ocean to see a sea monster (the monster represents his hidden destructive forces and callous trends). Curtains can be pulled down over the portholes if the sight of the monster is too disquieting.

Symbols for the analytic situation may be a school, a laundry, a basement, an excavation. They may also take the form of espionage, kidnapping, being exposed and attacked. The analyst may ask the patient why the dream presents its meaning through the use of its particular symbols. "School" would be a symbol for a person who thinks of the analytic situation mainly as a process of learning. The patient who dreamt of analysis as an excavation had a fear of falling into an abyss. A patient who does not think of changing but of covering up may dream of hanging wallpaper or putting on slipcovers.

An example of symbolic self-representation is a patient's dream about wildcats. At first he associated wildcats with women, but then he realized that they were an aspect of himself. To him, wildcats represented something that cannot be tamed, and he was very proud of being indomitable.

Patients tend to be afraid that they will be blamed for their dreams. There is no moral responsibility, of course, and we should not convey reproach, but patients must accept their dreams as expressions of their own inner dynamics. We have to tell the patient that this is *his* dream so that he can say to himself, "I am responsible: this is my dream and I must recognize that this is going on in me." In this way he will become interested in his dreams and what they can tell him about himself.

It is important for the analyst to assist the patient in interpreting his dreams. He may wish to avoid doing this because he fears hurting the patient to help him, but even if he senses that the patient is vulnerable, he must not evade this responsibility.

ANXIETY DREAMS

Anxiety dreams are a great help in understanding our conflicts. A dream may not overtly contain the affect of anxiety but may hint at it through dim lighting or a setting of dark, deserted streets. When the dream contains openly felt panic in a dangerous situation, the dreamer may awaken with anxiety, or with an attack of asthma or some other affliction.

When analyzing anxiety dreams we have to ask the following questions: What is the endangering factor? What is endangered? In what ways does the dreamer feel helpless and why? When we try to determine the endangering factor, we may discover tendencies that endanger the dreamer's idealized image — sadistic impulses in a self-effacing person, for example, or dependency in an aggressive one. If feelings of true friendliness emerge in the course of analysis and are reflected in dreams, this may endanger the dreamer's detachment or his need to be callous and brutal, so that even what the analyst regards as progress may feel dangerous to the patient. Or the patient may feel that tendencies toward growth are endangered. One patient dreamed of two lovely boys who symbolized his constructive trends. One of the boys was perched on a branch, and, afraid the boy would fall, the dreamer awoke in a state of anxiety. A feeling of helplessness may result from the dreamer's sense of being caught in a neurotic conflict. In a severely self-alienated patient, it may be a sign that he is becoming aware of his problems but does not know what to do about them.

PATIENTS' ATTITUDES TOWARD DREAMS

Patient's attitudes toward their dreams vary considerably. Some patients describe their dreams casually and find no meaning in them. Others do not bring associations to their dreams. Often there is little awareness of unconscious forces and no understanding of them. There are patients who spend the whole session telling their dreams but leave little time to discuss them. Usually these are people who live extensively in imagination as, for instance, writers whose existence has little meaning for them outside of their writings. But not all patients who live in imagination do this. Detached patients often show great interest in dreams but remain "scientific." They want to solve the puzzle of the dream but not to apply the dream to their lives. There also are patients whose interest in dreams is primarily intellectual or who find their dreams to be a source of aesthetic delight. Some patients like to talk about dreams because this gives them something to report or because they associate beautifully. The discussion of dreams will be sterile if patients consider it only "their duty" or "obligation," feel that they "should understand," or fail to connect dreams with the rest of their lives. In some cases, patients who are otherwise productive in analysis may deal with their dreams in a cavalier fashion. They may be witty and interested in some trend but impatient with details.

In people who are given to shallow living, there may be a discrepancy between what is revealed by their dreams and the surface smoothness of their lives, and the analyst should call attention to this disparity. Only in dreams does the depth of their problems show. There may be self-destructive impulses and a whole set of conflicts of which they have no conscious awareness. The analyst's work might then be compared to the digging of an archeologist, who finds evidence of one culture at one level and of a completely different culture underneath.

There are those whose dreams appear seldom or not at all, and those who have frequent dreams while continuing to deny the existence of the unconscious. Some patients have scarcely any dreams at certain periods. Is there a fear of unconscious processes? Some patients dream rarely but in ample detail. A woman patient who was functioning fairly well and was quite productive in therapy was still unaware of the tyranny of the "shoulds" which kept her in bondage. She dreamt first of one prisoner and then, recurrently, of a whole row of prisoners, all connected with a rope which they wound around themselves, hiding one man. The dreamer felt only horror. She could not see that the dream was showing her how imprisoned she was by her inner demands. Only much later did she recognize and experience these demands, as well as the disorder in her own inner self, which was quite a contrast to the outward order in her life. Her strong dislike of seeing her inner condition explained the rarity of her dreams.

ANALYSIS OF DREAMS

In analyzing a dream, we must try to get the general meaning, work on details, and seek to understand what provoked the dream and what solution it provides. Recall the dream in which the patient's schoolmate, who symbolized his sadistic self, jumped out the window. The patient himself suggested the general meaning. The dream was provoked by the previous analytic session in which the patient had seen his brutal egocentricity. He then tried to do away with it in the dream.

In addition, we should analyze the neurotic trends and inner conflicts that appear in the dream and connect them with the patient's life, with what is currently going on in him. The analyst can help in this process by asking questions, making suggestions, and offering tentative interpretations. All that is said in the same session may be related to the dream.

If attempts to understand the dream fail, do not pursue the matter but keep the dream in mind because later associations may throw light on it. Referring back to the dream gives the patient the feeling that you are vitally interested in it and inspires him to become interested also. If the dreamer does not bring many associations to the dream, do not ask in general, "What occurs to you about the dream?" but be specific. Ask: "Is there any part of the dream which made you think of something?" Or choose a specific symbol or theme and connect it with those of previous dreams.

There are many other questions to pursue. What are the feelings in the dream? Are they appropriate to its content? Feelings in dreams are most important, for such emotions as overwhelming sadness, nostalgia, anguish, and pity always come from the patient's depths. How is the dreamer symbolized? What is his goal? How far is he removed from himself? For example, the patient who dreamt of prisoners felt horror, but her self-destructiveness was still externalized. Where is she in the dream? She still does not recognize the tyranny she is imposing on herself. Is the dreamer passive or active? What is he doing in the dream? Is he aware of his role? The analyst should not be too easily satisfied. Ask what a particular symbol means to the dreamer, not what he thinks in general about Aunt Julie, who appeared in his dream. What is the attitude of the dreamer toward other figures in the dream? Is he distant, close, compliant, suspicious? Does he show much feeling for himself, or is he a spectator of the dream, regarding it as though it were a piece of fiction.

The analyst must try to feel himself into the dream in an effort to grasp its inner meaning. A patient who had experienced the impact of her pride while on vacation dreamed that she was in a car with her mother, a woman obsessed with prestige. They were going to visit a person whose main quality was healthy warmth. The analyst said, "Don't you mean to convey that healthy warmth is overcoming the need for prestige?" This was a shift in values which, until the dream, the patient had rejected as weakness.

We must not overlook the constructive forces in dreams. Ask yourself,

"What is really constructive in this dream and how constructive is it?" Even dreams which only present us with our problems are potentially constructive. Awareness of neurotic qualities is not constructive if the patient still invests pride in them. A patient may acknowledge his deceitfulness but still defend or glorify it. Awareness of neurotic qualities becomes constructive when the patient experiences disgust in the dream, and asks, in a sudden awakening, "What am I doing to myself?" Dreams are also constructive when a patient takes a stand or deals with anxiety or conflict.

Free Association

This lecture as reconstructed by Sara Sheiner was first published in the
American Journal of Psychoanalysis *27 (1967), 200–08. Dr. Sheiner's
notebooks, which are currently in my possession, indicate that the lecture was based on the courses Horney gave on psychoanalytic technique
in 1946 and 1952. Because it is partly derived from Horney's last course,
there is a fair amount of overlap with "Free Association and the Use of
the Couch" in* Final Lectures, *but there is also much material that cannot
be found there or anywhere else in Horney's writings. Except for* Self-
Analysis, *Horney's books and essays give little indication of the importance she ascribed to free association in the therapeutic process.*

Free associating means revealing oneself with utter frankness. It is telling
what one is thinking and feeling without selecting, preparing, figuring out, or
holding back. It requires the patient to be simultaneously relaxed and concentrated on experiencing his inner life. It is not the same as rambling, which also
involves saying whatever comes into one's mind but in a way that may be
superficial rather than connected to one's inner depths. Free association allows
the emergence of any kind of image, feeling, or memory without prejudgment.
It is a process of being attentive to one's inner self that leads to sincerity and
depth of feeling.

The word "associations" suggests a series of connections between individual images, feelings, and thoughts. As one association flows into another, we can see a unity and central meaning emerge. A group of associations constitutes a set, the components of which may be more clearly related to each other than to components of other sets. But these sets are not discrete entities. They are like a series of short stories, each of which has its own plot, theme, and characters and is separate from the other stories in the group, but each of which is also connected to the others in some way.

Characteristics of Free Association

Associations may take the form of anything at all that it is possible to experience consciously. They may be physical sensations such as hunger, or a wish, a fantasy, an image, a memory, an impulse to action, an idea, a word, or a phrase. A person known or unknown may come to mind, or a poem, or a melody. Associations may be responses to prior associations, to something the analyst has said, or to something he has done or not done. Although they are experienced in the present and are expressive of present states, they may refer to past, present, or future, or they may not be fixed in time at all. They may express intentions towards someone else, or they may go in the direction of self-exploration and a search for deeper meanings. While feeling a strong conflict about some decision, a person may recall a past event with stronger emotions than he had when the event actually occurred. Exploring the intensity of his feelings may lead to the clarification of his conflict.

When associations are "free," they are not constrained by self-judgment or concern for the impression made on the listener. We allow the emergence of inner states without regard to tact, organization, relevance, or logic. We are free of one kind of purposefulness in that no free association is consciously goal-directed as to content, form, or effect, sequence or coherence. At the same time, free association is purposeful in its dedication to letting things emerge and searching for the truth of oneself. Being "free" requires the courage to take a chance on oneself, the strength to tolerate anxiety, and a capacity to confront that which is unacceptable. It requires an ability to experience the reality of oneself and to cope with the analyst's response. While he is free associating, the patient can have no program or plan for dealing with specific issues but allows whatever comes to emerge. Even at times when the use of reason is valuable, allowing a free flow of associations may be more productive than highly focused thought.

Associating varies in its degree of freedom and spontaneity. Whatever a person says, planned or unplanned, has roots in unconscious processes and hence reflects and reveals these processes. A prepared series of self-observations or a rehearsed dream are not very "free" but are nonetheless revealing. Absolutely free associating would be the ideal, but it is not possible, of course. In any given hour a patient reports, reasons, free associates, makes connections. The ability to let go will vary from time to time and from person to person.

The Importance of Free Association

Patient and analyst are bound by an implicit agreement to work together in searching for the truth and fostering the patient's growth toward self-realization. Revealing himself to the analyst is fundamental to this mutual work and is one of the ways in which the patient fulfills his part of the contract. Free associating is a very important aspect of the self-revealing process. The most important data for the mutual work comes from what is going on in the patient, and the more freely he allows his associations to emerge, the more fully the analyst can grasp the inner dynamics of his personality. Allowing things to emerge helps the patient to overcome his impulse to withhold and select. It keeps the focus on what is going on in him and heightens his self-awareness.

The less controlled the patient's associations, the more productive they will be. They will lead the patient to a spontaneous recognition of the connections between his attitudes, his compulsions, and his behavior. The more he free associates, the more he participates in the work. Free associating puts a check on the patient's rambling or digressing in a search for something to say.

Educating the Patient to Free Associate

Educating the patient in the use, meaning, value, and purpose of free associating is a part of the analyst's work. Although many people come into psychoanalysis with some concept of free associating, it is valuable to make a simple statement about it at the beginning, in clear language. The analyst should mention that everyone has difficulties in letting go, but he should not overwhelm the patient with the difficulties. If the patient is not too anxious, it is advisable to explain during the first few sessions that analysis is a cooperative undertaking; that the analyst has an interest in everything the patient feels and thinks; that although he has training and experience, the analyst is an outsider to the patient, who has all the raw data; and that since it is the analyst's function to help the patient formulate and clarify the data, it is important for the patient to tell the analyst everything that comes to him without selecting. However, if the patient is anxious, it is best to say very little about free associating at first. In any event, a patient may grasp very little of what has been said at the beginning.

Simply pointing out that free association is desirable will not bring it about, nor will repeated injunctions to free associate. Through most of his analysis, the patient will have many blocks to free associating. These are the direct expression of the conflicts for the resolution of which he has come into psychoanalysis. Educating the patient as to the nature of these blocks is one way of helping him to free associate more effectively. Since associating freely is so difficult, the analyst needs to find ways to encourage the patient to express what comes from his depths in an uncontrolled way. One way is to show the patient that the sequence of emerging thoughts and feelings is full of meaning, perhaps by identifying the unifying theme that he infers to be present in seemingly disconnected associations. Or the analyst may associate to the patient's associations, and if his associations have meaning to the patient, this will help him see the value of allowing things to emerge freely.

The process of free association provides rich analytic material. When the patient expresses fears about saying something tactless or irrelevant, a search for an explanation of these fears may elicit previously unperceived aspects of the association. In the same way, fears of being indiscreet, hostile, or trivial may be explored for their meaning. It is often productive to ask what went on in the patient just prior to his recalling a particular event of his life.

The patient's responses to the idea of free association can be informative to the analyst. Some patients are overwhelmingly compliant. They may try to follow the principles of free association in a literal way, by discarding, for example, any thought that came to them on the way to the office, even though it recurs during the analytic hour. Others will not tell of any events or insights that have occurred between sessions on the premise that such reporting is not a "pure" association or not "absolutely" uncontrolled. Others show perfectionism in their attempts to follow up and elaborate on every association to an association, thus becoming lost in details. Others elaborate on how the association came to them and justify its occurrence or defend it.

The analyst can expect a good deal of resistance to the practice of free association. On hearing of free association, some patients dread a loss of control. They are afraid that they will be swept away if they speak in any but an organized way. Some patients avoid free associating by reporting on intervening events, or presenting an organized life history, or focusing on their responses to external stimuli, such as noises in the street. Some people brush aside free associating with a conscious feeling that such a method does not really pertain to them, either because they are above it or because they are too sick. Others think they are free associating while really editing and selecting, with the conscious belief that they are thereby improving upon what would otherwise be "scattered."

To What Must the Analyst Attend?

Although the patient may want to be cooperative and tries to free associate, he cannot do it well at the beginning. His conflicts and defenses, anxieties and compulsions, affect the free emergence of his thoughts and feelings. The skill of the analyst lies in identifying those of the patient's associations which will lead to what is most available for work at that time. Through his art, the analyst elicits the patient's interest in discovering the truth about himself and helps him overcome his blocks.

The analyst must train himself to attend to the following things: (1) the factual data that emerge; (2) the deviations from a free flow of associations; (3) the spirit in which a patient associates; (4) the sequences of associations; (5) the omission of certain areas of a patient's life; (6) contradictions, discrepancies, and inconsistencies.

1. *Factual Data.* Much that is important for the conduct of the analysis is inferred from the facts of the patient's life history. The order and the manner in which these facts are presented reveal much about the patient and about the availability of various aspects of his personality for work in analysis. The state of the patient's physical health, past and present, is significant. Factual data from the present include the patient's free associations and his responses to interpretations and other aspects of the analytic process.

2. *Deviations from Free Flow.* Deviations from a free flow give the analyst clues as to difficulties and blockages which may be either general or specific to currently emerging feelings.

Sometimes the analyst senses that the patient is holding back, consciously or unconsciously. Since the analyst may be wrong about this, he should be cautious about telling the patient that he believes he is withholding something. Withholding may be evidenced by silence, long pauses, a sudden shift in content to something which seems grossly disconnected. It may be inferred from the combination of a listless voice and visible anxiety. Or it may be inferred from the content of the associations, such as an association about a diplomat who deliberately withheld information. Sometimes it is productive to ask the patient simply if he is leaving something out.

A "flight of ideas" that sounds like free associating may be another deviation from a free flow. A flight of ideas may be indicated by a light tone of voice or by shallowness of language or feeling tone. It tends to be disjointed and superficial, and the patient is easily distracted by tangential issues. Sensitivity to his own responses can help the analyst to recognize a flight of ideas. For example, he may have a strong feeling that he is being told nothing of significance or a feeling that he can find no connecting theme. Generally there *is* no theme if the analyst has to strain to find one or comes up with something far-fetched. It may be productive to tell the patient he seems scattered. Flights of ideas may occur at the beginning of the analysis as a result of the patient's efforts to comply with the idea of free associating. They may be indicative of a weak sense of self or of general or current anxiety.

Some patients come to their sessions with fixed programs, having decided beforehand the order in which they are going to mention certain things, or the way in which they are going to develop their thoughts. Sometimes they bring notes on how a specific insight came to them. We may infer perfectionism and needs for rigid control from these behaviors. It may be helpful to remind the patient of the value of allowing things to emerge.

Others "report" thoughts, feelings, and events that have occurred between sessions, following a chronological order in their account. This is not the same as having a preplanned program, but may indicate a need for self-definition and identity through adherence to the concrete reality of time sequences, thus indicating alienation from self. Others who have a tendency to report have an onlooker attitude toward themselves. They are often excellent observers but have unconscious fears of experiencing feelings or of exploring their deeper significance. Some patients who report have a fear of letting go of conscious controls and allowing unconscious processes to manifest themselves. When it is timely and relevant, it is advisable to go into the implications of "reporting."

A tendency to theorize also interferes with free associating. This is frequent in patients who expect to be able to cope with life through reason and intellect. Or a person may be elusive, scattered, and jumpy in a way that is bewildering to the analyst. The associations appear to be connected, and the patient may move smoothly from one association to another, but a close examination of the connections shows that they are based on such superficial things as a tangential reference, a continuity in time, or a similarity of proper names. In such cases, the analyst often finds that although he felt he had comprehended the patient, he had not, for he cannot put his understanding into words. He may feel vague, left up in the air, or misled.

3. *Spirit of Free Associations.* The quality of the patient's interest in finding out about himself may be shown in *how* he associates. His associations may indicate a wanting to learn and be informed, or they may reveal that he regards analysis as just an entertaining form of intellectual exercise. He may avoid associating by asking theoretical questions and bringing in material for discussion which he has obtained from reading. When associating, he may jump

from topic to topic without much interest in any of them or respond with evasive moves if the analyst tries to focus on some particular point. He may be talking just for the sake of talking. He may be showing a spirit of docility, as though trying to live up to the analyst's expectations, and may ask how he is doing. He may act like he is a pupil at school. He may associate as though he is confessing and trying to gain absolution, or he may seem to be trying to defend himself against subtle self-recriminations. Such attitudes, which indicate little interest in genuine self-knowledge, show up in his posture, his tone of voice, and in the content and sequence of his associations. The analyst's personal feelings and associations may help him to become aware of the spirit of his patient's associations. When he is certain that there is a lack of interest, he should make the patient aware of this and try to discover the cause.

Changes in the spirit of associating are significant. Important questions are: When and under what circumstances is the patient systematic, scattered, reportorial, or spontaneous? When does he shift from one mode to another? Do these shifts occur in response to the analyst's comments or to an insight of his own?

Sometimes the spirit of the patient's associating is part of the dynamics of his relationship with the analyst. If the patient goes into great detail, it may indicate his need to impress the analyst with his perfection and the completeness of his observations, or it may indicate a need to show the analyst that he knows everything or has thought of everything himself. An expansive patient may be competing with the analyst or trying to prevent him from seeing anything.

Some patients have a need to organize and to figure things out. Their ideas may follow one another in an orderly progression. At first, figuring out may be helpful, but eventually the patient will confront things he cannot "understand." When the patient has a need to organize, it is good to keep his vulnerability and fragility in mind, while reminding him of the value of letting go.

It is important to develop a sensitivity to the continuity of associations, since this can lead the analyst not only to find themes in the patient's productions but also to recognize shifts in the quality and spirit of associations that indicate underlying needs. For example, what does it mean when a patient makes a quick transition from his own problem to the manifestation of that problem in some big generalization like "the democratic process?"

Similarly, an ear for the lucidity and pertinence of associations can help an analyst feel the "how" of the associations as well as help him see themes and connections. What are the needs behind a vague, diffuse, or evasive description of an event that was very important in the patient's life? What are the needs behind describing an irrelevant event in great detail?

The analyst should pay attention to what the patient is feeling and the degree to which he is feeling while he is associating, since this is just as important as the content of the association. Is the patient speaking under pressure? Does he sound as though he were fighting against resistances? Is he anxious or embarrassed?

Productivity in associating varies from patient to patient and hour to hour. The analyst must be attentive to how active the patient can be in his own behalf. At times some people can be very active in seeing connections and deeper meanings. Some are active between hours but not very productive during analytic sessions. Some say what is on their minds but seem uninterested in making connections, leaving that to the analyst, as though it were not their province to connect or see meanings. This indicates a passivity. Shifts from activity to passivity are significant, as are changes in productivity, and both might be analyzed.

Although repetitive themes are important aspects of the content of associations, their incidence is also pertinent to the spirit of associating. When some theme comes up over a number of hours, it is obviously important to the patient. It is helpful to note the varying forms the theme may take, the intensity with which it is brought up, the degree of personal involvement the patient feels with it. It is important to ask why the theme reappears so frequently. It may be related to the patient's need for safety or his pride, or he may be genuinely puzzled by some aspect of his life and be trying to gain insight into it. The repetition of something positive may indicate a need for reassurance or a desire to reinforce a feeling of hopefulness.

4. *The Sequences of Associations.* The movement from one theme to another can help the analyst draw conclusions as to underlying meanings of a train of associations. For example, in one hour, a man went through the following sequence of associations: his hatred for a group of dominating people; feelings of deadness; anger at an acquaintance who was inaccessible to reason and showed a cold and inhuman disregard for individuals; and conflict about going to a meeting, feeling that he did not want to go but considering himself a traitor if he did not. Hatred and anger stand out if one looks at the emotions only, but if one follows the sequence, one can see that it points toward the patient's feeling browbeaten by his own relentless suppression of his individual needs.

Sequences during one session can point to current problems. Sequences over a number of hours can illuminate a problem as it is being worked out over a period of time. Reviewing the sequences with the patient helps to involve him in the analytic work. It gives him a sense of his own continuity as well as a feeling for the ramifications of a problem.

5. *Omissions.* In any analysis, patients give some feelings and experiences

more attention than others. Some areas of life become glaring, however, by their omission. The patient omits, selects, and deemphasizes in accordance with what he is unconsciously defending or the anxieties he is avoiding. He may ignore factual data and dwell on fantasies, thoughts, and sensations. He may tell the analyst little about his life history. Or he may leave out specific areas of his life, such as work, education, parents, friends, interests, accomplishments, or failures. Some people identify no one by name, saying for example, "my oldest brother, you know, the one out West." Others may name their employer and co-workers but refer to the members of their immediate family as "the wife," "the boy," or "the girl." One man connected his development to the sociological structure of big cities, ignoring entirely the significant members of his family. Some patients may not mention specific people or people in general. Others may focus only on other people and events, ignoring themselves and their own feelings. Patients may avoid talking about their emotional lives in general or certain specific emotions such as love, anger, joy, or fear. One person may leave out aesthetic experience, another all moral concerns. A patient may talk about his feelings toward other people but omit any reference to his emotional response to the analyst. Some patients never mention anything constructive but focus only on suffering and pain.

In each instance, the analyst should try to determine the meaning of the omission. Is it consistent or inconsistent with other aspects of the patient's personality? What is he defending? What is he trying to gain?

6. *Contradictions, Discrepancies and Inconsistencies.* Just as sequences are illuminating, so are disparities between feelings, attitudes, and actions, as when a person is self-effacing with authorities and crudely violent when he is in power himself. One patient described himself as liking other people and wanting peace at any cost but was argumentative and defiant in his behavior. The term "discrepancy" implies a discordance in a person's feelings or attitudes. For example, a man experiencing intense panic telephoned his analyst out of a desperate need for help, but while dialing he felt himself swelling with arrogance. "Inconsistency" implies a lack of cohesion between elements that one would expect to fit together. One patient spoke consistently of the growth of his business and his pleasure in being successful, but his voice lacked conviction. He appeared pleased, however, when he occasionally mentioned that he was worried about not having enough money.

A sensitivity to contradictions, discrepancies and inconsistencies leads the analyst directly to the patient's conflicts and to his strategies for dealing with them. It is important to ascertain how aware the patient is of these conflicts. If aware, does he rationalize them and then feel satisfied? Which side of a conflict has the greater emotional force? Does he disregard one side as inconsequential? What are his responses when his conflicts are brought to his attention?

By focusing on free associations in the ways outlined above, the analyst can help the patient become involved with himself and make the therapeutic process one of ever-increasing self-awareness.

Evaluation of Change

This lecture as reconstructed by Ralph Slater was first published in the American Journal of Psychoanalysis *20 (1960), 3–7. The concluding lecture of Horney's 1952–53 course was to have been "Evaluating the Patient's Progress: Termination," but she did not live to deliver it. I have not found any discussion of the evaluation of change in Horney's notes for the courses she gave in the early 1950s, but she spoke on "Evaluating Changes in the Patient" in her 1946 course. I assume it is that lecture Dr. Slater has reconstructed.*

Our task as psychoanalysts is to help our patients change. We conceive of neurosis as a character disorder, a way of life in which a person is compulsively driven in an unhealthy direction by a variety of rigid and conflicting needs. This precarious way of life begins in childhood with basic anxiety and the development of defenses to cope with it. It continues with the person's desperate attempts to resolve the basic conflict between his defenses through the creation, with the help of imagination, of an idealized image of himself. Our therapeutic aim is to help our patients change from striving mainly to actualize their idealized images to striving mainly to actualize their real selves. Unless there is change in this direction, we cannot say that our therapeutic endeavors have been succesful. It is not enough that a patient acquire insight, that he become aware of something he did not know previously, since knowledge without inner change is sterile. It is essential that we evaluate the degree and nature of change in our patients if we are to assess accurately the effectiveness of our work. This is more easily said than done, since many factors make it difficult to evaluate change.

Difficulties in Evaluating Change

We are dependent to a large degree on what the patient communicates to us during the analytic hours. We do not have the opportunity to observe him at home and at work, among relatives, friends, and strangers. Also, we do not interview his wife, children, teachers, employers, employees, and peers. In short, we do not have the benefit of the observations of others, including people who see a good deal of him and who may have known him for a long period of time. It should be added, however, that the fact that the analyst does not see the patient as often as the members of his family and his close associates also has its advantages. A certain distance and objectivity may make it possible for the analyst to recognize and evaluate changes which are not perceived by those who live with the patient and see him daily.

The patient's own statements concerning the ways in which he has or has not changed are often unreliable. For one thing, some patients are unconsciously compelled to exaggerate the degree of their improvement; they bring in reports of how much they have progressed in much the same spirit as the pupil who presents his teacher with a shiny red apple. Some patients may exaggerate their progress because they are overly optimistic. There are other patients with equally powerful unconscious motives who are compelled to minimize or deny any change or improvement. Included in this group are patients who have to belittle the analyst and the therapeutic process, and those who have an intense aversion to change. In neither case can the analyst take at face value the patient's statements about his progress.

Another consideration is that the patient's and the analyst's concepts of progress often do not coincide. Thus, a patient may feel gratified because he has become more successful in taking revenge on those who hurt his pride or frustrate his claims. In such a case, the analyst will recognize that the patient has changed, but not in the direction of self-realization. He will make the same judgment about a patient whose change is a behavioral but not an inner one.

To the degree that they persist, the analyst's neurotic tendencies will warp his judgment and make it difficult or even impossible for him to estimate the extent and nature of the patient's change. Thus, the analyst in whom resignation has persisted as a way of life may be blind to evidences of change in the patient because resignation involves an aversion to change and a disbelief in it. The therapist who needs to cure all his patients and to do so as rapidly as possible may see more change than has in fact occurred. Even without such neurotic residuals in the therapist, it is inherently difficult to recognize changes in the patient, since they are often subtle and slow to develop.

External changes may affect the patient, making it difficult for the analyst to determine whether the person's improvement (or, for that matter, his worsening) is due to them, or to the therapeutic process, or to both in varying degrees. Such factors as marriage, divorce, the death of a relative or friend, and economic and occupational success or failure may bring about changes in a patient. Some patients are more disposed to attribute change in themselves to external factors than is actually warranted. Analysts are less likely to do so, since they are not compelled to externalize to the same degree. We can attempt to determine change in the patient by asking whether there is less of the neurotic in the patient. Is the person less driven by compulsions? Is he, for example, less pushed around by needs indiscriminately to please and placate others, to subordinate himself to others, to provoke abuse? Is he less compelled to belittle and disparage people, to prove himself superior and to triumph vindictively over them? Is he less coerced by a need to attain perfect freedom and self-sufficiency? Is he less anxious and less driven by an insatiable ambition? Does he make fewer irrational claims on people and on life? Is there a diminution in the rigidity and extent of his perfectionistic standards and of the severity of his self-contempt and self-accusation? Does he externalize less — that is, does he have less need to attribute his inner feelings and thoughts to people and institutions other than himself? Is there less need to pretend to virtues that he really does not possess? To the degree that the answer to these and similar question is "yes," we can feel that the patient has changed in the direction of increasing psychic health.

As examples of the diminution of the neurotic, I will mention two patients. The first had experienced giving Christmas presents to her fellow employees as a torture because her presents, as she put it, had to be "absolutely the best. I couldn't even consider the possibility of mine being other than the best." Some years later she was able to give a Christmas gift which was nice, although not the absolute best, and "it didn't kill me. Quite a relief." At the same time, this patient noted a decrease in her sensitivity to criticism. "Things don't bother me so much anymore — I'm less sensitive — I'm not hurt so deeply and so long by remarks." The other patient illustrates a decrease in unconscious pretense and self-deception. She said, "I'm not so sweet and self-sacrificing as I appear: underneath, I want quite a lot, and I want only expensive things, though I pretend otherwise.

In addition to asking if there is less of the neurotic, we may also try to determine if there is more evidence of healthy thinking, feeling, and acting in the patient. Does the patient sleep better, eat better, feel happier? Does he have more satisfying and enjoyable relationships with his fellows? Is he more spontaneous, more alive? Does he feel more deeply, and are his feelings appropriate and sustained? Is he able to express tender as well as angry feelings? Is he more honest with himself and others, more dependable, more courageous? Does he recognize and accept assets and limitations in himself and others? Is he able to work more creatively, in a more sustained and satisfying manner, and on his own initiative? Can he constructively criticize himself and others, and is he able to take criticism of himself and his work without undue upset? Can he enjoy both work and leisure? Can he take a stand, or yield, in accordance with his own inclinations and the requirements of his situation? Has he begun to question his values, to ask himself, for example, if it is really valuable, always, to be hard and tough and ready to do battle. To the degree that the answers to such questions are affirmative, we can feel convinced that the patient has changed in the direction of healthier living.

Evidence of increasing health may be found in the patient's dreaming. There may be a change in the pattern — thus, a person who rarely if ever dreams may begin to dream more, or rather, to remember more dreams, bring them in, and work on them. Conversely, a patient who has flooded the analyst with a superabundance of material may begin to bring in fewer dreams. (Exactly the same can be said about memories of childhood experiences.) There may be more interest in dreams and more productive associations to them. Also, change in the dream content may indicate change in the direction of increasing health. For example, dreams in which the person is a spectator of conflict may be replaced by dreams in which he is an active participant. Or something new, or growing and developing, may appear for the first time. Something living may appear where before there was deadness. Consider the dream of a woman who for a long time had complied with all demands, including unfair ones, while inwardly resenting the people whom she obeyed. She finally became able to say no to claims made on her, with a resultant decrease in resentment. In a dream she saw herself in a coffin. Suddenly her dead self in the coffin came to life and sat up, to everyone's surprise.

There may be evidence of change in the evolving therapist-patient relationship. Here the analyst's conclusions will be based on his own observations, feelings, and thoughts, as well as on the patient's words and actions, and they will be more valid than if they were based solely on the latter. In the beginning, the patient experiences the analyst as magic helper, adversary, and intruder. He may be unduly conciliatory, hostile, defensive, or secretive. If the analysis proceeds successfully, the patient's attitudes change, and this change is one that the analyst can see, hear, and sense. An over-effusive gratitude may gradually be replaced by an appropriate appreciation for help given. Defensiveness diminishes and the person becomes more honest and open. Fears of ridicule and contempt decrease, and the patient becomes more willing and able to expose what he has had to cover up to the analyst and to himself. Hostile tendencies to disparage and frustrate the analyst-adversary are gradually replaced by a sense of cooperation with another, helping human being in the effort of self-discovery. A hitherto frightened and timid person may become able to disagree with and even to criticize the therapist. Or a cold and withdrawn person may become able to feel and express positive feelings toward the analyst. As the patient's need for rigid self-control diminishes, his previously not-so-free associations become freer, and there is less compulsive intellectualizing and more letting go during the analytic hours.

It is evident, then, that the therapeutic relationship offers the analyst an excellent opportunity to observe and evaluate change in his patient. In addition to what I have mentioned, visible changes in the patient's appearance are also available to the analyst. I recall a young woman who always struck me as being poorly dressed; her clothes never seemed to hang right. During the analytic work she came to realize that she thought of herself as closely resembling a certain movie actress in appearance and physique. Actually, the actress was three or four inches taller than my patient. After the patient accepted the fact that she was really 5′ 2″ tall, not 5′ 6″, she bought clothes which fit properly, and there was a distinct change in her appearance, which became more pleasing. Similarly, there may be a change in a person's posture — for example, from bent-over and cringing to erect and confident. A person's eyes may change from dead and fishy to alive and warm. His voice may gain in assurance, while at the same time, there may be a noticeable decrease in restlessness and fidgeting. I could list many more such changes, but it is clear that the analyst can be guided in the task of evaluating change by observation of his patient's appearance and behavior.

In sum, the analyst who wants to assess the effectiveness of his therapy must attempt to evaluate change in his patient. He must do so with some regularity; otherwise, he may not do it at all. He will look for evidence that his patient is more spontaneous and less compulsive in his thinking, feeling, and acting. In doing this, he will pay attention to the totality of the patient's behavior: to what he says and how he says it, how he functions at work, how he gets along with people, what he dreams, how he dresses, and so on. And, of course, the analyst will also pay attention to his own feelings.

The analyst must try to determine whether or not a patient's progress is proportionate to the time and effort invested. In making this determination, his own experience is invaluable. If there has been no progress, or less than might reasonably have been expected, the analyst must ask himself what in the patient is obstructing his growth and how he can tackle the difficulty. Such questioning and evaluating is essential if we are to increase the effectiveness of therapy.

Mobilizing Constructive Forces

This lecture as reconstructed by Morton B. Cantor was first published in the American Journal of Psychoanalysis, *27 (1967), 188–99. Horney had scheduled two sessions on "Mobilizing Forces toward Self-Realization" in the syllabus for her 1952–53 course, but she did not get to this topic. The topic does not appear in the syllabus for the 1946 course, but there were sessions entitled "Mobilizing Constructive Forces" in 1950 and 1951. Dr. Cantor's reconstruction is based on the 1951 course.*

Neurosis is a special form of human development which blocks constructive forces and is antithetical to growth. In essence, the neurotic process and the growth process coexist, and we see evidences of both throughout life. Growing in a healthy way means liberating those evolutionary constructive forces inherent in man which urge him to realize his given potentialities. Although we can be very impressed with the evidence of the neurotic process, we must never forget that, however buried or apparently inactive, the potentiality for health is there. The essential goal of therapy is to help patients liberate and strengthen the constructive forces within them, while weakening the forces that are obstructive to growth. We want them to be as much as they can in terms of who they are as individuals.

The neurotic person is at war with himself. That the war exists is signaled to us by the presence of self-hate and all its destructive mechanisms. One set of conflicts is within the pride system itself. To the extent that a person is driven to actualize his idealized self, his life is dedicated to a search for glory. This leads him to become increasingly self-alienated and creates a basic uncertainty about his identity. Does he feel himself to be his proud, superhuman self and integrate himself around his expansive drives; or does he feel himself to be his subdued, guilty, despicable self and orient himself around his self-effacing drives? Both tendencies are present, with one being stronger than the other. The person oscillates between pride, when he feels that he is living up to his idealized image, and self-hate, when he feels that he has failed to do so.

There is a second and deeper conflict which I call the central inner conflict. This is between the pride system, which was developed to serve the idealized image, and the real self, from whence come all strivings toward healthy growth. This conflict is not apparent at the beginning of analysis but makes itself known as the pride system begins to be weakened and alienation from self is reduced. As the person begins to sense the existence of his real self, it becomes a threat to his pride, and his self-hate is directed against his emerging constructive forces, not simply against the limitations and shortcomings of his actual self.

Once we become aware of the fact that a war is on, we must try to understand not only our patient's illness, how it operates and its destructive potential, but also his real resources, the constructive forces with which he can fight against his illness. We must convey our understanding to the patient so that it has emotional meaning for him and motivates him to continue in his struggle to change. When we speak of helping the patient to liberate and strengthen his constructive forces, we are doing what a nation must do in war — mobilize its resources for active service in combat. To do this, we must recognize what these forces are, what we have on our side to help us.

Here we must remember that our patient differs from us in what he considers to be "constructive," since his goal at the beginning is different from ours. *He* initially views health as anything which seems to bring him closer to actualizing his idealized image, which minimizes anxiety and conflict, and which preserves an artificial harmony. *We* are seeking to elicit his real self, something of little or no interest to him initially.

It is by no means easy for either therapist or patient to see just what the real self is. When Peer Gynt shouted from the housetops that he was himself, he was referring to his expansive self, not his real self. In *The Moon and Sixpence,* Strickland's rebellious wanting to be himself was aimed at having a vindictive triumph, at showing others, at saying "to hell with them." Talking to the self-effacing person about being himself may have no appeal since to him it may mean embracing his repressed arrogant-vindictive tendencies. The "play-acting" person with no feeling of self may be merely interested in improving his performance and may not want to be pinned down to a single role. There is a great deal of resistance to getting in touch with the real self since that would pose a great danger to the neurotic strategies of the self-alienated person.

Identifying Constructive Forces

We should look for constructive forces when we evaluate the patient's past history. How has he responded to the conditions in his early environment that have hampered his development? He has adopted defensive strategies, of course, but has he also struggled to maintain his integrity, tried to replace what he has missed, and maintained his awareness of what was going on around him? Children whose real self has not been entirely crushed are more flexible and more resilient to physical and emotional setbacks. They can tolerate anxiety without collapsing, and they keep trying to learn more about life and to find ways to express their thoughts and feelings.

There may be constructive forces at work in the patient's desire for therapy, but initially they are weak, and the analyst must work with the motivations that are available, such as wanting to get rid of painful disturbances. Unreliable incentives such as mere intellectual curiosity, wanting to please or impress the analyst, or expectations of a magic cure will suffice at the beginning, although they will not carry the patient through upsetting periods of analytic work. But they will lead him to learn some things about himself that will help him develop a genuine desire for growth.

Constructive forces often manifest themselves in the changes that occur in the course of the therapeutic process. We have to be wary about accepting the patient's own evaluations of change, however, since his initial object is to actualize his idealized image, and a more effective neurotic functioning will seem like growth to him. He is more impressed by behavioral changes, while our focus is on what is going on inside of him. We are impressed with the external changes in the patient's life or with the diminution of symptoms only when they seem to be based on inner growth. We have to be wary about inner changes as well, however, since the patient may merely have adopted as his shoulds what the analyst seems to be promoting, while not appreciating that he pursues his new values in the same self-alienated and compulsive manner in which he had pursued his old ones. Later in analysis, as the patient begins to become aware of his real self and is struggling with his central inner conflict, he may be compelled to minimize or deny that he is improving. There may be an aversion to change, a desire to frustrate the analyst, or a fear of being abandoned because he has achieved "health."

Dreams often reveal constructive forces at work when they are hardly visible in any other way. In his dreams, the patient's real self may be showing him how divided he is, how he hates himself, and so on. This can be a step in the direction of health. Dreams often arise from disquieting problems (inner conflicts, the desire to feel things, to be free) and reflect the dreamer's efforts to find a solution. In his dreams we can begin to see the patient tapping his energies, feeling them as his own, and discovering what to do with them. They may show him acquiring freedom of choice and a sense of direction, accepting responsibility for himself and the consequences of his own actions, and developing an interest in self-evaluation and a sympathy for himself.

Mobilizing Constructive Forces

All that has been said about identifying constructive forces also has relevance to mobilizing them. In listening to the patient's account of his past and current situations, the analyst can try to make constructive elements more real by questioning, underlining, and clarifying what is being presented. The "facts" of the patient's life story, which he has been telling himself and others for years, may begin to acquire a new significance, and this, in turn, may stimulate his interest in making new connections and developing a new orientation. At the same time, the analyst welcomes constructive elements to which the patient may never have paid much attention because they were just "ordinary," not the glorious qualities demanded by his idealized image, and encourages their further development.

When the patient realizes how contradictory his attitudes have been and how many unconscious pretenses he has developed in order to blind himself to the existence of these contradictions, he begins to struggle for intellectual clarity. The analyst then helps him to clarify his goals in life and evaluate their desirability. He may say, for example: "You speak in glowing terms of independence. Fine! but merely doing as you please, being cynical or unconventional, does not make you independent. True independence entails being resourceful, assuming responsibilities, living by your convictions. Of course, it is up to you to decide whether you want true independence. But if you do, you will have to recognize and overcome all those factors in yourself that interfere with this goal, such as expecting too much of others, blaming them for your problems, and so forth." Discussing values in the context of analysis differs from reading books or talking with a friend in that it is combined with a scrutiny of what motivates one's beliefs. It is an example of the "philosophical help" the analyst can offer, which not only distinguishes between sound and unsound conceptions of such phenomena as "freedom," "independence," "honesty," or "love," but also applies such distinctions to the belief system of the patient.

Another way in which the analyst helps to mobilize constructive forces is through his general human help, his willingness to understand, his unflagging interest in the patient's growth, his faith in the patient's potentialities. In order to relinquish his defenses in the therapeutic relationship the patient must believe that the analyst has his best interests at heart.

Everything that I have talked about so far — identifying, questioning, underlining, clarifying, welcoming, encouraging, and general human help — comes into play during the "working through." In this process, we try to help the patient: (1) to become more aware of all the manifestations of his neurotic trends and conflicts; (2) to recognize the subjective value of his solutions; (3) to acknowledge the compulsiveness of his behavior; and (4) to feel the adverse consequences of his position. Only then can the patient experience how trapped he is in his vicious circles and how detrimental his defenses have been to his growth and happiness. He must develop an incentive to change that is powerful enough to overcome the retarding forces. Only when he feels that it is important to his health to change can he be become interested in his real self and be open to feeling its manifestations.

Mobilizing Constructive Forces in the Aggressive Person

Both patient and analyst may be shocked at fully experiencing the patient's vindictive and sadistic trends. Instead of being repelled by his violence and hostility, we must realize that we are dealing with compulsive phenomena that keep the patient functioning and therefore have a subjective value for him. Recognizing the compulsive quality of his vindictiveness also has a value for the patient. It may not diminish its intensity, but it does diminish the secret pride he takes in it, for he cannot be proud of behavior over which he has no control. At a time when constructive self-interest is barely present in the patient, a desire to change can be stimulated by focusing sharply on the adverse consequences which his vindictive and sadistic trends have for him. We must help him to see that these trends make him isolated and egocentric, absorb his energies, render him psychically sterile, and foreclose the possibility of resolving the difficulties that brought him into analysis. If he attains these realizations, he may stop glorifying his aggression and scorning healthy goals.

Mobilizing Constructive Forces in the Resigned Person

One of the analyst's greatest challenges is to mobilize constructive force in the predominately resigned person. This is not because the resigned person is necessarily sicker or more self-alienated than other neurotics; it is rather because of the nature of his particular solution. In addition to being detached from others and an onlooker at himself, in order to make his solution work the resigned person must avoid any serious striving for achievement, any goal-direction and planning, and any strong feelings or desires. His aversion to effort and change and his hypersensitivity to influence, pressure, and ties make all aspects of the analytic situation difficult. The first step for both patient and analyst is not to treat these behaviors as a constitutional or cultural peculiarity. Although so much in our culture favors resignation and shallow living, we are dealing with a specific neurotic disturbance. Despite all the patient's protesting that "This is the way I have always been," we can find earlier periods in life when there were active strivings, when the patient experienced emotional distress, felt a need for others, made plans and efforts, and sought to achieve his goals. During analysis we begin to find emotional depth and turbulence in dreams, fleeting emotional responses to emerging memories, nostalgia, and so forth. These can help us to mobilize the constructive energies within our resigned patients.

Mobilizing Constructive Forces in the Self-effacing Person

The self-effacing person is difficult to work with because he feels beyond repair and forgiveness, and, as his hopelessness becomes deeper, he develops the recklessness of a person who has nothing to lose. As long as this condition persists, it is impossible for him to assume a constructive attitude towards himself. Like the resigned person, the self-effacing person shrinks from making efforts and from changing, but for quite different reasons. He exaggerates his weakness, clinging to it tenaciously, instead of accepting difficulty as a challenge. He wants someone else to take care of him because he is so helpless. Compulsive unobtrusiveness and dependency lead him to withdraw when he is supposed to do something for himself. When he is faced with responsibility or risks, he may respond by procrastinating, by being overcome with fatigue, or by falling ill, having an accident, or wishing for one. His neurotic disturbances themselves may be used as an alibi, a fact which may retard therapy, since making progress would jeopardize his self-minimizing tendencies. We must be careful not to get carried away by interpreting this as an unwillingness to become well or a need for punishment. These patients want to get well but shrink from the prospect because it would mean taking an active stand and losing any excuse for not realizing their ambitions.

As we proceed in analysis we find the self-effacing patient using his insights into any difficulty that comes up to batter himself down, to maintain his way of life by cultivating his neurotic guilt feelings and self-accusations. The intensity of his self-torture comes into clearer focus as he dramatizes and exaggerates whatever is contrary to his idealized image of goodness and lovability. An emerging awareness of hostility makes him feel like a murderer. When he discovers his expectations of others, he feels like a predatory exploiter; when he realizes how disorganized he is about time and money, he feels that he is deteriorating. His self-hate and self-contempt are not more intense than in other kinds of neurosis, but he is more helpless about them, since he has no effective means to ward them off. He cannot fight in his own defense but takes every criticism lying down, and this intensifies his self-minimization.

When his self-accusations are aroused by his seeing one of his problems, his thoughts may immediately take him back to incidents or periods of his life when he actually was treated badly, and he may dramatize the wrongs done to him and dwell on them monotonously. Feeling victimized becomes a protection against self-hate, and this strategic position must be vigorously defended. He may provoke others to treat him badly, thus externalizing his self-hate and becoming the noble victim suffering in a cruel and ignoble world. His sense of martyrdom allows him to feel secretly superior to others and to legitimize his hostile aggressiveness, while expressing it in a disguised way through suffering.

During therapy, the self-effacing person is compulsively driven to negate all the constructive forces we may have identified in his past and present history. He distrusts people who are genuinely concerned about him and undermines his relationships with them. His self-belittling leads him to deny his real accomplishments, or not to enjoy them, or to prevent himself from achieving goals that are well within his reach. He has a way of turning everything in his life into something painful.

All the difficulties the patient has in his human relationships come into special focus with his analyst. Besides hindering the mobilizing of constructive forces, they may immobilize the analyst, who gets enmeshed in the patient's hypersensitivity to rejection, magical expectations, seductiveness, demonstrations of "love," draining demands, and vindictive attempts to make the analyst feel guilty. The analyst must be particularly aware of his own responses to the intensity of his patient's needs so that they do not further complicate an already complex and volatile situation.

While being fully aware of the psychopathology of the self-effacing patient, we must not forget that his needs to be close to others, to live in peace and work cooperatively, contain germs of healthy human attitudes. As difficult as it is, we must continually point to his healthy ambitions and show him how his way of life is leading to unhappiness and waste and how his feeling of being abused is bringing him closer to despair. Once he begins to recognize how he contributes to his own suffering and to accept his share as a matter of fact, without self-condemnation, the wrongs done to him begin to shrink to reasonable proportions and may even stop seeming to be wrongs at all.

At some point, the self-effacing patient will begin to see contradictions in himself. When he becomes aware of his contempt for others, his rage at being a "sucker," his envy of others, and his desire to rebel against being "nice," we can accept these real and important parts of his personality in a way which shows that we regard them as aspects of being human and that we do not accept him the less. The realization of his contradictory trends comes as a shock to him, but as he grows stronger though analytic work, we can help him to take satisfaction from the fact that he is beginning to work at his conflicts.

Mobilizing Constructive Forces in the Face of Hopelessness

The patient's hopelessness constitutes a hindrance, of course, to the treatment of any severe neurosis. We can do nothing without the constructive energy that urges the patient toward inner freedom, and it is this invaluable force which is paralyzed by a condition of hopelessness. Some therapists are so overwhelmed by the patient's hopelessness that they become hopeless themselves. This is fatal to the therapeutic process because the patient senses that the analyst has given up on him. Or, if the analyst does not take the patient's hopelessness seriously enough and merely gives him encouragement, this will be insufficient because the patient knows deep down that his hopelessness is not just a mood that can be dissipated by well-meant words.

The analyst must realize and explicitly convey to the patient that his situation is hopeless only so long as the status quo persists and is felt to be unchangeable. He might say, "Of course the situation is difficult. But what makes it hopeless is your own attitude toward it. If you would consider changing your claims on life, there would be no need to feel hopeless." This statement implies that the analyst takes the hopelessness seriously but that he sees it as a consequence of the patient's specific neurotic process and believes that the patient can change.

Dealing with the Central Inner Conflict

As the patient begins to acquire real knowledge of his defensive strategies and their consequences, he begins to question his version of reality, his way of life, and his values. This disillusioning process does not in itself cure the patient, but it helps to liberate the constructive forces of the real self. As he comes to feel that the way he has lived is not really desirable, the patient begins to ask, "What do I want? What do I stand for? Who am I?" As he begins to relinquish his defenses, there is the terrible realistic fear of not being able to cope with life without all the neurotic props which have seemingly stood him in good stead and have given him a sense of integrity and identity. To give up this familiar known for a mysterious, emerging unknown is frightening, yet the healthy drives within him keep urging him ahead. He is held back, however, by his continuing need for self-idealization, since being what he can be will not give him the glory which has hitherto been the meaning of his life. He is now caught in central inner conflict between his real and his proud selves.

As the patient swings violently between self-idealization and self-realization, it is important that the analyst not become bewildered by the movements toward health and the relapses back into illness. If he has a clear vision based on his own constructiveness and is an unambiguous ally of the endangered self, he will be able to support his patient at this most trying time. The patient will be less helpless against the turmoil of his growing pains if he is helped to realize the predictability of the forces operating within him. The analyst can also offer support by conveying the fact that the patient is engaged in a final battle and by showing him the odds against which, and the goals for which, he is struggling. Each time the patient understands the meaning of a relapse, he comes out of it stronger than before. The relapses become shorter and less intense and the good periods become more constructive. The prospect of his changing and growing becomes a tangible possibility, and the new sense of his own authentic direction gives him a feeling of strength and unity. Any move he makes toward being himself gives him a sense of fulfillment different from anything he has known before. Seeing himself live better without pretense and the illusion of magical powers gives him more faith in himself and his genuine resources. Beginning to feel at one with himself and with life gives the patient the greatest incentive to continue to work at his growth.

References

Benedek, E. P. 1991. Discussion of "The Goals of Analytic Therapy": Some Thoughts on Karen Horney's Contributions. *American Journal of Psychoanalysis* 51: 227–30.

Fink, P. J. 1991. Discussion of "The Goals of Analytic Therapy." *American Journal of Psychoanalysis* 51: 231–34.

Garofalo, D. 1996. The Clinical Application of Karen Horney's Theory to Group Psychoanalysis. *American Journal of Psychoanalysis* 56: 193–202.

Kelman, H. 1948. Group Therapy: A Psychoanalytic Viewpoint. *American Journal of Psychoanalysis* 8: 44–54.

———. 1971. *Helping People: Karen Horney's Psychoanalytic Approach.* New York: Science House.

Kohut, Heinz. 1977. *The Restoration of the Self.* New York: International Universities Press.

Laing, R. D. 1965. *The Divided Self.* Baltimore: Penguin Books.

Lapponi, E. 1996. Psychodynamic and Systematic Paradigms: An Attempted Integration in the Light of Personal Experience with Groups. *American Journal of Psychoanalysis* 56: 177–85.

Maiello, S. 1996. Epistemological Contribution of the Horney Theory to Group Psychoanalysis. *American Journal of Psychoanalysis* 56: 187–92.

Maslow, Abraham. 1970. *Motivation and Personality.* 2d ed. New York: Harper and Row.

Masterson, James. 1985. *The Real Self.* New York: Brunner/Mazel.

Miller, Alice. 1981. *Prisoners of Childhood: The Drama of the Gifted Child and the Search for the True Self.* Translated by Ruth Ward. New York: Basic Books.

———. 1983. *For Your Own Good: Hidden Cruelty in Child-rearing and the Roots of Violence*. Translated by Hildegarde and Hunter Hannum. New York: Farrar, Straus, Giroux.

Paris, B. J. 1994. *Karen Horney: A Psychoanalyst's Search for Self-Understanding*. New Haven: Yale University Press.

Quinn, S. 1987. *A Mind of Her Own: The Life of Karen Horney*. New York: Summit Books.

Rose, S. 1953. Applications of Karen Horney's Theories to Group Analysis. *American Journal of Psychoanalysis* 13: 270–79.

———. 1956. A Philosophy of Group Analysis. *American Journal of Psychoanalysis* 16: 32–41.

Rubins, J. L. 1978. *Karen Horney: Gentle Rebel of Psychoanalysis*. New York: The Dial Press.

Schachtel, Ernest. 1959. *Metamorphosis: On the Development of Affect, Perception, Attention, and Memory*. New York: Basic Books.

Stern, Daniel N. 1985. *The Interpersonal World of the Infant*. New York: Basic Books.

Winnicott, D. W. 1965. Ego Distortions in Terms of True and False Self. In *The Maturational Processes and the Facilitating Environment*. New York: International Universities Press.

———. 1987. *The Spontaneous Gesture: Selected Letters of D. W. Winnicott*. Ed. F. Robert Rodman. Cambridge: Harvard University Press.

Writings of Karen Horney

1915. *Ein kasuistischer Beitrag Zur Frage der traumatischen Psychosen* [A case history contributing to the question of traumatic psychoses]. Doctoral thesis. Berlin: H. Bode.

1917. Die Tecknik der psychoanalytischen Therapie. *Zeitschrift für Sexualwissenschaft* 4. The Technique of Psychoanalytic Therapy. *American Journal of Psychoanalysis* 28 (1968): 3–12. In this volume.

1923. Zur Genese des weiblichen Kastrationskomplexes. *Internationale Zeitschrift für Psychoanalyse* 9: 12–26. On the Genesis of the Castration Complex in Women. *International Journal of Psycho-analysis* 5 (1924): 50–65. Also in *Feminine Psychology,* ed. H. Kelman, New York: W. W. Norton, 1967, pp. 37–53.

1925. Review of *Zur Psychologie der weiblichen Sexualfunktionen* by Helene Deutsch. *Internationale Zeitschrift für Psychoanalyse* 11: 388–94. Review of *On the Psychology of Female Sexual Functioning* by Helene Deutsch. *International Journal of Psycho-analysis* 7 (1926): 92–100.

1926a. Die Flucht aus der Weiblichkeit. *Internationale Zeitschrift für Psychoanalyse* 12: 360–74. The Flight from Womanhood: The Masculinity Complex in Women as Viewed by Men and by Women. *International Journal of Psycho-analysis* 7: 324–39. *Feminine Psychology,* pp. 54–70.

1926b. Gehemmte Weiblichkeit: Psychoanalytischer Beitrag zum Problem der Fridigität. *Zeitschrift für Sexualwissenschaft* 13: 67–77. Inhibited Femininity: Psychoanalytical Contribution to the Problem of Frigidity. *Feminine Psychology,* pp. 54–70.

1927a. Der Männlichkeitskomplex der Frau *Archive für Frauenkunde* 13: 141–54. The Masculinity Complex in Women. In *The Unknown Karen Horney.*

1927b. Psychische Eignung und Nichteignung Zur Ehe. *Die Ehe: Ihre Physiologie, Psychologie, Hygiene und Eugenik*, ed. M. Marcuse. Berlin: Marcus & Weber, pp. 192–203. Psychological Fitness and Unfitness for Marriage. In *The Unknown Karen Horney*.

1927c. Über die psychischen Bestimmungen der Gattenwahl. *Die Ehe: Ihre Physiologie, Psychologie, Hygiene und Eugenik*, ed. M. Marcuse. Berlin: Marcus & Weber, pp. 470–80. On the Psychological Determinants of Choice of a Marriage Partner. In *The Unknown Karen Horney*.

1927d. Über die psychischen Wurzeln einiger typishcer Ehekonflikte. *Die Ehe: Ihre Physiologie, Psychologie, Hygiene und Eugenik*, ed. M. Marcuse. Berlin: Marcus & Weber, pp. 481–91. On the Psychological Roots of Some Typical Marriage Problems. In *The Unknown Karen Horney*.

1927e. Diskussion der Laienanalyse. *Internationale Zeitschrift für Psychoanalyse* 13: 203–06. Discussion on Lay Analysis. *International Journal of Psycho-analysis* 8: 255–59 [with S. Freud, E. Jones, H. Sachs, C. Oberndorf, J. Rickman, A. Brill, S. Jelliffe, F. Alexander, C. Muller-Brunschweig, T. Benedek, T. Reik, G. Roheim, H. Nunberg, F. Deutsch, W. Reich, E. Simmel, R. Waelder].

1928a. Die monogame Forderung. *Internationale Zeitschrift für Psychoanalyse* 13: 397–407. The Problem of the Monogamous Ideal. *International Journal of Psycho-analysis* 9 (1928): 318–31. Reprinted in *Feminine Psychology*, pp. 84–98.

1928b. The Problem of the Monogamic Statute. *Psychoanalytic Review* 15: 92–93.

1930a. Die specifische Problematik der Zwangneurose im Lichte der Psychoanalyse [Specific problems of compulsion neurosis in light of psychoanalysis]. *Archiv für Psychoanalyse* 91: 597–601.

1930b. Die einrichtungen der lehranstalt: Zur Organisation [The establishment of the educational program: On organization]. *Zehn Jahre Berliner Psychoanalytisches Institute*. Wein: Internationaler Psychoanalytischer Verlag, pp. 48–52.

1931a. Das Misstrauen zwischen den Geschlechtern. *Die Ärztin* 7: 5–12. The Distrust between the Sexes. In *Feminine Psychology*, pp. 107–18.

1931b. Die prämenstruellen Verstimmungen. *Zeitschrift für pscyhoanlytische Pädagogik* 5: 1–7. Premenstrual Tension. In *Feminine Psychology*, pp. 99–106.

1931c. Der Kampf in der Kultur: Einige Gedanken und Bedenken zu Freuds Todestreib und Destruktionstreib in *Das Problem der Kultur und die ärztliche Psychologie* [The problem of civilization and medical psychology]. *Vortrage Institut für Geschichte der Medizin, University of Leipzig* 4: 105–18. Thieme-Verlag, Leipzig. Culture and Aggression: Some Thoughts and Doubts about Freud's Death Drive and Destruction Drive. *American Journal of Psychoanalysis* 20 (1960): 130–38. Reprinted in *The Unknown Karen Horney* under the title Culture and Aggression: Some Thoughts and Doubts about Freud's Theory of Instinctual Drives toward Death and Destruction.

1932a. Die Angst vor der Frau: Über einen spezifishen Unterscheid in der männlichen und weiblichen Angst vor dem anderen Geschlecht. *Internationale Zeitschrift für Psychoanalyse* 18: 5–18. The Dread of Woman: Observations on a Specific Difference in the Dread Felt by Men and by Women for the Opposite Sex. *International Journal of Psycho-analysis* 13: 348–60. Reprinted in *Feminine Psychology*, pp. 133–46.

1932b. Zur Problematik der Ehe. *Psychoanalytische Bewegung* 4: 212–23. Problems of Marriage. In *Feminine Psychology*, pp. 119–32.

1932c. On Rank's *Modern Education: A Critique of Its Fundamental Ideas* (Review). *Psychoanalytic Quarterly* 1: 349–50. Reprinted in *The Unknown Karen Horney.*

1933a. Die Verleugnung der Vagina: Ein Beitrag Zur Frage der spezifish weiblichen Genitalangst. *Internationale Zeitschrift für Psychoanalyse* 19: 372–84. The Denial of the Vagina: A Contribution to the Problem of Genital Anxieties in Women. *International Journal of Psycho-Analysis* 14: 57–70. Reprinted in *Feminine Psychology*, pp. 147–61.

1933b. Psychogenic Factors in Functional Female Disorders. *American Journal of Obstetrics and Gynecology* 25: 694–703. Reprinted in *Feminine Psychology*, pp. 162–74.

1933c. Maternal Conflicts. *American Journal of Orthopsychiatry* 3: 455–63. Reprinted in *Feminine Psychology*, pp. 175–81.

1933d. The Misuse of Psychoanalysis. In this volume.

1933e. Common Deviations in Instinct Development: Homosexual Women and Boy Crazy Girls (lecture). In *The Unknown Karen Horney,*

1933f. The Problem of Frigidity (lecture). In *The Unknown Karen Horney.*

1933g. Psychogenic Factors in Menstrual Disorders (lecture). In *The Unknown Karen Horney.*

1933h. Psychogenic Factors in Problems Relating to Pregnancy (lecture). In *The Unknown Karen Horney.*

1933i. The Uses and Limitations of Analytic Knowledge in Gynecological Practice (lecture). In *The Unknown Karen Horney.*

1933? Illness and Suffering as a Form of Gratification. In *The Unknown Karen Horney.*

1934a. The Overvaluation of Love: A Study of a Common Present-Day Feminine Type. *Psychoanalytic Quarterly* 3: 605–38. *Feminine Psychology*, pp. 182–213.

1934b. Restricted Applications of Psychoanalysis to Social Work. *The Family* 15 (6): 169–73. In this volume.

1934c. Concepts and Misconcepts of the Analytic Method. *Archives of Neurology and Psychiatry* 32: 880–81.

1935a. The Problem of Feminine Masochism. *Psychoanalytic Review* 22: 241–57. *Feminine Psychology*, pp. 214–33.

1935b. Personality Changes in Female Adolescents. *American Journal of Orthopsychiatry* 5: 19–26. *Feminine Psychology* pp. 234–44.

1935c. Conceptions and Misconceptions of the Analytical Method. *Journal of Nervous and Mental Disease* 81: 399–410. In this volume.

1935d. Certain Reservations to the Concept of Psychic Bisexuality [Abstract of paper presented at the American Psycho-analytic Association meeting]. *International Journal of Psycho-analysis* 16: 510–11.

1935e. On Difficulties in Dealing with the Transference. *The News-Letter of the American Association of Psychiatric Social Workers* 5 (2): 1–5. In this volume.

1935f. Woman's Fear of Action [a talk delivered to the National Federation of Professional and Business Women's Club in July 1935]. In Bernard J. Paris, *Karen Horney: A Psychoanalyst's Search for Self-Understanding.* New Haven: Yale University Press, pp. 232–38. In *The Unknown Karen Horney.*

1936a. The Problem of the Negative Therapeutic Reaction. *Psychoanalytic Quarterly* 5: 29–44. In this volume.

1936b. Culture and Neurosis. *American Sociological Review* 1: 221–30. In *The Unknown Karen Horney.*

1937a. *The Neurotic Personality of Our Time.* New York: W. W. Norton.

1937b. Das neurotische Liebesdurfnis. *Zentralblatt für Psychotherapie* 10: 69–82. The Neurotic Need for Love. *Feminine Psychology,* pp. 245–58.

1938a. Understanding Personality Difficulties in a Period of Social Transition. In *The Unknown Karen Horney.*

1938b. The Achievement of Freud. In *The Unknown Karen Horney,*

1939a. *New Ways in Psychoanalysis.* New York: W. W. Norton.

1939b. Can You Take a Stand? *Journal of Adult Education* 11: 129–32. In *The Unknown Karen Horney.*

1939c. What Is a Neurosis? *American Journal of Sociology* 45: 426–32. Reprinted in *The Unknown Karen Horney.*

1939d. Children and the War. *Child Study* 17: 9–11. In *The Unknown Karen Horney.*

1941. Letter to American Psychoanalytic Association by Five Resigning Members of the New York Psychoanalytic Society. *American Journal of Psychoanalysis* 1: 9–10 [with H. Ephron, S. Kelman, B. Robbins, C. Thompson]. In *The Unknown Karen Horney.*

1942a. *Self-Analysis.* New York: W. W. Norton.

1942b. Understanding of Individual Panic [Summary of contribution to a Symposium on Panic at the New School for Social Research] *American Journal of Psychoanalysis* 2: 40–41. In *The Unknown Karen Horney.*

1942c. Remarks made at a meeting of the Auxiliary Council of the Association for the Advancement of Psychoanalysis in 1942. In Dedication (to the Twentieth Anniversary of the Karen Horney Clinic). *American Journal of Psychoanalysis,* (1975) 35: 99–100.

1942?. Psychological Remarks on Hoarding. In *The Unknown Karen Horney.*

1945a. *Our Inner Conflicts.* New York: W. W. Norton.

1945b. Overemphasis on Love. In *The Unknown Karen Horney,*

1946a. Karen Horney, ed. *Are You Considering Psychoanalysis?* New York: W. W. Norton.

1946b. Introduction to *Are You Considering Psychoanalysis?* New York: W. W. Norton, pp. 9–13.

1946c. What Does the Analyst Do? In *Are You Considering Psychoanalysis?* New York: W. W. Norton, pp. 187–209. In *The Unknown Karen Horney.*

1946d. How Do You Progress After Analysis? In *Are You Considering Psychoanalysis?* New York: W. W. Norton, pp. 235–57. In *The Unknown Karen Horney.*

1946e. The Role of Imagination in Neurosis [Abstract of paper presented at meeting of the Association for the Advancement of Psychoanalysis]. *American Journal of Psychoanalysis* 6: 56. In *The Unknown Karen Horney.*

1946f. Criteria for Dream Interpretation [Abstract of paper presented at meeting of the Association for the Advancement of Psychoanalysis]. *American Journal of Psychoanalysis* 6: 57. In *The Unknown Karen Horney.*

1946g. The Future of Psychoanalysis [Summary of an address celebrating the fifth anniversary of the Association for the Advancement of Psychoanalysis]. *American Journal of Psychoanalysis* 6: 66–67. In *The Unknown Karen Horney.*

1946h. Sadistic Love [Summary of lecture]. Pamphlet of the Auxiliary Council to the Association for the Advancement of Psychoanalysis. In *The Unknown Karen Horney.*

1946? Enslavement in Marriage. In *The Unknown Karen Horney.*

1947a. Inhibitions in Work. *American Journal of Psychoanalysis* 7: 18–25. In *The Unknown Karen Horney.*

1947b. Foreword to Gertrud Lederer-Eckardt, "Gymnastics and Personality." *American Journal of Psychoanalysis* 7: 48–49. In *The Unknown Karen Horney.*

1947c. Self-hate and Human Relations [Abstract of paper presented at meeting of the Association for the Advancement of Psychoanalysis]. *American Journal of Psychoanalysis* 7: 65–66. In *The Unknown Karen Horney.*

1947d. Pride and Self-hate in Psychoanalytic Therapy [Abstract of paper presented at meeting of the Association for the Advancement of Psychoanalysis]. *American Journal of Psychoanalysis* 7: 68–69. In this volume.

1947e. Maturity and the Individual [Contribution to a Symposium on Mature Attitudes in a Changing World]. *American Journal of Psychoanalysis* 7: 85–87. In *The Unknown Karen Horney.*

1947f. Pride and Self-Hatred: Influence on Human Relations (lecture). In *The Unknown Karen Horney.*

1947g. Pride and Self-Hatred: Influence on Love-Life (lecture). In *The Unknown Karen Horney.*

1947h. Pride and Self-Hatred: Influence on Sex-Life (lecture). In *The Unknown Karen Horney.*

1947i. Pride and Self-hatred in Freud (lecture). In *The Unknown Karen Horney.*

1947j. Pride and Self-hatred in Literature: The Devil's Pact. In *The Unknown Karen Horney.*

1947k. Pride and Self-Hatred: Solution in Therapy (lecture). In this volume.

1948a. The Value of Vindictiveness. *American Journal of Psychoanalysis* 8: 3–12. In *The Unknown Karen Horney.*

1948b. On Self-Effacing Attitudes [Abstract of paper presented at meeting of the Association for the Advancement of Psychoanalysis (see also abstract of the discussion of this paper with Karen Horney as moderator, same journal issue, pp. 81–82)]. *American Journal of Psychoanalysis* 8: 75–77. In *The Unknown Karen Horney.*

1948c. The Meaning of Neurotic Suffering—I [Abstract of paper presented at meeting of the Association for the Advancement of Psychoanalysis]. *American Journal of Psychoanalysis* 8: 78–79. In *The Unknown Karen Horney.*

1948d. The Meaning of Neurotic Suffering—II [Abstract of paper presented at meeting of the Association for the Advancement of Psychoanalysis]. *American Journal of Psychoanalysis* 8: 79–80. In *The Unknown Karen Horney.*

1949a. Finding the Real Self: A Letter with a Foreword by Karen Horney. *American Journal of Psychoanalysis* 9: 3–7. In this volume.

1949b. Shallow Living as a Result of Neurosis [Abstract of paper presented at meeting of the Association for the Advancement of Psychoanalysis]. *American Journal of Psychoanalysis* 9: 84–86. In *The Unknown Karen Horney.*

1949c. Man as a Thinking Machine [Abstract of paper presented at meeting of the

Association for the Advancement of Psychoanalysis] *American Journal of Psychoanalysis* 9: 94–95. In *The Unknown Karen Horney.*

1950a. *Neurosis and Human Growth: The Struggle toward Self-Realization.* New York: W. W. Norton.

1950b. A Morality of Evolution. *American Journal of Psychoanalysis* 10: 3–4. (Reprint of the Introduction to *Neurosis and Human Growth*).

1950c. Contribution to a Symposium on Psychoanalysis and Moral Values. *American Journal of Psychoanalysis* 10: 64–65. In *The Unknown Karen Horney.*

1950d. Neurotic Disturbances in Work [Abstract of paper presented at a meeting of the Association for the Advancement of Psychoanalysis]. *American Journal of Psychoanalysis* 10: 80–82. In *The Unknown Karen Horney.*

1950e. Responsibility in Neurosis [Abstract of paper presented at meeting of the Association for the Advancement of Psychoanalysis]. *American Journal of Psychoanalysis* 10: 84–85. In *The Unknown Karen Horney.*

1950f. Psychotherapy [Abstract of a conference talk at the Institute of Living]. *Digest of Neurology and Psychiatry* 18: 278–79. In this volume.

1950g. The Search for Glory. Part I. *Pastoral Psychology* 1: 13–20.

1950h. The Search for Glory. Part II. *Pastoral Psychology* 1: 31–38.

1950i. Karen Horney on Work, Art, Creativity, and Neurosis [Condensation of a March 1950 lecture by Karen Horney at the New York Academy of Medicine] *Newsweek,* March 20, 1950, pp. 44–46. Reprinted in *American Journal of Psychoanalysis* 51 (1991): 245–47. In *The Unknown Karen Horney.*

1951a. Tenth Anniversary [Address to the Association for the Advancement of Psychoanalysis]. *American Journal of Psychoanalysis* 11: 3–4. In *The Unknown Karen Horney.*

1951b. On Feeling Abused. *American Journal of Psychoanalysis* 11: 5–12. In *The Unknown Karen Horney.*

1951c. The Individual and Therapy [Contribution to a Symposium on Psychoanalysis and the Constructive Forces in Man]. *American Journal of Psychoanalysis* 11: 54–55. In this volume.

1951d. Ziele der analytischen Therapie. *Psyche: Eine Zeitschrift für Tiefenpsychologie und Menschenkunde in forschung und Praxis* 5 (7): 463–72. The Goals of Analytic Therapy. *American Journal of Psychoanalysis* 51 (1991): 219–26. In this volume.

1952a. The Paucity of Inner Experiences. *American Journal of Psychoanalysis* 12: 3–9. In *The Unknown Karen Horney.*

1952b. Human Nature Can Change [Contribution to a Symposium]. *American Journal of Psychoanalysis* 12: 67–68. Reprinted, with additions, in *The Unknown Karen Horney.*

1952c. Values and Problems of Group Analysis [Contribution to a Symposium on Group Analysis: Some Problems and Promises]. *American Journal of Psychoanalysis* 12: 80–81. In this volume.

1952d. [Abstract of remarks by Karen Horney as Moderator to a panel discussion on Neurotic Anxiety at meeting of the Association for the Advancement of Psychoanalysis]. *American Journal of Psychoanalysis* 12: 89–90. In *The Unknown Karen Horney.*

1953a. Abstract of remarks by Karen Horney as moderator to a round table discussion on Constructive Forces in the Therapeutic Process at meeting of the American Psychiatric Association. *American Journal of Psychoanalysis* 13: 4.

1953b. Abstract of remarks by Karen Horney as Moderator to a discussion of Dr. Kondo's paper on Morita Therapy at meeting of the Association for the Advancement of Psychoanalysis. *American Journal of Psychoanalysis* 13: 87–88.

1956a. Evolutionary Psychotherapy [An interview of Karen Horney by Werner Wolff on the "Therapy of Interpersonal Relationships"]. In Werner Wolff, *Contemporary Psychotherapists Examine Themselves.* Springfield, Ill.: Charles C. Thomas, pp. 84–90.

1956b. Aims of Psychoanalytic Therapy [compiled by Ralph Slater from lectures on psychoanalytic technique given by Karen Horney at the American Institute for Psychoanalysis during 1946, 1950, 1951, and 1952]. *American Journal of Psychoanalysis* 16: 24–25. Edited version in this volume.

1956c. Understanding the Patient as the Basis of All Technique [compiled by Emy A. Metzger from lectures on psychoanalytic technique given by Karen Horney at the American Institute for Psychoanalysis during 1946, 1950, 1951, and 1952]. *American Journal of Psychoanalysis* 16: 26–31. Edited version in this volume.

1956d. Blockages in Therapy [compiled by Joseph Zimmerman from lectures on psychoanalytic technique given by Karen Horney at the American Institute for Psychoanalysis during 1946, 1950, 1951, and 1952]. *American Journal of Psychoanalysis* 16: 112–17. Edited version in this volume

1956e. Interpretations [compiled by Ralph Slater from lectures on psychoanalytic technique given by Karen Horney at the American Institute for Psychoanalysis during 1946, 1950, 1951, and 1952]. *American Journal of Psychoanalysis* 16: 118–24. Edited version in this volume.

1957a. The Analyst's Personal Equation [compiled by Louis A. Azorin from lectures on psychoanalytic technique given by Karen Horney at the American Institute for Psychoanalysis during 1946, 1950, 1951, and 1952]. *American Journal of Psychoanalysis* 17: 34–38. Edited version in this volume.

1957b. The Initial Interview, Part I [compiled by Morton B. Cantor from lectures on psychoanalytic technique given by Karen Horney at the American Institute for Psychoanalysis during 1946, 1950, 1951, and 1952]. *American Journal of Psychoanalysis* 17: 39–44. Edited version in this volume.

1958. Dreams. Part I: Theoretical Considerations [compiled by Wanda Willig from lectures on psychoanalytic technique given by Karen Horney at the American Institute for Psychoanalysis during 1946, 1950, 1951, and 1952]. *American Journal of Psychoanalysis* 18: 127–37. Edited version in this volume.

1959. The Quality of the Analyst's Attention [compiled by Morton B. Cantor from lectures on psychoanalytic technique given by Karen Horney at the American Institute for Psychoanalysis during 1946, 1950, 1951, and 1952]. *American Journal of Psychoanalysis* 19: 28–32. Edited version in this volume.

1960. Evaluation of Change [compiled by Ralph Slater from lectures on psychoanalytic technique given by Karen Horney at the American Institute for Psychoanalysis during 1946, 1950, 1951, and 1952]. *American Journal of Psychoanalysis* 20: 3–7. Edited version in this volume.

1967a. *Feminine Psychology*, Ed. Harold Kelman. New York: W. W. Norton.

1967b. Mobilizing Constructive Forces [compiled by Morton B. Cantor from lectures on psychoanalytic technique given by Karen Horney at the American Institute for Psychoanalysis during 1946, 1951, and 1952]. *American Journal of Psychoanalysis* 27: 188–99. Edited version in this volume.

1967c. Free Association [compiled by Sara Sheiner from lectures on psychoanalytic technique given by Karen Horney at the American Institute for Psychoanalysis during 1946, 1951, and 1952]. *American Journal of Psychoanalysis* 27: 200–08. Edited version in this volume.

1980. *The Adolescent Diaries of Karen Horney,* ed. Marianne Eckardt. New York: Basic Books.

1987. *Final Lectures,* ed. Douglas H. Ingram. New York: W. W. Norton.

1999. *The Therapeutic Process,* ed. Bernard J. Paris. New Haven: Yale University Press.

2000b. *The Unknown Karen Horney: Essays on Women, Culture, and Psychoanalysis,* ed. Bernard J. Paris. New Haven: Yale University Press.

Index